MW01593886

English 5

Writing & Grammar Worktext

Third Edition

bju **press**®

Greenville, South Carolina

ENGLISH 5: Writing and Grammar Student Worktext
Third Edition

Writers
Bethany J. Davis, MA
Lois Oldenburg, MS
Karin L. Wiley, MEd

Biblical Worldview
Chris Collins, MDiv
Bruce Ostrom, PhD
Bryan Smith, PhD

Academic Integrity
Jeff Heath, EdD

Academic Oversight
Rebecca del Toro, MEd
Rachel Santopietro, MEd

Editors
Kristina Albert
Rebekah Meyer

Designer
Elizabeth Matías

Cover and Concept Design
Ciara Chafin

Cover Illustrator
Timothy Banks

Illustrators
Timothy Banks
Daniela Geremia
Juanbjuan Oliver
Aleksandar Sotirovski
Dana Thompson

Production Designers
Sarah Centers
Jennifer Stuhl

Permissions
Maria Andersen
Carrie Hanna

Project Coordinator
Abby Ray

Postproduction Liaison
Peggy Hargis

Photo credits appear on page 385.

Text acknowledgments appear on page 386.

The text for this book is set in Adobe Minion Pro, Adobe Myriad Pro, Alana by Laura Worthington Type, Apple Color Emoji, Arial, Avenir, Avenir Next, Baroque Text JF by Jason Walcott, Calibri by Monotype, Dolce by Elena Albertoni, Eds Market by Laura Worthington Type, Epicursive by Crystal Kluge, Eskapade by Alisa Nowak, Filmotype Maxwell by Charles Gibbons, Helvetica, Korolev Condensed by Rian Hughes, LiebeGerda by Ulrike Rausch, Merriweather by Eben Sorkin, Museo Sans by Exljbris, Peachy Keen JF by Jason Walcott, Roc Grotesk by Kostic Type Foundry, Rockwell by Monotype, Snicker Bold by Mark Simonson Studio, Symbol, Termina by Mattox Shuler, Times, Times New Roman PSMT, Usual by Rui Abreu, Wingdings, and Wingdings 2.

© 2023 BJU Press
Greenville, South Carolina 29609
First Edition © 1985 BJU Press
Second Edition © 2005 BJU Press

ISBN 978-1-64626-374-5

15 14 13 12 11 10 9 8 7 6 5 4 3 2 1

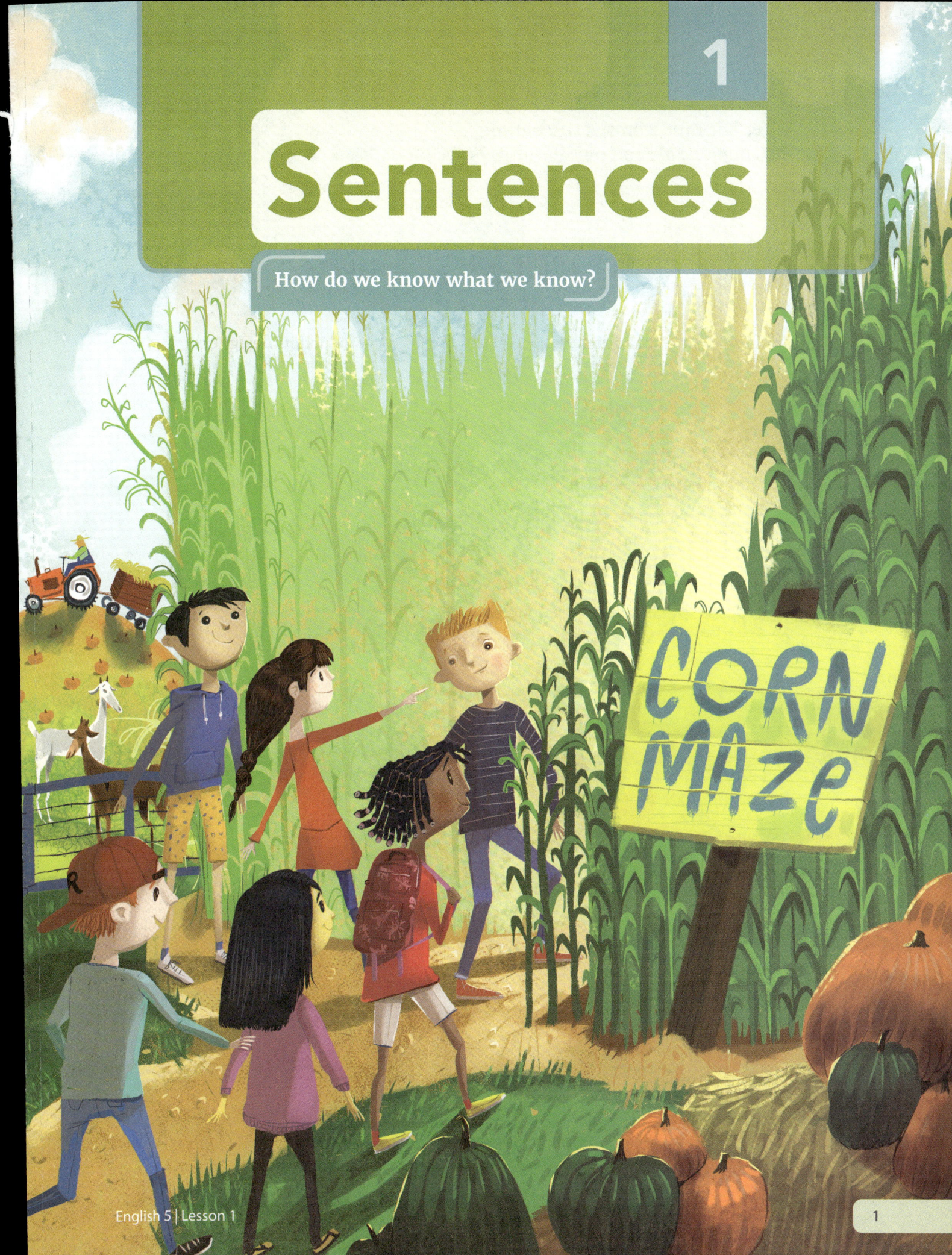

Sentences

How do we know what we know?

1

CORN MAZE

Mentor Text

Excerpt from *Eat Your Words: A Fascinating Look at the Language of Food* by Charlotte Foltz Jones

Bread and Butter Pickles

Dill pickles are flavored with dill. Sweet pickles are sweetened with sugar. Watermelon pickles are made from watermelon rind. So, are bread and butter pickles made from bread and butter?

Actually, no.

Sometime around 1900, a homemaker (some say her name was Mrs. Fanning) made jars and jars of sweet pickles using her own special recipe. She had more than her family could eat, so she opened a roadside stand and sold her pickles to passersby. She called them bread and butter pickles, since the money she earned provided the family with bread and butter, as well as other necessities.

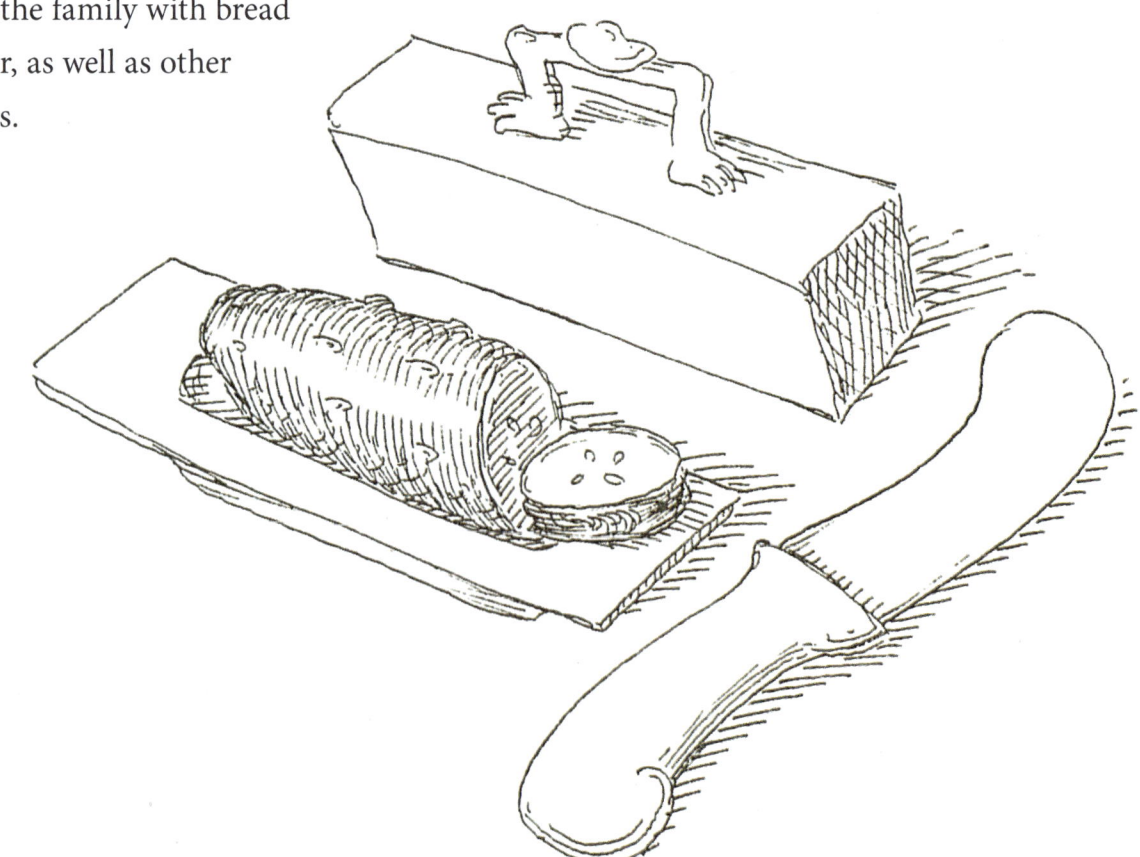

Nouns and Verbs

A **noun** names a person, place, thing, or idea.

Mr. Jones rode his motorcycle across America.
His new book describes his adventures.

A **verb** tells what something does or is.

Mr. Jones wrote the book last year.
A picture of his motorcycle is on the cover.

Underline the nouns in the sentence.

1. Mom bakes bread every Saturday.

2. The whole family helps in the kitchen.

3. First, Grayson measures the ingredients.

4. Then Mom mixes the dough in a large bowl.

5. The dough must rise for several hours.

6. Later, Ava shapes the dough into round loaves.

7. Dad will wash the dishes while the bread is in the oven.

Underline the verb twice.

8. Thomas picked strawberries from the berry patch.

9. The berries were perfectly ripe.

10. Thomas's mother made strawberry jam that afternoon.

11. Homemade strawberry jam is Thomas's favorite biscuit topping.

12. Sometimes his mother also makes strawberry pie.

13. Thomas and his mother enjoy strawberry pie with whipped cream.

Underline the nouns in the sentence.

14. Jayden and Camilla live on a farm.

15. Camilla feeds the chickens and collects eggs in the morning.

16. Jayden weeds and waters the garden.

17. Mr. Walker raises wheat in the fields.

18. The children enjoy riding the tractor with their father.

19. On the weekends, Mrs. Walker sells homemade bread at the market.

20. Many people want to buy fresh, healthy food from local farmers.

Underline the verb twice.

21. Chickens sit on their eggs for three weeks.

22. The mother hen turns the eggs regularly.

23. The hen's body keeps the eggs warm.

24. Each egg is full of food for the baby chick.

25. Adult chickens eat grains, insects, and seeds.

26. Chicken eggs are usually white or brown.

27. One type of chicken from South America lays blue eggs.

Prepositions

A **prepositional phrase** begins with a preposition and ends with the object of the preposition.

> A **preposition** shows the relationship between a noun or pronoun and other words in the sentence.

> The noun or pronoun that comes after the preposition is called the **object of the preposition**.

> *The farmer planted barley in long rows across his field.*

Common Prepositions					
about	at	by	inside	on	to
above	before	down	into	out	under
across	behind	for	near	outside	until
after	below	from	of	over	up
around	beside	in	off	through	with

Underline each preposition in the sentence.

1. Boaz, a landowner, gazed across his barley field.

2. At harvest time, reapers were hired.

3. Their job included putting the cut grain into bundles.

4. Reapers did not harvest the corners of the field.

5. The barley in the corners was left for the poor.

Circle each object of the preposition.

6. Ruth and her mother-in-law were widows with nothing.

7. Naomi sent Ruth to Boaz's field for grain.

8. Ruth gathered barley in the field and met Boaz.

Put parentheses around each prepositional phrase.

9. Ruth gathered barley in Boaz's field.

10. At mealtime Ruth sat beside the reapers.

11. Ruth worked until dusk.

12. Joyfully she walked through the city.

13. Naomi saw Ruth walking with the full basket.

14. She called Ruth into the house.

Barley

Ephesians 4:32 tells us to be kind to others. Describe an act of kindness you have seen displayed at home or at school. Circle any prepositions that you use.

Ephesians 4:32
And be ye kind one to another, tenderhearted, forgiving one another, even as God for Christ's sake hath forgiven you.

15. _____

_____

_____

Underline each preposition in the sentence.

16. Boaz was a kinsman or relative of Ruth.

17. Boaz was kind to Ruth.

18. She could gather barley in his fields.

19. She worked with the women until evening.

20. They sifted the grain through a sieve.

Circle each object of the preposition.

21. Faithfully, Ruth returned home with the grain.

22. Ruth cared for Naomi because she loved her.

23. Boaz paid for the land.

24. After the land purchase, Boaz married Ruth.

Put parentheses around each prepositional phrase.

25. Boaz also cared for Naomi.

26. God blessed Boaz and Ruth with a son named Obed.

27. Over the years, Obed brought great joy to his family.

28. Obed became the grandfather of David.

29. Boaz and Ruth were in the family of Christ.

Ruth

Boaz

Obed

Jesse

David

Jesus

Using Prepositional Phrases

Prepositional phrases make a sentence more interesting. They can be used in the beginning, in the middle, or at the end of a sentence.

Each phrase begins with a **preposition** and ends with an **object of the preposition**.

Americans love snacking (on fluffy popcorn.)

Approximately 1,600 kernels (of unpopped popcorn) fill one cup.

A little bit (of moisture)(in a popcorn kernel) makes it pop.

Put parentheses around each prepositional phrase.

1. Field corn, sweet corn, and popcorn are the three basic kinds of corn.

2. Popcorn is harvested in autumn.

3. Native Americans popped popcorn in pots.

4. They heated the pots over a fire.

5. Today, people make popcorn on the stove or in the microwave.

Add a prepositional phrase to expand the sentence.

6. The popcorn popped.

_____

7. The boy ate popcorn.

_____

8. Mom found popcorn kernels.

_____

Put parentheses around each prepositional phrase.

9. After the harvest, popcorn is best stored on the cob.

10. The popcorn kernels are taken off the cob and put into a package.

11. Popcorn packages are best stored inside a cabinet.

12. Popcorn lasts around eighteen months.

13. Moisture is trapped inside the hard kernel.

14. When the kernels are heated, the moisture turns into steam.

15. The pressure of the steam makes it pop!

16. We can pop the kernels on the stove or in a microwave.

17. The popped kernels taste good with caramel.

18. Kettle corn is made with sugar.

19. I like the sweet and salty taste of these two flavors.

20. For an extra special treat, drizzle chocolate over the popcorn.

Imagine that you have just finished a long search for a lost pet. Write sentences about where you searched. Use the prepositions given.

21. Behind: _____

_____

22. Below: _____

_____

23. Inside: _____

_____

24. Under: _____

_____

Subjects and Predicates

A sentence is a group of words that expresses a complete thought. Every sentence has a subject and a predicate.

AfterSchoolHelp

Simple Subjects & Predicates

The subject tells whom or what the sentence is about. All the words in the subject part of the sentence make up the **complete subject**.

The predicate tells what the subject does or is. All the words in the predicate part of the sentence make up the **complete predicate**.

The main noun or pronoun in the complete subject is the **simple subject**.

The main verb in the complete predicate is the **simple predicate**.

The bread bakers in Rome|had special privileges.
They|baked bread every morning.

Underline the simple subject once and the simple predicate twice. Draw a line between the complete subject and the complete predicate.

1. Wheat is a very important crop.

2. Farmers in Asia grew wheat for the first time thousands of years ago.

3. We make flour from the grain of wheat.

4. People around the world use flour for bread and other baked foods.

5. This bakery sells bread, bagels, cookies, cakes, and pastries.

6. The busy bakers arrive early in the morning.

7. They work hard every day.

Write a complete subject or a complete predicate to finish the sentence.

8. _____ bakes the most delicious bread.

9. The customers at the bakery _____.

Underline the simple subject once and the simple predicate twice. Draw a line between the complete subject and the complete predicate.

10. Pastor James Allen taught us about the feast of the Passover.

11. The feast includes bread without yeast.

12. The Israelite priests offered the bread to God.

13. The book of Exodus tells about bread made from wheat.

14. The Jewish people made bread in big bowls.

15. Yeast made the dough rise.

16. Women shaped the dough into round cakes.

17. The bread baked on a hearth.

18. Pharaoh ordered the people out of Egypt.

19. The people of Israel carried the bowls on their shoulders.

20. They made the dough without yeast before the journey.

21. The finished bread was a thin, hard cake.

Write a complete subject or a complete predicate to finish the sentence.

22. _____ tastes delicious.

23. The new cookie recipe _____.

24. _____ liked the cookies we gave them.

25. _____ send special packages to college students.

26. Sophia's favorite bread _____.

Sentences and Fragments

A **fragment** is a group of words that does not express a complete thought.

Some fragments are missing a subject or a predicate.

Sentence: *Rice was used as a food for more than 4,000 years.*

Fragment: *Contains vitamins and minerals.*

Other fragments are dependent clauses. A dependent clause has a subject and a predicate, but it does not express a complete thought.

Fragment: *Although rice was brought to America.*

Write *S* if the group of words is a sentence. Write *F* if the group of words is a fragment.

_____ 1. The farmer's crop.

_____ 2. Farmers grow rice throughout Asia.

_____ 3. Eats rice for many meals.

_____ 4. Because rice may have originated in Asia.

_____ 5. You can boil, bake, or fry rice.

_____ 6. For two-thirds of the world's population.

_____ 7. Protein and fiber.

_____ 8. Rice does not contain any fat.

_____ 9. A bag of yellow rice in the grocery store.

_____ 10. Tasted delicious last night.

Choose a fragment from the previous exercise and rewrite it as a complete sentence.

11. _____

_____

AfterSchoolHelp

Sentences & Fragments

Write *S* if the group of words is a sentence. Write *F* if the group of words is a fragment.

_____ 12. Many different types of rice.

_____ 13. For thousands of years.

_____ 14. Rice is grown in muddy fields called paddies.

_____ 15. Before farmers used special irrigation techniques.

_____ 16. Ships brought rice to North America.

_____ 17. The gold rush of 1849.

_____ 18. Was important to the immigrants.

_____ 19. Grew rice in the early 1900s in California.

_____ 20. Rice is the world's favorite grain.

_____ 21. Served in many restaurants.

_____ 22. Can be eaten with chopsticks.

Rice paddies in Indonesia

Choose two fragments from the previous exercise and rewrite them as complete sentences.

23. _____

_____

24. _____

_____

Practice

Match the underlined word or words with the correct term.

A	preposition	C	simple subject	E	complete subject
B	prepositional phrase	D	simple predicate	F	complete predicate

_____ 1. Famous Apples is a popular orchard <u>in</u> North Carolina.

_____ 2. The orchard <u>has</u> twenty-five acres of apple and peach trees.

_____ 3. Thirty different <u>varieties</u> of apples can be picked.

_____ 4. <u>The number and kind of apples available</u> are dependent on the weather.

_____ 5. Customers <u>can pick apples off the trees or select pre-picked apples</u>.

_____ 6. We picked a whole bushel <u>of apples</u>.

Add a prepositional phrase to expand the sentence.

7. Phillip picked a great big apple.

_____

8. He took a big bite.

_____

9. Soon Phillip's basket will be full.

_____

10. The whole family enjoys apple picking.

_____

Write _S_ if the group of words is a sentence. Write _F_ if the group of words is a fragment.

_____ 11. Climbed up a ladder.

_____ 12. Phillip reached the highest apple.

_____ 13. Lying on the ground under the tree.

_____ 14. Shiny, red Honey Crisp apples.

_____ 15. These apples are his favorite.

_____ 16. They are nice and crunchy.

_____ 17. A dozen Granny Smith apples.

_____ 18. His mom likes those the best for baking.

_____ 19. Known for their tart flavor.

_____ 20. Some bakers like Golden Delicious apples.

_____ 21. Because they are not too tart and not too sweet.

Choose two fragments from the previous exercise and rewrite them as complete sentences.

22. _____

_____

23. _____

_____

Types of Sentences

A **declarative sentence** makes a statement that gives information and ends with a period.

> *Oats are an important grain crop in the United States.*

An **interrogative sentence** asks a question and ends with a question mark.

> *How are most of our oats used?*

An **imperative sentence** gives a command or makes a request and usually ends with a period. When a command is given with strong feeling, it ends with an exclamation mark.

> *Please feed oats to the cows.*
>
> *Close the gate before the cow gets out!*

An **exclamatory sentence** shows strong feeling and ends with an exclamation mark.

> *My mom makes the best oatmeal!*

An **interjection** is a word that expresses feelings, agreement or disagreement, greetings, politeness, or hesitation.

> *Ouch! The hot oatmeal burned my tongue!*
>
> *Oh, drink some nice, cool water right away.*

AfterSchoolHelp

Types of Sentences

Label the sentence with the correct abbreviation. Write the correct end punctuation mark. Circle any interjections.

Dec. declarative   **Int.** interrogative   **Imp.** imperative   **Exc.** exclamatory

_____ 1. Oats provide fiber in our diet ____

_____ 2. Don't forget the oat flour in the recipe ____

_____ 3. What a cute calf that is ____

_____ 4. Oats originated in Asia ____

_____ 5. Do you ever eat oatmeal for breakfast ____

_____ 6. Help me feed the horses after school ____

_____ 7. Oh, our stallion is running loose ____

_____ 8. Catch him before he gets away ____

Write a four-sentence commercial convincing people to eat oatmeal. Include one sentence of each type: declarative, interrogative, imperative, and exclamatory. Circle any interjections that you use.

EVERYONE SHOULD TRY THIS OATMEAL!

9. _____

_____

_____

_____

_____

Label the sentence with the correct abbreviation. Write the correct end punctuation mark. Circle any interjections.

Dec. declarative   **Int.** interrogative   **Imp.** imperative   **Exc.** exclamatory

_____ 10. Our family ate breakfast together on Saturday ____

_____ 11. What was that loud noise ____

_____ 12. We looked out the window ____

_____ 13. Wow! Lightning struck the barn ____

_____ 14. Quick, call the fire department ____

_____ 15. Get the animals out ____

_____ 16. What a frightening time this is for everyone ____

_____ 17. Finally! Here come the fire trucks ____

Subjects of Imperative Sentences

An **imperative sentence** gives a command or makes a request. In an imperative sentence, *you* is the subject. The word *you* may or may not be in the sentence.

Declarative Sentence:

Drew makes delicious marshmallow treats.

Exclamatory Sentence:

Wow, these treats taste good!

Imperative Sentence:

Make some marshmallow treats.

Keep the heat low while you heat the marshmallows!

Write the simple subject of the sentence. Mark the correct sentence type.

_____ 1. I cleaned the table and the kitchen counters.

○ imperative ○ declarative

_____ 2. Wow, the kitchen sparkles!

○ imperative ○ exclamatory

_____ 3. Find a large mixing bowl, a rectangular pan, and a saucepan.

○ imperative ○ declarative

_____ 4. Spray cooking spray into the rectangular pan.

○ imperative ○ exclamatory

_____ 5. Find the measuring cup.

○ imperative ○ exclamatory

_____ 6. Daniel can bake the brownies tonight.

○ imperative ○ declarative

What do you eat for breakfast? Write several imperative sentences telling someone how to make your breakfast. Check your sentences to see whether *you* is understood to be the subject.

7. _____

_____

_____

_____

Write the simple subject of the sentence. Mark the correct sentence type.

_____ 8. Melt three tablespoons of margarine in the saucepan.

     ○ imperative   ○ declarative

_____ 9. Don't let the margarine burn!

     ○ imperative   ○ exclamatory

_____ 10. Mom warned me not to eat all the marshmallows.

     ○ imperative   ○ declarative

_____ 11. Add one package of marshmallows to the margarine.

     ○ imperative   ○ declarative

_____ 12. Add six cups of crisp rice cereal.

     ○ imperative   ○ declarative

_____ 13. Press the mixture into a rectangular pan.

     ○ imperative   ○ declarative

_____ 14. I cut the cooled treats into small squares.

     ○ imperative   ○ declarative

_____ 15. Our family enjoyed the crispy marshmallow treats for dessert.

     ○ imperative   ○ declarative

Compound Subjects and Predicates

A **compound subject** has two or more simple subjects that share the same predicate. Conjunctions *and* or *or* connect the simple subjects.

> *Dad* and *I love Grandma's apple pie.*

A **compound predicate** has two or more simple predicates that share the same subject. Conjunctions *and* or *or* connect the simple predicates.

> *Grandma slices or cubes the apples.*

Underline the simple subject once and the simple predicate twice.

1. On Fridays the Rivera family makes and eats pizza.

2. Mom or Emma mixes the pizza dough.

3. Liam shreds and spreads the cheese.

4. Ham and pineapple are the family's favorite toppings.

5. The pizza smells and tastes delicious!

6. Later Emma and Liam clean the kitchen.

AfterSchoolHelp

Compound Subjects & Predicates

Make a compound subject or predicate by combining the sentences. Use the conjunction *and* or *or*.

7. The chef rolled the pizza dough. The chef tossed it into the air.

_____

8. Pepperoni is a popular pizza topping. Sausage is a popular pizza topping.

_____

Write a sentence about your favorite food. Use a compound subject or a compound predicate.

9. _____

_____

Underline the simple subject once and the simple predicate twice.

10. Workers plow and plant the fields.

11. Rain and sunshine make tall and healthy cornstalks.

12. The farmer dries and grinds the corn to make cornmeal.

13. Cornbread and tortillas include this ingredient.

14. Some cooks make grits and polenta from boiled cornmeal.

15. People in the South cook and serve grits with shrimp.

Make a compound subject or predicate by combining the sentences. Use the conjunction *and* or *or*.

16. The Garcias grow pumpkins. The Garcias sell pumpkins.

   _____

17. Pumpkin pie tastes wonderful. Pumpkin bread tastes wonderful.

   _____

18. Nyla visits the pumpkin patch every year. Damian visits the pumpkin patch every year.

   _____

19. Mom cuts the pumpkin. Mom removes the seeds.

   _____

20. Nyla toasts the seeds in the oven. Damian toasts the seeds in the oven.

   _____

Compound Sentences

A **simple sentence** gives one complete thought. A simple sentence can have a compound subject or predicate.

> The apple orchard opens in September.
> Apples and peaches grow in this orchard.
> People pick and buy fruit here.

A **compound sentence** contains two or more simple sentences joined together by a comma and the conjunction *and*, *or*, or *but*.

> Grandma wanted to bake apple pies today, but she forgot to buy the apples.

Underline each simple subject once and each simple predicate twice. Write *S* if the sentence is a simple sentence. Write *C* if the sentence is a compound sentence.

_____ 1. Max looks for fireflies and glowworms in the backyard.

_____ 2. Fireflies and glowworms are both beetles.

_____ 3. Fireflies have wings, but glowworms are flightless.

_____ 4. These beetles produce yellow, orange, or green light, and one beetle produces red light.

_____ 5. Max catches some fireflies and puts them in a jar.

Write a compound sentence using a comma and a conjunction.

> Remember to use a comma before the conjunction.

6. Max's family keeps dairy cows. Lily's family raises goats.

_____

_____

7. Lily feeds the goats. Lily's brother does the milking.

_____

_____

8. The family can drink the milk. They can make goat cheese.

_____

_____

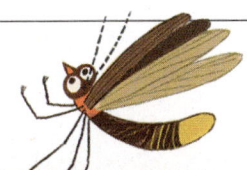

Write a compound sentence about a farm animal.

9. _____

_____

Underline each simple subject once and each simple predicate twice. Write _S_ if the sentence is a simple sentence. Write _C_ if the sentence is a compound sentence.

_____ 10. Wild rabbits ruin gardens, but some farmers raise rabbits.

_____ 11. Rabbits are useful for meat or for scientific research.

_____ 12. Many children keep rabbits as pets.

_____ 13. Lily and her dad built a hutch for her pet rabbit.

Dutch dwarf rabbit

_____ 14. She feeds her rabbit every day, and she cleans the hutch regularly.

_____ 15. Some people collect rabbit fur and spin it into yarn.

_____ 16. Last summer Lily learned how to spin yarn, and she learned how to dye it.

_____ 17. Lily's mom makes beautiful yarn, and the family sells it at the farmers' market.

Write a compound sentence using a comma and a conjunction.

18. Baby rabbits are called kits. They are called bunnies.

_____

_____

19. The Flemish Giant rabbit has enormous ears. The Lionhead rabbit has a very furry face.

_____

_____

20. The Dutch rabbit has a white stripe on its face. Its ears are black or brown.

_____

_____

Using Commas

Commas make writing clearer. If a sentence is read aloud, the reader should pause at a comma to help the listener understand what is being said.

1. Add commas in a series.

   We saw butterflies, moths, and dragonflies.

2. Add a comma after introductory words such as **yes**, **no**, and **well**.

   Yes, I will come.
   No, I cannot come.
   Well, I will try to come.

3. Add a comma after long introductory phrases of five or more words.

   In the tall grass beside the parking lot, Stanley found a grasshopper.

4. Use commas to separate an appositive from the word that it renames.

   Mr. Stanley, the historian, works at the museum.

5. Use a comma in a compound sentence before the conjunction.

   Chloe likes furry animals, but she does not like insects.

Mark the sentence that uses commas correctly.

1. ○ Dragonflies live near water, but moths need dry places.
   ○ Dragonflies live near water but moths need dry places.

2. ○ Yes I know, that dragonflies eat mosquitoes.
   ○ Yes, I know that dragonflies eat mosquitoes.

3. ○ The monarch an orange and black butterfly migrates hundreds of miles.
   ○ The monarch, an orange and black butterfly, migrates hundreds of miles.

Use ⌃ to add commas where they are needed.

4. In the butterfly house at the museum we could observe live insects.

5. Monarch caterpillars have yellow black and white stripes.

AfterSchoolHelp

Using Commas

Answer the question with a complete sentence using the introductory word _yes_ or _no_.

6. Do you like insects? Why or why not?

_____

_____

7. Have you ever caught a butterfly or moth? Describe it or explain where you saw it.

_____

_____

Mark the sentence that uses commas correctly.

8. ○ No that is not a twig.
   ○ No, that is not a twig.

9. ○ This insect, a walking stick, looks like a twig.
   ○ This insect a walking stick looks like a twig.

10. ○ Young walking sticks are green but older ones are brown.
    ○ Young walking sticks are green, but older ones are brown.

Use ⌃ to add commas where they are needed.

11. Liam Jack and Aiden are working on an insect collection.

12. Mr. Simmons the science teacher taught the boys how to pin the insects.

13. After school and on the weekends the boys hunt for insects in their neighborhood.

14. Yes the librarian helped the boys find a field guide to identify the insects.

15. The boys research each insect and they carefully write labels.

Practice

Match the sentence with the sentence type. Write the correct end punctuation mark.

_____ 1. Have you been to Famous Apples in the fall ____

_____ 2. The leaves are absolutely gorgeous this time of the year ____

_____ 3. Sometimes the weather can be chilly ____

_____ 4. Plan to take a sweater or a jacket ____

> **A** declarative
> **B** interrogative
> **C** imperative
> **D** exclamatory

Make a compound subject or predicate by combining the sentences. Use the conjunction _and_ or _or_.

5. Apple butter can be purchased at the orchard. Apple pies can be purchased at the orchard.

_____

6. Our family devours the hot apple cider donuts. Our family sips on the hot cider.

_____

Write _S_ if the sentence is a simple sentence. Write _C_ if the sentence is a compound sentence.

_____ 7. The orchard offers other activities for a family to do.

_____ 8. Sometimes they offer hayrides, and sometimes they offer cooking lessons.

_____ 9. Ducks can be seen swimming in the orchard pond, or peacocks can be seen spreading their feathers.

_____ 10. You can venture through the pumpkin patches and even buy a carved pumpkin.

Write a compound sentence using a comma and a conjunction.

11. Dad and I helped Mom peel the apples. We also cut them all up.

_____

_____

12. I learned how to make applesauce. I like making the apple turnovers the best.

_____

_____

13. For dessert, we could choose to share a piece of warm apple pie. We could choose to eat a whole candied apple.

_____

_____

Mark the sentence that uses commas correctly.

14. ○ On our kitchen pantry shelves, Mom has stocked many jars of applesauce and canned apples for future apple pies.

○ On our kitchen pantry shelves Mom has stocked many jars of applesauce and canned apples for future apple pies.

15. ○ Eating the hot apple cider donuts, sipping the cider, and feasting on the hot apple pie were my favorite memories.

○ Eating the hot apple cider donuts sipping the cider and feasting on the hot apple pie were my favorite memories.

16. ○ Famous Apples the apple orchard will definitely be a place we will visit again.

○ Famous Apples, the apple orchard, will definitely be a place we will visit again.

Chapter 1 Review

Match the underlined word or words with the correct term.

_____ 1. Austin <u>has a new pair of roller skates</u>.

_____ 2. He skates every day <u>after</u> school.

_____ 3. His mom <u>reminds</u> him about his helmet.

_____ 4. <u>Oh</u>, he went down the hill faster than all the other boys!

_____ 5. <u>Austin's friend James</u> is saving his money for a new bicycle.

_____ 6. James, Cameron, and Austin meet <u>at the track</u> every Saturday.

_____ 7. The <u>boys</u> race around the track until lunchtime.

> **A** preposition
> **B** prepositional phrase
> **C** simple subject
> **D** simple predicate
> **E** complete subject
> **F** complete predicate
> **G** interjection

Add a prepositional phrase to expand the sentence.

8. The family ate lunch.

_____

Write *S* if the group of words is a sentence. Write *F* if the group of words is a fragment.

_____ 9. We planted an herb garden.

_____ 10. Used glass jars for the plants.

_____ 11. Gets plenty of sunlight on the windowsill.

_____ 12. Amanda watered the plants this morning.

_____ 13. Until the seeds sprout.

Rewrite the fragment as a complete sentence.

14. Amanda and her sister.

_____

15. Carefully fills the watering can.

_____

Match the sentence with the sentence type.

_____ 16. Popcorn balls are a delicious treat in the winter!

_____ 17. Did you wash your hands?

_____ 18. The butter, sugar, and syrup need to simmer together on the stove.

_____ 19. Add the popcorn to your mixture and shape a popcorn ball.

A	declarative
B	interrogative
C	imperative
D	exclamatory

Make a compound subject or predicate by combining the sentences. Use the conjunction _and_ or _or_.

20. Avery is taking a pottery class. Michael is taking a pottery class.

_____

21. The students shape the clay. The students wait for it to dry.

_____

Write _S_ if the sentence is a simple sentence. Write _C_ if the sentence is a compound sentence.

_____ 22. Bitter almonds are poisonous, but sweet almonds are a healthy food.

_____ 23. Almond milk and almond butter are made from almonds.

_____ 24. Some people are allergic to cow's milk, but they can drink almond milk.

_____ 25. People with wheat allergies can use almond flour.

Write a compound sentence using a comma and a conjunction.

26. My church is having a special meal. Everyone will bring food.

_____

27. Mom will make a cake. She will make oatmeal cookies.

_____

Mark the sentence that uses commas correctly.

28. ○ The school library is open on Mondays Tuesdays, and Thursdays.
    ○ The school library is open on Mondays, Tuesdays, and Thursdays.

29. ○ The librarian, Mrs. Lee, is very helpful.
    ○ The librarian Mrs. Lee is very helpful.

Journal

Write about a time when your perception turned out to be wrong. Use complete sentences.

_____

_____

_____

_____

_____

_____

_____

_____

_____

_____

_____

_____

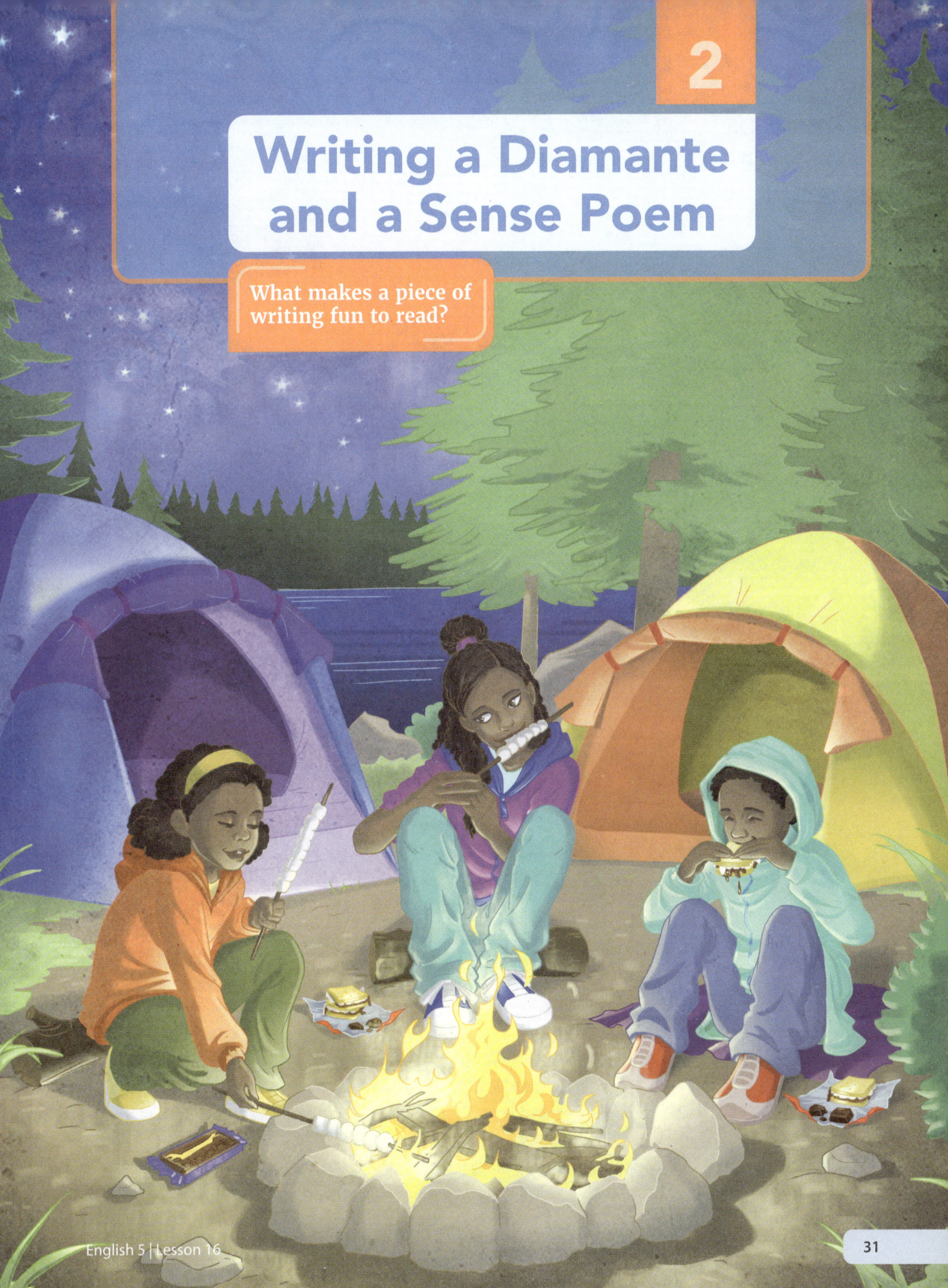

2

Writing a Diamante and a Sense Poem

What makes a piece of writing fun to read?

Mentor Text

"Tent" and "Dragon" from
Words with Wings by Nikki Grimes

Tent

Say "tent,"
and I run my fingers
over the velvety moss
near my sleeping bag,
and I feel
the cool night air
ripple the hair
on my arms,
and I hear
the cricket chorus
while my cousins and I
melt marshmallows
and scarf down s'mores
round a campfire,
stuffing ourselves
with gooey goodness
under the stars.

Dragon

Say "dragon,"
and I raise my shield,
fend off the fire
of his mighty breath.
Then, when he's not looking,
I scramble onto his back,
grab a handful of scale,
and ride him across the sky
till the sun dives
into the sea.

Using a Thesaurus

A **thesaurus** gives common words and then lists synonyms for those words. It may list antonyms as well.

A thesaurus helps a poet find the most appropriate words.

> The right word must have the meaning that best expresses the poet's ideas.

> The word must fit the sounds and rhythm of the poem as well.

> **funny** *adjective*
> **causing laughter; humorous**
> *The funny joke made us laugh.*
> amusing, comical, entertaining, hilarious, humorous, jolly, laughable, silly **antonyms: boring, sad, serious**

Compare the two poems. Answer the questions and choose the poem they describe. Underline some of the words that give that poem its appeal.

> Which poem uses more interesting words?

> Which poem has more sound and rhythm as a result of its words?

Seashells

Shattered castles around my feet,
Fragments of royal homes.
Pieces of palaces borne on the tide,
Washed to the shore in foam.

Surely a king must have stored his jewels
In this tunnel of polished pearl.
And maybe that scalloped ivory cup
Belonged to a duke or an earl.

Surely a queen must have lined her walls
With these delicate speckled tiles.
Who built the homes that the reckless sea
Has smashed and scattered for miles?

Seashells

Broken castles around my feet,
Broken pieces of royal homes.
Bits of castles carried on the water,
Washed to the shore in the water.

Maybe a king kept his jewels
In this smooth hollow shell.
And maybe this white cup
Belonged to an important ruler.

Surely a queen lined her walls
With these small spotted tiles.
Who built the homes that the sea
Has broken and left lying on the shore?

Use the Thesaurus on Handbook pages 358–71 to find a more interesting or unusual word to replace the underlined word. Write the new word.

1. We need to <u>change</u> the way we eat. _____

2. I am reading about a <u>famous</u> musician. _____

3. Today is an <u>important</u> day in our history. _____

4. This would be a <u>nice</u> time for a walk in the park. _____

5. The earth was <u>wet</u> after the rainstorm. _____

Use the Thesaurus on Handbook pages 358–71 to find an appropriate word to replace the underlined word. Write the new word.

6. The leaves stay green
   On the juniper tree
   Though the <u>cold</u> wind
   Blows restlessly.

   _____

7. The <u>big</u> bear
   lumbers into the forest,
   climbing over logs.

   _____

8. Crack of wooden bat!
   Voices <u>shouting</u> cheers;
   Clap of fans' hands—
   Spring is here!

   _____

Write one or two sentences telling something you like about a friend. Use the Thesaurus on Handbook pages 358–71 to find at least one interesting word to use in your sentence. You might want to try a rhyming couplet.

9. _____

_____

_____

Diamantes

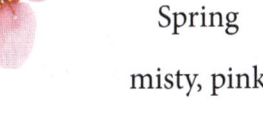

Spring

misty, pink

thawing, warming, budding

flowers, rainbows, crickets, bonfires

changing, cooling, falling

colorful, hazy

Fall

Ant

busy, tiny

crawling, working, carrying

crumbs, dirt, mountaintops, talons

rising, soaring, crying

immense, watchful

Eagle

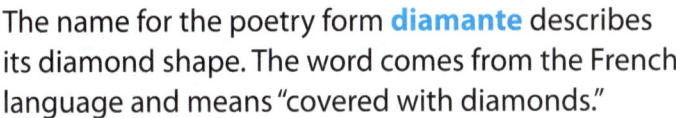

The name for the poetry form **diamante** describes its diamond shape. The word comes from the French language and means "covered with diamonds."

A diamante contrasts two nouns that are opposites. The poem begins with one opposite and ends with the other.

The first half of the poem describes one opposite, and the second half describes the other.

Each line of the poem uses a certain type and number of words.

Line 1 Spring (one noun)

Line 2 misty, pink (two adjectives)

Line 3 thawing, warming, budding (three action words ending in *-ing*)

Line 4 flowers, rainbows, crickets, bonfires (four nouns)

Line 5 changing, cooling, falling (three action words ending in *-ing*)

Line 6 colorful, hazy (two adjectives)

Line 7 Fall (one noun)

List adjectives, *-ing* action words, and nouns that you could use to describe the two opposites *day* and *night*.

First word: _Day_   **Second word:** _Night_

Adjectives	Adjectives

-ing action words	*-ing* action words

Nouns	Nouns

Diamante: Plan and Draft

A diamante contrasts two unlike people, places, things, or ideas. Ideas are harder to describe than other kinds of nouns. Imagining or drawing pictures can help the writer think of words for each noun.

Think about the picture that you see in your mind when you hear or read the word.

Ask yourself questions about the picture.

If a picture does not come immediately to mind, try drawing a picture while you think about the word.

Are there any people or animals in the picture? What are they doing?

Is it an indoor or outdoor scene?

What colors are in the picture?

Choose two nouns to contrast in your diamante. Write your nouns in the blanks. Then draw a picture that goes with each noun.

Possible Noun Pairs		
People	grandmother/grandfather	teacher/student	parent/child
Places	ocean/desert	earth/space	North Pole/equator
Things	roof/basement	hat/shoe	mouse/elephant
Ideas	fear/courage	sadness/happiness	rebellion/obedience

Plan your diamante by listing adjectives, *-ing* action words, and nouns that go with each of your opposites.

First word: _____   Second word: _____

Adjectives	Adjectives

-ing action words	*-ing* action words

Nouns	Nouns

Use the words from your planning chart to draft your diamante. Follow the drafting guide, checking off each line of the diamante as you write.

Drafting Guide		
Line 1	One noun	
Line 2	Two adjectives	
Line 3	Three action words ending in *-ing*	
Line 4	Four nouns	
Line 5	Three action words ending in *-ing*	
Line 6	Two adjectives	
Line 7	One noun	

Diamante: Revise and Proofread

In a peer conference, writers can exchange encouraging comments and suggestions for improvement.

Remember:

Consider using these sentence starters:

"I really liked ..."   *"Do you think ..."*

"I had a question about ..."   *"It might be clearer to say ..."*

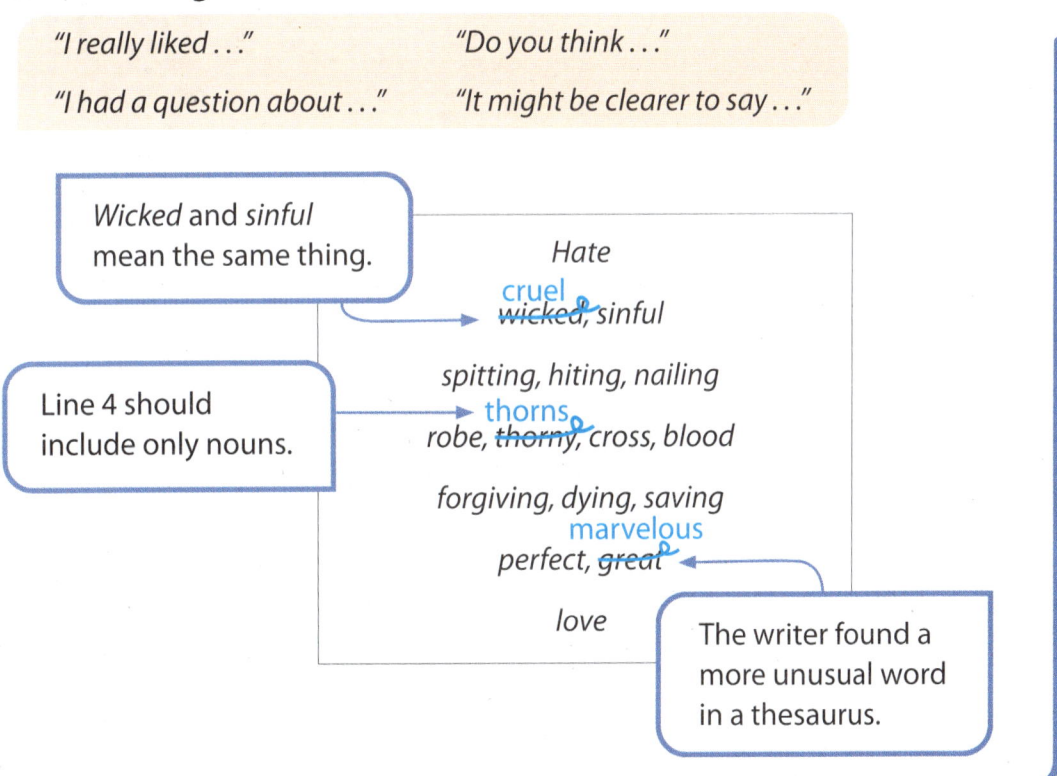

Wicked and *sinful* mean the same thing.

Line 4 should include only nouns.

The writer found a more unusual word in a thesaurus.

Hate

cruel
~~wicked,~~ sinful

spitting, hiting, nailing
thorns
robe, ~~thorny,~~ cross, blood

forgiving, dying, saving
marvelous
perfect, ~~great~~

love

Use the following checklist as you revise your diamante.

Revising Checklist
My diamante clearly contrasts two opposite nouns.
My diamante follows the correct form.
My diamante uses interesting, unusual words.

Proofreading Marks

∧∨ Add
⤶ Delete
≡ Capital letter
/ Lowercase
⟳→ Move

Since a diamante is an organized list of words rather than a sentence, there are no rules for its punctuation and capitalization. When proofreading, make sure that the punctuation and capitalization you use make sense.

Hate

cruel, sinful

hitting
spitting, biting, nailing

robe, thorns, cross, blood

forgiving, dying, saving

perfect, marvelous

love

Use the following checklist as you proofread your diamante.

Proofreading Checklist	
My diamante uses correct spelling.	
My diamante uses capitalization and punctuation in a way that makes sense.	

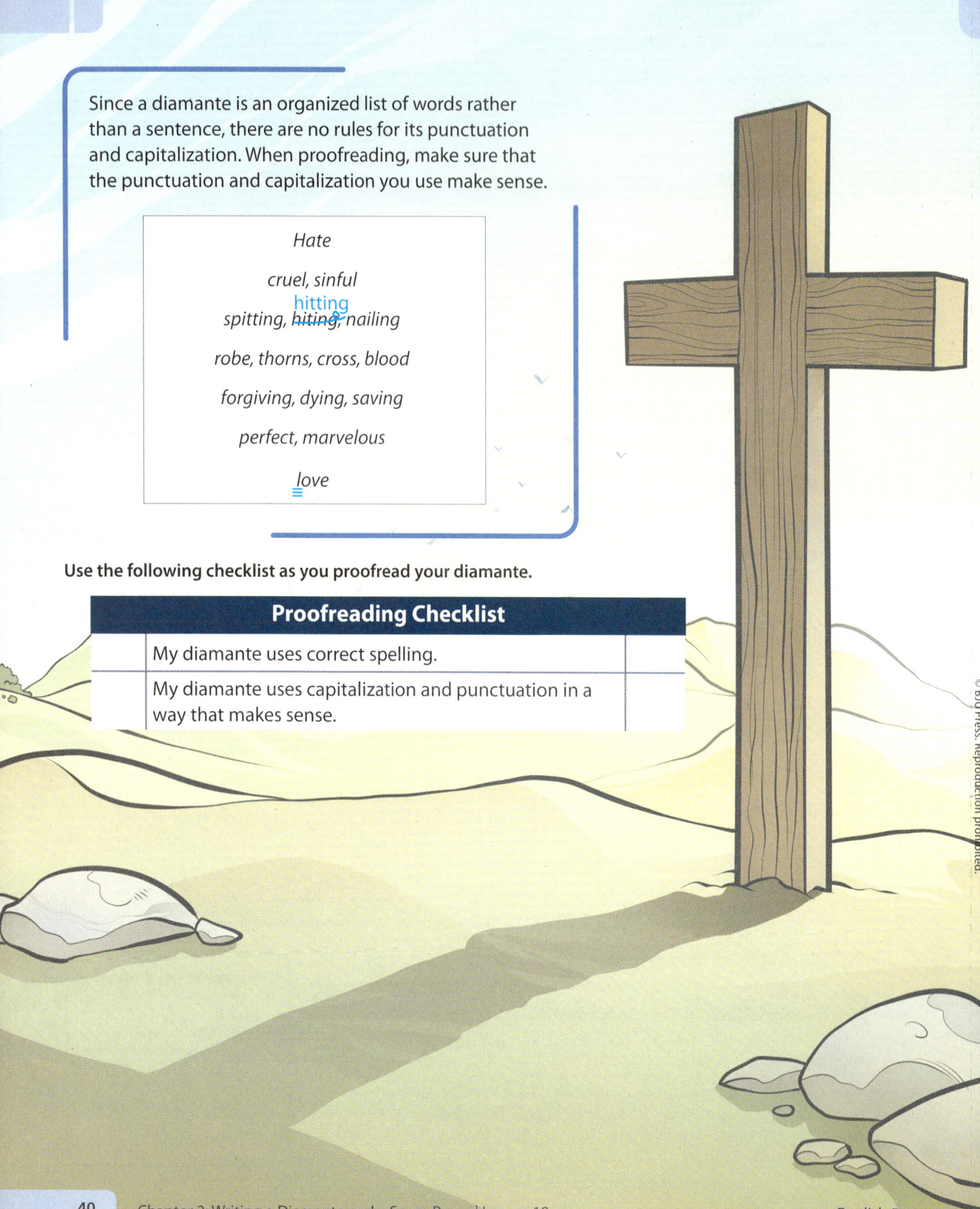

Sense Poems

Christmas

Looks like lights shining everywhere
Sounds like carols playing on the radio
Tastes like oranges, cinnamon, and sugar
Smells like gingerbread cookies baking
Feels like a cozy wool blanket

Getting Up

Sounds like an alarm beeping in my ear
Looks like fuzzy pictures, out of focus
Feels like getting off a roller coaster ride
Smells like Mom's coffee dripping
Tastes like eggs and bacon!

Sense poems describe a topic, using the five senses. Each line deals with one of the five senses. The senses may occur in any order.

The topic is important in a sense poem. It should be a topic that can be experienced by all five senses.

The order of the lines can help express the writer's ideas about the topic. For example, the poem may end with a line that sums up all of the ideas in the poem.

Work with your teacher to draft a sense poem about one of the following topics. In the chart below, list the impressions the topic makes on each sense.

> **Possible Topics**
> a picnic
> snowflakes
> a basketball game

Looks like	Smells like	Sounds like	Tastes like	Feels like

Sense Poem: Plan and Draft

To begin planning a sense poem, choose a topic that appeals to all five senses.

your birthday	*a season*	*a trip to the zoo*
the ocean	*a hike in the woods*	*your favorite kind of pizza*

Then form a word web.

| First, write your topic in an oval. | Next, list the five senses in ovals around your topic. | Complete the web by writing your ideas in ovals around each sense. |

Choose a topic for your sense poem. On your own paper, list each of the five senses in ovals around your topic. Complete your word web by writing sensory impressions in smaller ovals around each sense oval.

Use ideas from the word web to draft the sense poem.

  Pick the details that best express each sense in your poem. One impression for each sense may be enough.

  Consider adding descriptive words.

  You may arrange the lines in any order, but be sure to include all five senses. It is often effective to place the strongest line last in a poem.

> Christmas
>
> *Looks like lights shining everywhere*
>
> *Sounds like carols*
>
> *Tastes like oranges cinaman, and sugar*
>
> *Feels like a wool blanket*
>
> *smells like gingerbread cookies baking*

Use the drafting guide and your word web to draft your sense poem. Ask yourself the questions as you look at your word web.

Drafting Guide	
Choose the best sensory impressions for your poem.	
Which sensory impressions in my web should I include on each line of the poem?	
Is there one that expresses that particular sense better than the ideas in the other ovals?	
Should I list all the impressions for any of the senses?	
Decide on an order for the five senses.	
In what order should I arrange the five lines?	
Should I arrange the senses in an order that achieves a certain effect?	
Is there one sense that best expresses the meaning of the whole poem?	
Draft your sense poem.	

Sense Poem: Revise and Proofread

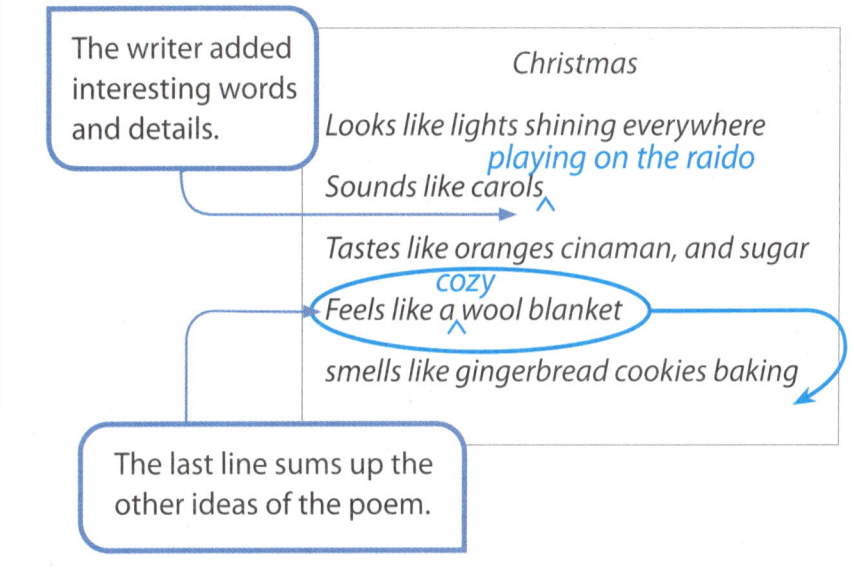

The writer added interesting words and details.

Christmas

Looks like lights shining everywhere
playing on the raido
Sounds like carols
∧

Tastes like oranges cinaman, and sugar
cozy
Feels like a wool blanket
∧

smells like gingerbread cookies baking

The last line sums up the other ideas of the poem.

Proofreading Marks

∧∨ Add
↩ Delete
≡ Capital letter
/ Lowercase
⭕→ Move

Use the following checklist as you revise your sense poem.

Revising Checklist	
My sense poem follows the correct form.	
My sense poem organizes the lines in an order that makes sense.	
My sense poem is vivid because of its interesting, unusual words.	
My sense poem includes details that communicate my pleasure to the reader.	

> Christmas
>
> *Looks like lights shining everywhere*
>
> *Sounds like carols playing on the ~~raido~~* radio
>
> *Tastes like oranges, ~~cinaman,~~ and sugar* cinnamon
>
> *smells like gingerbread cookies baking*
>
> *Feels like a cozy wool blanket*

The series of nouns needed another comma.

Capitalization and punctuation should make sense.

Use the following checklist as you proofread your sense poem.

Proofreading Checklist	
My sense poem uses correct spelling.	
My sense poem uses capitalization and punctuation in a way that makes sense.	

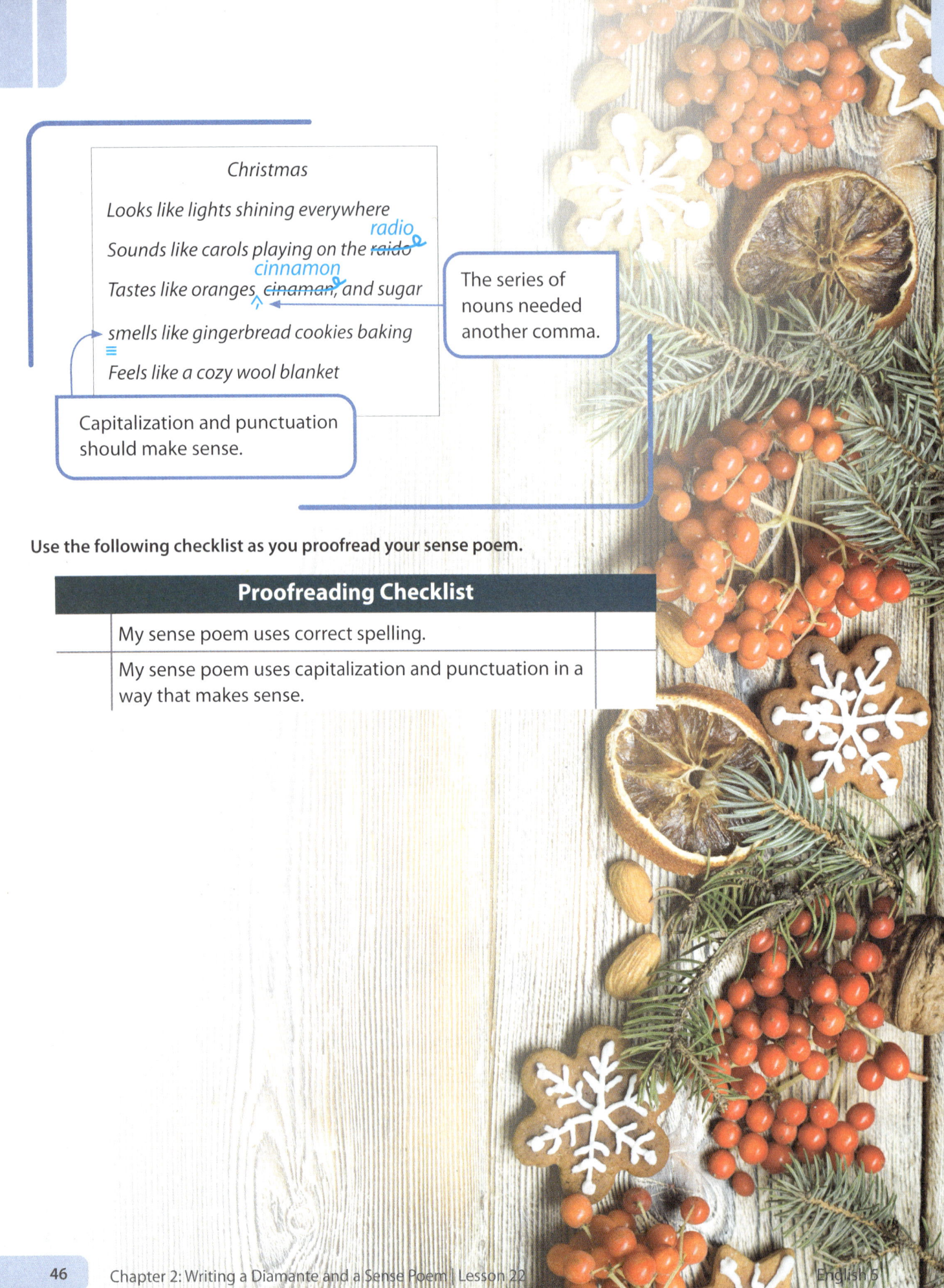

Reflection

A writer can take pleasure in crafting a poem.

Think about writing your poem and answer the question.

1. What did you find enjoyable about writing your diamante?

_____

_____

_____

_____

2. What did you find enjoyable about writing your sense poem?

_____

_____

_____

_____

Cumulative Review

Put parentheses around each prepositional phrase.

1. I lay in the grass and observed nature around me.

2. At the sound of flapping wings, a small rabbit froze.

3. My dog excitedly ran to me with a large stick.

4. We played fetch until suppertime.

5. Totally exhausted, we headed into the house for supper.

Add a prepositional phrase to expand the sentence.

6. I watched the horses.

_____

Underline the simple subject once and the simple predicate twice. Draw a line between the complete subject and the complete predicate.

7. Sometimes, we fish in the lake on my grandma's property.

8. I caught a pretty big trout there one time.

9. Rainbow trout are covered with spots.

10. Thankfully, my dad cleaned the fish for me.

11. The next evening, Mom cooked it for supper.

Write a complete subject or a complete predicate to finish the sentence.

12. My goal _____.

13. _____ will fall apart or will wear out.

Write *S* if the group of words is a sentence. Write *F* if the group of words is a fragment.

_____ 14. Tells about treasures.

_____ 15. All Christians should seek heavenly treasure.

_____ 16. When earthly things break and rust.

_____ 17. Christians cannot take their earthly things to heaven.

Choose a fragment from the previous exercise and rewrite it as a complete sentence.

18. _____

Label the sentence with the correct abbreviation. Write the correct end punctuation mark. Circle any interjections.

Dec.	declarative
Int.	interrogative
Imp.	imperative
Exc.	exclamatory

_____ 19. Daniel decided not to eat the king's meat _____

_____ 20. What did Daniel do when he was tempted _____

_____ 21. Be faithful to God in every situation _____

_____ 22. How deceitful Satan is _____

_____ 23. Wow! Satan is like a roaring lion seeking whom he can devour _____

Write an imperative sentence reminding yourself of something you need to do.

24. _____

_____

Underline each simple subject once and each simple predicate twice. Write *S* if the sentence is a simple sentence. Write *C* if the sentence is a compound sentence.

_____ 25. Isaac and Rebekah had twin sons.

_____ 26. Esau loved the outdoors, but Jacob preferred staying at home.

_____ 27. Esau and Jacob wanted a blessing from Isaac before his death.

_____ 28. Jacob tricked his father, and Isaac blessed Jacob rather than Esau.

_____ 29. Esau took a tasty meal to Isaac, but Isaac had given Jacob the blessing.

Write a compound sentence using a comma and a conjunction.

30. Jacob was afraid of Esau's anger. He ran away.

_____

31. Jacob fell asleep at Bethel. God spoke to him in a dream.

_____

Use ⌃ to add commas where they are needed.

32. After lying on the hard ground he had a vivid dream of a ladder reaching up to heaven.

33. Yes Jacob used a stone for a pillow.

3

Nouns

How important are details?

Mentor Text

Excerpt from *This Strange Wilderness: The Life and Art of John James Audubon* by Nancy Plain

Audubon sat in a small cave, watching a grayish brown bird, an eastern phoebe, as she sat on her nest. At first, her mate had tried to chase him away, darting and scolding. But he had returned every morning until both birds had grown used to him. Now he was able to peek at the first newly laid egg. . . . Soon five eggs hatched, and five baby birds jostled each other in the nest. They allowed Audubon to touch them. When they were old enough, he picked up each one and gently tied a silver thread around a tiny leg. The phoebes would fly south for the winter, but the threads would show him if any came back to the same spot in the spring.

The next April he heard cries of "fee-bee, fee-bee!" . . . He searched for silver-threaded birds and found two nesting nearby. The experiment had worked. This was the first time that birds were banded in America. No older than twenty, Audubon had just made a major contribution to the study of bird migration and to *ornithology*, or the study of birds, in general.

Eastern Phoebe

Types of Nouns

A **noun** names a person, place, thing, or idea.

A **common noun** is a general name of a person, place, or thing.

mayor   business   backpack

A **proper noun** names a specific person, place, or thing. Proper nouns are often more than one word.

Columbia Zoo   Mrs. Parker   Lake Thunderbird

An **abstract noun** names an idea.

courage   liberty   happiness

A **collective noun** names a group of people or things.

family   herd   flock

Underline the nouns in the sentence.

1. Eva likes to learn about dinosaurs with her class.

2. The Museum of Natural History has several reconstructed skeletons of dinosaurs.

3. Paleontologists look for fossils from all over the world.

4. The students showed politeness to the workers at the museum.

5. The man who led the tour was full of enthusiasm.

Write a proper noun for the common noun.

6. teacher _____

7. school _____

Write a common noun for the proper noun.

8. Mrs. Simmons _____

9. Oregon _____

adventure	crowd	freedom	peace	team

Choose an abstract noun from the box above and use it in a sentence.

10. _____

_____

Choose a collective noun from the box above and use it in a sentence.

11. _____

_____

Underline the nouns in the sentence.

12. Zane saw dolphins at Sea World.

13. No one felt boredom during the show.

14. Landon met one of the trainers later.

15. Mr. Bailey studies and identifies whales.

16. The blue whale is the largest mammal on earth.

17. Blue whales are sometimes seen off the coast of California.

18. Would you feel fear if you were close to a live whale?

Write a proper noun for the common noun.

19. country _____

20. man _____

Write a common noun for the proper noun.

21. *American Heritage Dictionary* _____

22. White House _____

Singular and Plural Nouns

Singular nouns name one person, place, thing, or idea.

Plural nouns name more than one person, place, thing, or idea.

| Most nouns are made plural by adding -**s**.

> dog   cat
> dogs   cats

| If the noun ends in **ch**, **sh**, **s**, **x**, or **z**, add -**es**.

> match   box
> matches   boxes

| If the noun ends in a **consonant** + **y**, change the **y** to **i** and add -**es**.

> city   bully
> cities   bullies

| If the noun ends in a **vowel** + **y**, add -**s**.

> boy   day
> boys   days

> ch, sh, s, x, z
> Add an s behind an e.
> Not just s,
> Not just e,
> es does it accurately!

Write the plural form of the singular noun.

1. puppy _____

2. donkey _____

3. wish _____

4. bus _____

5. fox _____

6. country _____

Mark the sentence that is written correctly.

7. ○ The blue jayes flew off.
   ○ The blue jays flew off.

8. ○ The days grow shorter in the fall.
   ○ The dais grow shorter in the fall.

9. ○ Josh dries the dishs after Kaylee washes them.
   ○ Josh dries the dishes after Kaylee washes them.

AfterSchoolHelp

Common Nouns: Singular and Plural

Look around the room. Write a sentence about what you see. Use at least one singular and one plural noun.

10. _____

_____

Write the plural form of the singular noun.

11. key _____ 15. rock _____

12. tax _____ 16. daisy _____

13. cherry _____ 17. quiz _____

14. batch _____ 18. eyelash _____

Mark the sentence that is written correctly.

19. ○ John and I enjoy hiking more than visiting citys.
    ○ John and I enjoy hiking more than visiting cities.

20. ○ We drove through deep valleys to get to the trail.
    ○ We drove through deep vallies to get to the trail.

21. ○ There were no houss for miles.
    ○ There were no houses for miles.

22. ○ The waterfall was hidden by the bushs.
    ○ The waterfall was hidden by the bushes.

23. ○ A few raies of light shone through the clouds.
    ○ A few rays of light shone through the clouds.

24. ○ Logan saw flashes of lightning.
    ○ Logan saw flashs of lightning.

25. ○ The boies went back to the car.
    ○ The boys went back to the car.

Write a sentence about a family activity. Use at least one singular and one plural noun.

26. _____

_____

Special Plurals

There are special rules for forming the plurals of some nouns.

| For a noun ending in a **vowel + o**, add **-s**.

> rodeo   studio
> rodeos   studios

AfterSchoolHelp

**Common Nouns:
Special Plurals**

| For a noun ending in a **consonant + o**, add **-s** or **-es**.

> potato   tomato   echo   silo   hero   piano
> potatoes tomatoes echoes siloes heroes pianos

| For some nouns ending in **f** or **fe**, change the **f** to **v** and add **-es**.

> calf   half   knife
> calves halves knives

| Some plural nouns have a special form that does not end in **-s**.

> woman   man   child   foot   goose   ox
> women   men   children feet   geese   oxen

| Some nouns do not change form at all when they are made plural.

> sheep   deer   moose   elk   scissors   trout   fish

Write the plural form of the singular noun.

1. piano _____   3. leaf _____

2. woman _____   4. mouse _____

Mark the sentence that is written correctly.

5. ○ Three deer ran across the field.
   ○ Three deers ran across the field.

6. ○ The wolfs howled at the moon.
   ○ The wolves howled at the moon.

7. ○ The wagons were pulled by oxen.
   ○ The wagons were pulled by oxes.

Choose an animal from the word bank. Write one sentence that uses the animal's name as a singular noun and one sentence that uses it as a plural noun.

deer   elk   fish   sheep   trout

8. Singular: _____

_____

9. Plural: _____

_____

Write the plural form of the singular noun.

10. child _____

11. hero _____

12. tomato _____

13. half _____

14. hoof _____

15. goose _____

16. man _____

17. piano _____

18. moose _____

19. mouse _____

20. foot _____

21. potato _____

Mark the sentence that is written correctly.

22. ○ Mike enjoys attending rodeos with his family.
    ○ Mike enjoys attending rodeoes with his family.

23. ○ Mom reminds the bois not to wander off by themselves.
    ○ Mom reminds the boys not to wander off by themselves.

24. ○ The brothers watch the cowboys rope the calves.
    ○ The brothers watch the cowboys rope the calfs.

25. ○ The horses have metal shoes on their feets.
    ○ The horses have metal shoes on their feet.

26. ○ The mans who win the events will receive prizes.
    ○ The men who win the events will receive prizes.

Singular Possessive Nouns

A **singular possessive noun** is a singular noun that has or owns something. Singular nouns are made possessive by adding -'s to the end of the noun.

> the shell that Riley has → *Riley's* shell
>
> the telescope that belongs to the museum → the *museum's* telescope
>
> the feathers on the bird → the *bird's* feathers

AfterSchoolHelp

Possessive Nouns: Singular & Plural

Underline the possessive noun in the sentence.

1. I like looking at my friend's rock collection.

2. This rock's surface has been worn smooth.

3. That book's title is *Gems and Minerals*.

4. Some rocks are formed by a volcano's heat.

5. My brother's favorite hobby is rock hunting.

Rewrite the phrase using a singular possessive noun.

6. the price of the cup _____

7. the size of the shirt _____

8. the arms of the starfish _____

9. the souvenir belonging to Mark _____

Mark the sentence that is written correctly.

10. ○ This animal's fur is thick.
    ○ This animals fur is thick.

11. ○ The whales mouth is huge.
    ○ The whale's mouth is huge.

Change the underlined words to phrases with possessive nouns and combine the sentences to make a sentence with a compound subject.

12. The father of Caleb works for the museum.

The brother of Elena works for the museum.

_____

Underline the possessive noun in the sentence.

13. We visited the museum's store.

14. Our group's favorite part was the book section.

15. This snake's markings show that it is poisonous.

16. The telescope's lenses are powerful.

17. You can see the bird's feathers clearly with binoculars.

18. The stuffed dinosaur's tail is made of cloth.

Coral snake

Rewrite each phrase using a singular possessive noun.

19. the light belonging to the star _____

20. the history of the fossil _____

21. the name of the dinosaur _____

22. the design of the basket _____

23. the colors that the dragonfly has _____

Mark the sentence that is written correctly.

24. ○ This museums curator greeted us.
    ○ This museum's curator greeted us.

25. ○ The world's largest cut white diamond is the 530-carat Star of Africa.
    ○ The worlds largest cut white diamond is the 530-carat Star of Africa.

26. ○ It became part of the Crown Jewels during King Edward's reign.
    ○ It became part of the Crown Jewel's during King Edwards reign.

27. ○ Visitor's to the Smithsonian Institution can see the blue Hope Diamond.
    ○ Visitors to the Smithsonian Institution can see the blue Hope Diamond.

Plural Possessive Nouns

A **plural possessive noun** is a plural noun that has or owns something.

> If the plural noun already ends in **-s**, add an apostrophe after the **-s**.
>
> *the hats of the boys* → *the boys' hats*
>
> If the plural noun does not end in **-s**, add **-'s**.
>
> *the cars belonging to the policemen* → *the policemen's cars*

Underline the plural possessive noun in the sentence.

1. The scientists' ideas were correct.

2. Ian went to the biologists' meeting.

3. The butterflies' wings are beautiful.

4. The teacher listened to the children's presentations.

5. They explained how butterflies drink the flowers' nectar.

Mark the sentence that is written correctly.

6. ○ The two museums' exhibits were similar.
   ○ The two museum's exhibits were similar.

7. ○ There were sketches of the trees leaves in the book.
   ○ There were sketches of the trees' leaves in the book.

8. ○ The guide told us about several plants' leaves.
   ○ The guide told us about several plant's leaves.

Rewrite the phrase using a plural possessive noun.

9. the trunks that the elephants have _____

10. the noses of the oxen _____

11. the names of the men _____

12. the dens belonging to the lions _____

AfterSchoolHelp

Possessive Nouns: Singular & Plural

Change the underlined words to phrases with plural possessive nouns and combine the sentences to make a compound sentence.

13. <u>Wool from sheep</u> is spun to make yarn.

    <u>Skins of calves</u> are tanned to make leather.

    _____

    _____

Underline the plural possessive noun in the sentence.

14. Some animals' teeth are made of a special material.

15. Elephants' tusks are made of ivory.

16. Ivory was carried from Africa in merchants' ships.

17. The ivory trade threatened the animals' survival.

18. Scientists' research has provided substitutes for ivory.

Mark the sentence that is written correctly.

19. ○ The meadow was the deerses' favorite grazing place.
    ○ The meadow was the deer's favorite grazing place.

20. ○ The geeses' flight formed a V shape.
    ○ The geese's flight formed a V shape.

21. ○ Leopards' spots hide them from view.
    ○ Leopards's spots hide them from view.

22. ○ The peacock's tails are beautiful.
    ○ The peacocks' tails are beautiful.

Rewrite the phrase using a plural possessive noun.

23. the tails belonging to the sheep _____

24. the necks of the geese _____

25. the plans of the women _____

26. the houses owned by the men _____

27. the yokes of the oxen _____

28. the holes that the mice have _____

Practice

ability   band   bunch   childhood   choir   friendship   happiness   tribe

Choose an abstract noun from the box above and use it in a sentence.

1. _____

   _____

Choose a collective noun from the box above and use it in a sentence.

2. _____

   _____

Write a common noun for the proper noun.

3. Spanish _____

4. Pepsi _____

5. *Misty of Chincoteague* _____

Write a proper noun for the common noun.

6. airport _____

7. car _____

8. city _____

Mark the sentence that is written correctly.

9. ○ My art class made paintings using potatoes.
   ○ My art class made paintings using potatos.

10. ○ We put on aprons to protect our clothes.
    ○ We put on aprones to protect our clothes.

11. ○ My design looked like a bunch of mouses with long tails.
    ○ My design looked like a bunch of mice with long tails.

12. ○ Sarah painted some gooses flying through the air.
    ○ Sarah painted some geese flying through the air.

13. ○ Our art teacher says that our lifes can be artistic reflections of Christ.
    ○ Our art teacher says that our lives can be artistic reflections of Christ.

Write the plural form of the singular noun.

14. video _____

15. person _____

16. zero _____

17. calf _____

18. monkey _____

19. tooth _____

Rewrite the phrase using a singular possessive noun.

20. the love of God _____

21. the car belonging to my brother _____

22. the shoes belonging to Josie _____

23. the book the library owns _____

24. the lessons given to the class _____

Rewrite the phrase using a plural possessive noun.

25. the rattles belonging to the babies _____

26. the necks of the giraffes _____

27. the classes of the teachers _____

28. the courage of the heroes _____

29. the colors of the many fish _____

Capitalizing Proper Nouns

AfterSchoolHelp

Proper Nouns: Capitalization Rules

A **proper noun** names a specific person, place, or thing.

Proper nouns can be more than one word. Each main word in a proper noun begins with a capital letter.

Abigail Adams

Philadelphia, Pennsylvania

Declaration of Independence

Use 🔲 to mark the letters that should be capitalized.

1. herbert lang and james chapin explored africa in 1909.

2. The men traveled from new york to the belgian congo in africa.

3. james chapin visited chief okonda's village.

4. The explorers returned to the united states in november 1915.

5. chapin worked for the american museum of natural history.

6. I learned the museum's history at the young naturalists' club last christmas.

See Capitalizing Proper Nouns on Handbook page 374.

Write a sentence about a sports team. Use a proper noun.

7. _____

_____

Write a sentence about a place you like to visit. Use a proper noun.

8. _____

_____

Use  **to mark the letters that should be capitalized.**

9. My school is called reidsville academy.

10. The school is on brookside avenue.

11. Mrs. lee taught us about a famous ship called the USS *constitution*.

12. The ship is nicknamed old ironsides.

13. oliver wendell holmes wrote a poem about it.

14. People can still see this ship in boston, massachusetts.

15. Our class visited the aquarium in atlanta, georgia.

16. georgia and south carolina are on the coast of the atlantic ocean.

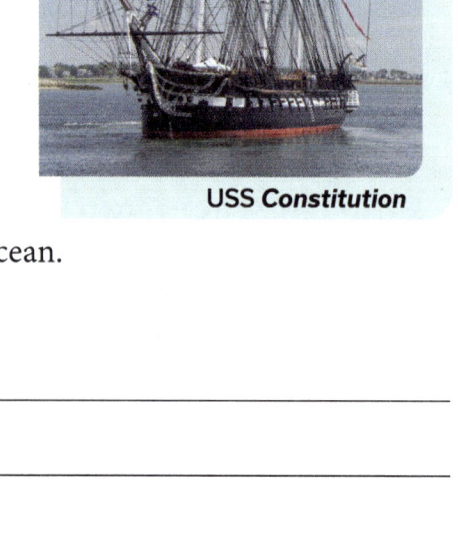

USS *Constitution*

Write a sentence about your favorite holiday. Use a proper noun.

17. _____

_____

Write a sentence about a business. Use a proper noun.

18. _____

_____

Write a sentence about an ocean, river, or lake. Use a proper noun.

19. _____

_____

Lake Michigan

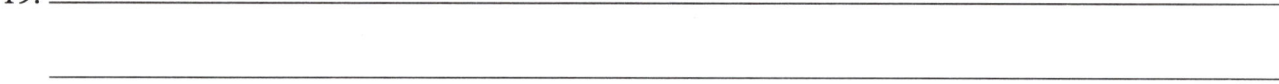

Capitalizing Titles

The titles of books, newspapers, magazines, stories, poems, and songs are proper nouns.

Capitalize the first, last, and all important words of these titles.

Underline or italicize the title of a book, newspaper, or magazine. Place quotation marks around the title of a song, poem, or story.

Sarah, Plain and Tall   "Cinderella"   Orangeburg Daily Observer

Mark the title that is written correctly.

See Capitalizing Titles on Handbook page 375.

1. ○ (poem) "The Sunset"
   ○ (poem) *The Sunset*

2. ○ (book) "The Search for the Silver Eagle"
   ○ (book) *The Search for the Silver Eagle*

3. ○ (magazine) Military kid's life
   ○ (magazine) *Military Kid's Life*

4. ○ (newspaper) Dave's Daily News
   ○ (newspaper) "Dave's Daily News"

5. ○ (song) "We Gather Together"
   ○ (song) We Gather Together

Write the title correctly.

6. wildlife of alaska (book) _____

7. the tale of custard the dragon (poem) _____

8. ranger rick (magazine) _____

9. the sword in the stone (story) _____

10. american haven (book) _____

11. the king and the shirt (story) _____

Imagine that you have published a book of stories and poems. Invent a title for your book and titles for some of the stories and poems that it includes. Write them correctly.

12. _____

_____

_____

_____

Mark the title that is written correctly.

13. ○ (story) "The Beginning Of The Armadillos"
    ○ (story) "The Beginning of the Armadillos"

14. ○ (book) *In search of Honor*
    ○ (book) *In Search of Honor*

15. ○ (poem) <u>Wynken, Blynken, and Nod</u>
    ○ (poem) "Wynken, Blynken, and Nod"

16. ○ (newspaper) *Richmond Report*
    ○ (newspaper) "Richmond Report"

17. ○ (song) "We three Kings"
    ○ (song) "We Three Kings"

18. ○ (story) "Vasko's Christmas Rescue"
    ○ (story) *Vasko's Christmas Rescue*

Write the title correctly.

19. birds of the african savanna (book) _____

20. young rider (magazine) _____

21. old ironsides (poem) _____

22. king solomon's ring (story) _____

23. mountain born (book) _____

Confusing Proper Nouns

Some words can be **common nouns** or **proper nouns**. Common nouns that show family relationships become proper nouns when they are used as a name or part of a name.

> *My aunt and my uncle live in California.*
>
> *Aunt Katie and Uncle Patrick live in California.*

Common nouns that describe a geographic feature become proper nouns when they are used as a name or part of a name.

> *The river is at the bottom of the valley.*
>
> *The Hudson River is at the bottom of the Hudson Valley.*

Compass words become proper nouns when they are used to refer to a region.

> *My family travels west every summer.*
>
> *We watched a news broadcast about wildfires in the West.*

Titles of respect are capitalized when they are used with a person's name.

> *The pastor preached a gospel message.*
>
> *Pastor Reynolds preached a gospel message.*

Mark the sentence that is written correctly.

1. ○ The Senator visited our school.
   ○ The senator visited our school.

2. ○ José lives near the Rocky Mountains.
   ○ José lives near the Rocky mountains.

3. ○ Drive three miles south on Ridgedale Road.
   ○ Drive three miles South on Ridgedale Road.

Write one sentence with *lake* used as a common noun and another sentence with *Lake* used as a proper noun.

4. Common: _____

   _____

5. Proper: _____

   _____

Mark the sentence that is written correctly.

6. ○ My uncle bought me a telescope from the museum shop.
   ○ My Uncle bought me a telescope from the museum shop.

7. ○ Mom and dad saw the meteor shower.
   ○ Mom and Dad saw the meteor shower.

8. ○ Did you ask aunt Mary to bring a warm coat?
   ○ Did you ask Aunt Mary to bring a warm coat?

9. ○ My dad recognized the North Star.
   ○ My Dad recognized the North Star.

10. ○ I like reading about president Adams.
    ○ I like reading about President Adams.

11. ○ The Civil War was fought between the north and the south.
    ○ The Civil War was fought between the North and the South.

12. ○ The Thompson family goes to the coast every summer.
    ○ The Thompson family goes to the Coast every summer.

13. ○ The Cascade Mountains are located in North America.
    ○ The Cascade mountains are located in North America.

Write one sentence with *doctor* used as a common noun and another sentence with *Doctor* used as a proper noun.

14. Common: _____

_____

15. Proper: _____

_____

Abbreviations

An **abbreviation** is a short way of writing a word.

| Most abbreviations end with a period.

| Abbreviations for proper nouns begin with a capital letter.

Months	Jan. Feb. Mar. Apr. Aug. Sept. Oct. Nov. Dec. *May*, *June*, and *July* are not abbreviated.
Days	Sun. Mon. Tues. Wed. Thurs. Fri. Sat.
Titles	Mr. Ms. Mrs. Rev. Dr. Jr. Sr.

Times		Metric Measurement Units		Customary Measurement Units	
*a.m.	morning	m	meter(s)	in.	inch(es)
*p.m.	afternoon, night	cm	centimeter(s)	ft.	foot (feet)
BC	before Christ	mm	millimeter(s)	yd.	yard(s)
*AD	after Christ's birth	g	gram(s)	lb.	pound(s)
min(s).	minute(s)	kg	kilogram(s)	oz.	ounce(s)
sec(s).	second(s)	l or L	liter(s)	gal.	gallon(s)
hr(s).	hour(s)	ml or mL	milliliter(s)		

*Latin.   a.m. = ante meridiem, "before noon."
          p.m. = post meridiem, "after noon."
          AD = anno Domini, "in the year of our Lord."

Write the correct abbreviation for the underlined word.

1. Monday, May 22 _____

2. last Wednesday _____

3. October 1 _____

4. Jim Beadle, Senior _____

5. 3 meters _____

6. Mister Hanson _____

7. 30 feet long _____

8. 300 milliliters _____

See Abbreviations on Handbook pages 376–78.

Underline the abbreviation that is written correctly.

9. Reverend (Rev., Ren.) Kenneth Smith spoke about
   Jerusalem in the 7:00 post meridiem (PM, p.m.)
   service. He told us that Jerusalem was destroyed in
   anno Domini (a.d., AD) 76.

Write the correct abbreviation for the name of the month or day.

10. April _____

11. March _____

12. November _____

13. August _____

14. December _____

15. February _____

16. Tuesday _____

17. Wednesday _____

18. Thursday _____

Write the correct abbreviation for the unit of measurement.

19. second _____

20. kilogram _____

21. yard _____

22. centimeter _____

23. millimeter _____

24. gram _____

25. hour _____

26. meter _____

27. foot _____

28. pound _____

29. minute _____

30. liter _____

Underline the abbreviation that is written correctly.

31.

Come Join Naturalists' Club!

Meet at the museum on Tuesday (Tues., Tue.) and Thursday (Thur., Thurs.) at 6:00 post meridiem (p.m., P.M.).

Doctor (Doc., Dr.) Bradshaw is coming to speak on September (Sept., Sep.) 20th. A harvest party in honor of Mister (Mst., Mr.) Carlton is scheduled after the speech.

Be sure to arrive a few minutes (min., mi.) early so you can see the displays. Jacob Woods, Junior (Jun., Jr.), President (Presid., Pres.)

Using Commas

Commas are an important part of letters, addresses, and dates.

1. Use commas after the greeting and closing in letters.
   Dear Skyler,   *Sincerely,*
2. Use a comma between the city and the state.
   Columbus, Georgia
3. Use a comma between the day and year in a date.
   July 20, 1969

AfterSchoolHelp

Using Commas

Write the date with the correct abbreviation and punctuation.

1. October 31 1517 _____

2. December 16 1773 _____

3. July 4 1776 _____

Unscramble Everly's address. Use correct capitalization, punctuation, and abbreviations to write it on the lines below.

| 53 | 02108 | Applewood | Boston | Everly | Harris | Lane | Massachusetts |

4. _____

_____

_____

Write a short note of encouragement to someone that you know. Include a greeting and a closing. Use correct punctuation.

5. _____

_____

_____

_____

_____

Write the date with the correct abbreviation and punctuation.

6. March 4 2015 _____

7. January 1 2001 _____

8. April 9 2022 _____

Unscramble Mateo's address. Use correct capitalization, punctuation, and abbreviations to write it on the lines below.

| 80123 | 93 | Colorado | Denver | Garcia | Junior | Mateo | Raccoon | Road |

9. _____

_____

_____

Practice

Use to mark the letters that should be capitalized.

1. I play hockey for the lindville lions.

2. Most of our games are in january and february.

3. mom and aunt louisa are coming to our next game.

4. coach jennings believes that we can honor the lord by being good sports.

5. Our team memorized james 4:6, a bible verse encouraging us to act with humility.

Write the title correctly.

6. the eagle (poem) _____

7. moses and joshua (story) _____

8. medallion (book) _____

9. the new york post (newspaper) _____

10. the farmer in the dell (song) _____

11. answers in genesis (magazine) _____

Write the correct abbreviation for the underlined word.

12. 450 <u>before Christ</u> _____   15. 3 <u>inches</u> _____

13. <u>August</u> 18 _____   16. <u>Reverend</u> Patrick Hall _____

14. Jim Beadle, <u>Junior</u> _____   17. 300 <u>gallons</u> _____

Write the date with the correct abbreviation and punctuation.

18. September 11 2012 _____

19. April 1 1957 _____

20. May 25 2001 _____

Unscramble Jake's address. Use correct capitalization, punctuation, and abbreviations to write it on the lines below.

| 201 | 85030 | Arizona | Drive | Elm | Greenwood | Jake | Matthews |

21. _____

_____

_____

Write a short thank you note to someone for a kind deed. Include a greeting and a closing. Use correct punctuation.

22.

Chapter 3 Review

Mark the sentence that is written correctly.

1. ○ This atlas has information about cities mentioned in the Bible.
   ○ This atlas has information about citys mentioned in the Bible.

2. ○ Baby Moses sailed down the Nile in a basket made of bulrushes.
   ○ Baby Moses sailed down the Nile in a basket made of bulrushs.

3. ○ Mila is looking for facts about Arctic foxs.
   ○ Mila is looking for facts about Arctic foxes.

4. ○ These tomatoes came from our garden.
   ○ These tomatos came from our garden.

5. ○ Pioneers traveled across America in covered wagones.
   ○ Pioneers traveled across America in covered wagons.

6. ○ Grandpa will sharpen the kitchen knifes for Mom.
   ○ Grandpa will sharpen the kitchen knives for Mom.

7. ○ Olivia has new eyeglasses.
   ○ Olivia has new eyeglasss.

8. ○ Our cat keeps mouses out of the house.
   ○ Our cat keeps mice out of the house.

Rewrite the phrase using a possessive noun.

9. the words of the books _____

10. the classroom of the children _____

11. the age of the scroll _____

12. the faith of Abraham _____

Use ▤ to mark the letters that should be capitalized.

13. lake ontario is on the border between the united states and canada.

14. Marcus goes to grace baptist church.

15. His church has services in english and in spanish.

16. Pastor martinez preached a sermon about the holy spirit.

Lesson 38

Mark the title that is written correctly.

17. ○ (book) "A Question of Yams"
    ○ (book) *A Question of Yams*

18. ○ (newspaper) *The centerville Star*
    ○ (newspaper) *The Centerville Star*

19. ○ (story) "The Boy who cried Wolf"
    ○ (story) "The Boy Who Cried Wolf"

20. ○ (poem) "Mother Doesn't Want a Dog"
    ○ (poem) Mother Doesn't Want a Dog

Mark the sentence that is written correctly.

21. ○ The school board elected a new president.
    ○ The school board elected a new President.

22. ○ We will visit grandmother Wallace this summer.
    ○ We will visit Grandmother Wallace this summer.

23. ○ Have you been to the Pacific ocean?
    ○ Have you been to the Pacific Ocean?

Write one sentence with *uncle* used as a common noun and another sentence with *Uncle* used as a proper noun.

24. Common: _____

    _____

25. Proper: _____

    _____

Write the correct abbreviation.

26. minutes _____   28. President _____

27. before Christ _____   29. ounces _____

Unscramble Malachi's address. Use correct capitalization, punctuation, and abbreviations to write it on the lines below.

| 85 | 21117 | Acorn | Baltimore | Malachi | Maryland | Mister | Reed | Lane |

30. _____

    _____

    _____

Journal

Think of a task that requires precision that you do regularly. Describe the ways that details and accuracy are important for this task.

1. _____

_____

_____

_____

What would happen if you ignored details and accuracy in this task? Keep in mind what you learned about precision from a biblical worldview as you write your answer.

2. _____

_____

_____

_____

Cumulative Review

Write _S_ if the group of words is a sentence. Write _F_ if the group of words is a fragment.

_____ 1. Strong Christians read their Bibles, pray, and obey God's commands.

_____ 2. About heavenly treasures in the Bible.

_____ 3. Christians should not worry about food or clothing.

_____ 4. The Lord provides for all their needs.

_____ 5. God's faithful servants.

Choose a fragment from the previous exercise and rewrite it as a complete sentence.

6. _____

_____

Put parentheses around each prepositional phrase.

7. In captivity Daniel was an obedient man of God.

8. He faithfully prayed on his knees from his open window.

9. Daniel was respectful to King Darius and earned his favor.

Add a prepositional phrase to expand the sentence.

10. I read my Bible. _____

Underline each simple subject once and each simple predicate twice.

11. Daniel's coworkers disliked Daniel and made a plan of revenge.

12. His coworkers dishonestly influenced the king.

Write a compound sentence using a comma and a conjunction.

13. Daniel understood the new law. He still remained faithful to God.

_____

_____

14. The coworkers saw Daniel praying. They went and told the king.

_____

_____

Use ⌃ to add commas where they are needed.

15. The king liked Daniel but he could not go against his royal decree.

16. Down in the dark lion's den Daniel trusted God.

17. God protected Daniel and Daniel came out of the den alive.

Rewrite the phrase using a possessive noun.

18. a multi-colored coat belonging to Joseph _____

19. the ark of Noah _____

20. the sacrifices of the priests _____

21. the altars of the Israelites _____

Mark the sentence that is true.

22. ○ A thesaurus helps the user find all the definitions and pronunciations of words.

    ○ A thesaurus helps the user find the most appropriate words.

23. ○ An antonym is a word that means the opposite of another word.

    ○ An antonym is a word that means the same as another word.

Match the phrase with the correct term.

_____ 24. Improving your writing

_____ 25. Finding and correcting mistakes in your writing

_____ 26. Getting ready to write

_____ 27. Writing your ideas in sentences

_____ 28. Sharing your writing with someone

A planning
B drafting
C revising
D proofreading
E publishing

Write the plural form of the singular noun.

29. candy _____   32. tornado _____

30. loaf _____   33. box _____

31. watch _____   34. goose _____

4

Verbs

What makes each person unique?

Mentor Text

Excerpt from *Mistakes That Worked: The World's Familiar Inventions and How They Came to Be* by Charlotte Foltz Jones

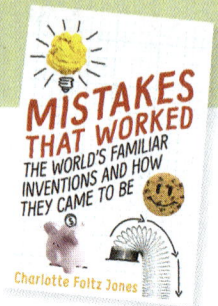

Levi's Jeans

The invention of men's pants was certainly no accident.

And Levi Strauss's success at making what we now know as blue jeans was no accident either.

However, Levi Strauss did not leave New York in 1853 hoping to become the biggest and most successful blue jeans manufacturer in the world. He didn't even intend to manufacture blue jeans.

Levi Strauss went to San Francisco in 1853 intending to sell dry goods. The California Gold Rush of 1849 had attracted thousands of prospectors, and Levi planned to sell canvas for tents and Conestoga wagon covers. But as Levi talked to the prospectors, they told him, "Shoulda brought pants. Pants don't wear worth a hoot in the diggin's!" So Levi had a tailor make some pants from his brown canvas. Word quickly spread about the quality of "those pants of Levi's," or simply "Levi's jeans."

When his supply of canvas was gone, Levi switched to another sturdy fabric, made in Nîmes, France. It was called *serge de Nîmes* (now known as denim). Levi improved his pants—changing the color to a deep blue and adding arcuate (arched) stitching and rivets to the pockets to prevent the weight of the gold nuggets from ripping them.

Levi Strauss's pants are still worn all over the world, and in 1976, a pair of Levi's jeans were put on display at the Smithsonian Institution in Washington, DC, as part of the permanent collections in the National Museum of American History.

Fun Facts about Jeans!

Why do we call them jeans? "Gene" was a form of the word "Genoese," meaning "from Genoa, Italy." In the late 1500s, sailors' pants were made of a cotton twill fabric made in Genoa. Those pants were often called genes, which was later changed to jeans.

The average American college student owns five to six pairs of jeans.

Each year, 1.2 billion pairs of jeans are sold around the world.

Verb Tenses

A **verb** tells what the subject is or does.

A **present-tense verb** tells about something that is happening now or is continuing to occur.

> *The textile company constructs a new building.*

A **past-tense verb** tells about what has already happened.

> *The textile company constructed a new building.*

A **future-tense verb** tells about a time in the future. The helping verb *will* is used to form future-tense verbs.

> *The textile company will construct a new building.*

AfterSchoolHelp

Verb Tense

constructs

will construct

constructed

Underline the simple subject once and the verb twice. Write *present*, *past*, **or** *future* **to identify the verb tense.**

_____ 1. For centuries textiles helped people live normal lives.

_____ 2. Everyone needs clothing and household fabrics.

_____ 3. Textiles will fill many needs in years to come.

_____ 4. Most ancient people colored fabrics with natural dye.

_____ 5. The indigo plant is a natural dye.

Wild indigo

Write a sentence about something that is happening now. Use a present-tense verb.

6. _____

_____

Write a sentence about something that happened last week. Use a past-tense verb.

7. _____

_____

Write about something that will happen next week. Use a future-tense verb.

8. _____

_____

Underline the simple subject once and the verb twice.
Write *present*, *past*, or *future* to identify the verb tense.

> Look for the verb first. Ask *who* or *what* to find the simple subject.

_____ 9. Scientists found linen, cotton, silk, and wool in old ruins.

_____ 10. First, scholars examine the material fragments.

_____ 11. Next, they determine the types of fibers.

_____ 12. The style of the thread will show the origin of the fabric.

_____ 13. Scholars learned many facts about ancient weaving practices.

_____ 14. Unusual weaving instruments provide another means of identification.

_____ 15. They discovered specific weaving methods for wool.

_____ 16. The type of wool will tell the scientists about the time and place when the fabric was created.

Ancient weaving method

Subject-Verb Agreement

A **singular subject** requires a **singular verb**. In the present tense, a singular verb usually ends in *-s* or *-es*.

> The *mill makes* cotton cloth.
> A *truck carries* fabric to the factory.

A **plural subject** and the pronouns *I* and *you* require a plural form of a verb. Most plural verbs do not end in *-s* or *-es*.

> The *mills make* cotton cloth.
> *Trucks carry* fabric to the factories.
> *You make* gifts from cotton cloth.
> *I choose* fabric for our next project.

A **compound subject** joined by *and* uses the **plural form of a verb**.

> The *worker and the manager attend* the meeting.

When a **compound subject** is joined by *or*, the **verb form** agrees with the subject closer to it.

> The *manager or the workers attend* the meeting.
> The *workers or the manager attends* the meeting.

> The verb in a sentence must **agree** with subject of the sentence.

Mark the sentence that is written correctly.

1. ○ Electricity run the machine.
   ○ Electricity runs the machine.

2. ○ Textile factories produce many types of fabrics.
   ○ Textile factories produces many types of fabrics.

Underline the simple subject once. Write the correct present-tense verb to complete the sentence.

3. Textile mills _____ fabric for many uses.
   _{manufacture}

4. The mechanic _____ the broken machinery.
   _{fix}

5. The designer and I _____ patterns and colors.
   _{select}

6. The manufacturers or the purchaser _____ the fabrics
   _{choose}
   for furniture.

AfterSchoolHelp

Present-Tense Verbs

Think of products that are made from textiles. Write one sentence about a textile product, using a singular subject and a present-tense verb.

7. _____

_____

Think of another textile product. Write one sentence using a plural subject and a present-tense verb.

8. _____

_____

Mark the sentence that is written correctly.

9. ○ The factory or the stores sells the textiles.

○ The factory or the stores sell the textiles.

10. ○ The couch and the chairs need reupholstering.

○ The couch and the chairs needs reupholstering.

11. ○ My parents and I purchase a new recliner.

○ My parents and I purchases a new recliner.

12. ○ The workers or the salesman carries the chair to our van.

○ The workers or the salesman carry the chair to our van.

Underline the simple subject once. Write the correct present-tense verb to complete the sentence.

13. Mr. and Mrs. Brown _____ a furniture store.

own

14. Mr. Brown or Mrs. Brown _____ each customer.

help

15. The store _____ furniture and rugs.

sell

16. Multicolored yarns _____ together in this beautiful rug.

blend

17. The Browns _____ more chairs from a factory.

order

18. An upholsterer _____ the chairs with fabric.

cover

19. Then a dock worker _____ the new chairs onto trucks.

load

Consistent Verb Tenses

The tense of the verb tells when the action is happening. You should avoid changes in verb tenses that could be confusing to the reader.

Maria **plays** *soccer. Her team* ~~*practiced*~~ *practices every day after school. They* **work** *hard to get ready for each game.*

Mark the correct verb form to complete the sentence.

1. This morning my class learned about tapestry. In the Middle Ages, weavers _____ colorful tapestries on the loom.

   ○ make   ○ made

2. Large, beautiful tapestries hung on the walls of castles and palaces. Small tapestries _____ furniture.

   ○ cover   ○ covered

3. Today, museums _____ tapestries from the Middle Ages. Visitors can see them on display.

   ○ preserve   ○ preserved

The following paragraph should be written in present tense. Circle the three incorrect verbs in the paragraph. Write the correct verb form to improve the paragraph.

The ermine is a small animal with several names. People called it the ermine, the stoat, or the short-tailed weasel. This animal lives in the cold northern parts of Europe, North America, and Asia. Ermine fur is brown in the summer, but it turned white in the winter. White ermine fur are a symbol for wealth, royalty, and purity.

4. _____

5. _____

6. _____

Ermine

Write several sentences about a castle. Use consistent verb tenses.

7. _____

_____

_____

_____

Mark the correct verb form to complete the sentence.

8. George V built the Marienburg Castle in 1867. It ____ a gift for his wife, Queen Marie. Conrad Wilhelm designed the castle for them.

   ○ is   ○ was

9. George and Marie fled the country when a war began. Their children ____ eighty years later and opened the castle to visitors.

   ○ returns   ○ returned

10. The castle still stands in Lower Saxony, Germany. Many tourists ____ there every year.

   ○ travel   ○ traveled

The following paragraph should be written in past tense. Circle the three incorrect verbs in the paragraph. Write the correct verb form to improve the paragraph.

Caden and Mila visited the castle last year. Mila enjoys the guided tour. The tour guide wears a historical costume. Caden and his dad climb the stairs to the top of the tower. The view from the top was beautiful.

11. _____

12. _____

13. _____

Marienburg Castle

Irregular Verbs

Verbs that change spelling and do not add -ed in the past tense are **irregular verbs**.

The helping verbs *have*, *has*, and *had* are used with a verb form called the **past participle**. Irregular verbs often change spelling in the past participle form.

	Present Tense	Past Tense	Past Participle
catch	catch, catches	caught	caught
come	come, comes	came	come
do	do, does	did	done
eat	eat, eats	ate	eaten
fall	fall, falls	fell	fallen
find	find, finds	found	found
give	give, gives	gave	given
go	go, goes	went	gone
ride	ride, rides	rode	ridden
run	run, runs	ran	run
say	say, says	said	said
see	see, sees	saw	seen
take	take, takes	took	taken
think	think, thinks	thought	thought
wear	wear, wears	wore	worn
write	write, writes	wrote	written

Mark the sentence that is written correctly.

1. ○ Francis Cabot Lowell finded a place for his new mill.
   ○ Francis Cabot Lowell found a place for his new mill.

2. ○ He had come with a design for a new weaving loom.
   ○ He had came with a design for a new weaving loom.

3. ○ Amazed people had saw the speed of his new machine.
   ○ Amazed people had seen the speed of his new machine.

4. ○ Lowell had thought he could change the way factories operated.
   ○ Lowell had thinked he could change the way factories operated.

AfterSchoolHelp

Irregular Verbs

Choose a verb from the chart. Use the past-tense form in a sentence.

5. _____

_____

Choose another verb from the chart. Use the past-participle form in a sentence.

6. _____

_____

Mark the sentence that is written correctly.

7. ◯ Soon many young girls had come to the factory for work.
   ◯ Soon many young girls comed to the factory for work.

8. ◯ These girls had ran all the machinery in the factory.
   ◯ These girls ran all the machinery in the factory.

9. ◯ The workers finded factory life hard.
   ◯ The workers found factory life hard.

10. ◯ The factory had given the "mill girls" rooms in a boarding house.
    ◯ The factory had gave the "mill girls" rooms in a boarding house.

11. ◯ The girls eaten and stayed at the boarding house at least one year.
    ◯ The girls ate and stayed at the boarding house at least one year.

12. ◯ Most of the girls thought the work hours were too long.
    ◯ Most of the girls had thinked the work hours were too long.

13. ◯ Some girls caught lung diseases from poor working conditions.
    ◯ Some girls catched lung diseases from poor working conditions.

14. ◯ They written letters about changes in factory conditions.
    ◯ They wrote letters about changes in factory conditions.

15. ◯ More people saw the hardships of factory life.
    ◯ More people seen the hardships of factory life.

16. ◯ Child labor laws done change slowly.
    ◯ Child labor laws did change slowly.

More Irregular Verbs

AfterSchoolHelp

Irregular Verbs

Verbs that do not add -ed when changed to the past tense are called **irregular verbs**.

The helping verbs *have*, *has*, and *had* are used with a verb form called the **past participle**. Irregular verbs often change spelling in the past-participle form.

Verb	Present Tense	Past Tense	Past Participle
begin	begin, begins	began	begun
blow	blow, blows	blew	blown
break	break, breaks	broke	broken
choose	choose, chooses	chose	chosen
fly	fly, flies	flew	flown
freeze	freeze, freezes	froze	frozen
grow	grow, grows	grew	grown
know	know, knows	knew	known
ring	ring, rings	rang	rung
sing	sing, sings	sang	sung
speak	speak, speaks	spoke	spoken
steal	steal, steals	stole	stolen
swim	swim, swims	swam	swum
tear	tear, tears	tore	torn

Mark the sentence that is written correctly.

1. ○ The American Thread Company began in 1898.
   ○ The American Thread Company had began in 1898.

2. ○ Many people do not know that Velcro was invented at this company.
   ○ Many people do not knowed that Velcro was invented at this company.

3. ○ Thomas Edison chosen the American Thread Company as the first factory to place his new invention of electric lighting.
   ○ Thomas Edison chose the American Thread Company as the first factory to place his new invention of electric lighting.

4. ○ People speaked highly of this company for years.
   ○ People spoke highly of this company for years.

Choose a verb from the chart. Use the past-tense form in a sentence.

5. _____

_____

Choose another verb from the chart. Use the past-participle form in a sentence.

6. _____

_____

Mark the sentence that is written correctly.

7. ○ Work at the mill had grown harder over the years.
   ○ Work at the mill grown harder over the years.

8. ○ Dust blown around the workers constantly.
   ○ Dust blew around the workers constantly.

9. ○ Children had knew the hardships of long hours of work.
   ○ Children knew the hardships of long hours of work.

10. ○ Workers spoke out about the abuses of the company and went on strike.
    ○ Workers speaked out about the abuses of the company and went on strike.

11. ○ Many people had chosen to strike for improved working conditions.
    ○ Many people had chose to strike for improved working conditions.

12. ○ In the summer of 1925, some workers live in tents.
    ○ In the summer of 1925, some workers lived in tents.

13. ○ The company had breaked up a strike.
    ○ The company had broken up a strike.

14. ○ In 1985 the company chose relocation.
    ○ In 1985 the company had chose relocation.

15. ○ The old mill buildings were later occupied as offices.
    ○ The old mill buildings were later occupy as offices.

Mixing Verb Tenses

Sometimes a change in verb tenses is necessary to show the order of events, a shift in time, or conditions for something to happen.

William borrowed a book from Xavier. Xavier has read the book already.

William will return the book when he finishes with it.

Mark the correct verb form to complete the sentence.

1. Our class learned that a silkworm _____ a type of caterpillar.
   - ○ is
   - ○ was

2. Chinese people have produced silk for thousands of years. Legend says that an emperor's wife _____ silk and taught others about it.
   - ○ discovers
   - ○ discovered

3. A female silk moth lays hundreds of eggs before she _____.
   - ○ dies
   - ○ died

4. The silkworm spins a cocoon from one long fiber. Workers _____ the cocoon to get the fibers.
   - ○ unraveled
   - ○ unravel

5. The workers clean and _____ the fibers into thread. Then they dye the thread. After the thread dries, the workers weave it into beautiful silk fabric.
   - ○ spin
   - ○ will spin

6. The silk-making process _____ a secret for many years. Now silk is made in many countries.
   - ○ is
   - ○ was

Mark the correct verb form to complete the sentence.

7. The Silk Road is a name for a system of trade routes between China and the Middle East. Traders _____ along these routes in ancient times.
   - ○ travel
   - ○ traveled

8. Middle Eastern and European people bought silk, paper, and gunpowder from China. Historians _____ these inventions today.
   - ○ study
   - ○ studied

9. Silk has been a symbol of royalty and wealth in some societies. In some places, common people _____ not allowed to wear silk.
   - ○ were
   - ○ will be

10. Archeologists _____ silk while they were visiting the burial sites of ancient Egyptian kings.
    - ○ have found
    - ○ has found

11. Silk production _____ to Europe after the Crusades, and weavers in Italy and France sold their silk to other countries.
    - ○ comes
    - ○ came

12. After the Industrial Revolution, many factories _____ cotton fabric. Silk became too expensive for most people.
    - ○ produce
    - ○ produced

13. Polyester and nylon are imitation silk fabrics. Silk _____ still an expensive fabric today.
    - ○ is
    - ○ was

14. The Bible _____ silk in several places. The woman in Proverbs 31 uses silk to make clothes.
    - ○ mentions
    - ○ will mention

Practice

Write the correct progressive form of the verb to complete the sentence.

1. Noah and his family _____ in the ark for one year. **past**
   float

2. The rain _____ for forty days. **past**
   fall

3. Today, many creation scientists _____ evidence for Noah's flood. **present**
   find

4. We _____ some of the evidence at the museum. **future**
   see

Write a sentence about an animal you might see on Noah's ark. Use a past progressive verb in your sentence.

5. _____

_____

Mark the sentence that is written correctly.

6. ○ The animals ate the food Noah had stored on the ark.
   ○ The animals eaten the food Noah had stored on the ark.

7. ○ A dove flown out of the ark to look for dry land.
   ○ A dove flew out of the ark to look for dry land.

8. ○ We have saw the faith of Noah through the Bible story.
   ○ We have seen the faith of Noah through the Bible story.

9. ○ We can know that the promises of God are true.
   ○ We can known that the promises of God are true.

Write a sentence with the verb *give*. Use the past-tense form in a sentence.

10. _____

_____

Write a sentence with the verb *choose*. Use the past-participle form in a sentence.

11. _____

_____

Label the underlined verb *present perfect*, *past perfect*, or *future perfect*.

_____ 12. The Bible <u>has recorded</u> the fact that Noah took all the animals God commanded.

_____ 13. By the time you leave the Ark Encounter, you <u>will have learned</u> many things about God's Word.

_____ 14. Researchers <u>have estimated</u> around 7,000 animals were on the Ark.

_____ 15. With God's instruction, Noah <u>had planned</u> enough space for his family, all the animals, and all their supplies.

Write a sentence in the present-perfect tense using the verb *speak*.

16. _____

_____

Write a sentence in the past-perfect tense using the verb *go*.

17. _____

_____

Mark the correct verb form to complete the sentence.

18. Noah's wife traveled with him in the ark. She might ____ Noah to care for all those animals.

    ◯ have helped   ◯ has helped

19. Even though Noah was quite old, God ____ Noah and his wife with three sons: Shem, Ham, and Japheth.

    ◯ blesses   ◯ blessed

20. Through Noah's sons, God ____ the earth after the Flood.

    ◯ has repopulated   ◯ repopulated

21. Scientists estimate that by 2050, the world population ____ over 9 billion.

    ◯ will have reached   ◯ had reached

Chapter 4 Review

Underline the simple subject once and the complete verb twice. Write *present*, *past*, or *future* to identify the verb tense.

_____ 1. During the Middle Ages, many English people raised sheep.

_____ 2. English farmers sold their wool to weavers in Flanders, a place in Belgium.

_____ 3. Several wars and high taxes hurt the English wool trade.

_____ 4. Today, Spain dominates the world's trade in wool.

_____ 5. We will learn more about the Hundred Years' War in our history class.

Mark the sentence that is written correctly.

6. ○ Merino sheep come from Spain.
   ○ Merino sheep comes from Spain.

7. ○ Their wool are very soft.
   ○ Their wool is very soft.

8. ○ The farmer or his son shears the sheep once a year.
   ○ The farmer or his son shear the sheep once a year.

Underline the simple subject once and the correct helping verb twice.

9. That Merino sheep (does, do) have horns.

10. The craft store (has, have) advertised some yarn made from Merino wool.

11. Today, Merino sheep (is, are) raised in Spain, Australia, New Zealand, and the United States.

12. One breed (was, were) developed in Vermont.

Choose a helping verb from the word bank and use it in a sentence.

| am   has   is   might   should |

13. _____

    _____

Write the correct progressive form of the verb to complete the sentence.

14. We _____ to see my grandparents this summer. **present**
    go

15. Grandpa _____ me about the Industrial Revolution. **past**
    tell

16. We _____ a museum together. **future**
    visit

Mark the sentence that is written correctly.

17. ○ Grandpa knows a lot about American history.
    ○ Grandpa known a lot about American history.

18. ○ I found a newspaper article about an old mill in my town.
    ○ I have find a newspaper article about an old mill in my town.

19. ○ I will taken the article with me the next time I visit them.
    ○ I will take the article with me the next time I visit them.

Label the underlined verb *present perfect*, *past perfect*, or *future perfect*.

_____ 20. My family has planned a trip to New Zealand next year.

_____ 21. My brother will have graduated from high school by that time.

_____ 22. Dad's family had lived in New Zealand for many years.

Mark the correct verb form to complete the sentence.

23. Emily and Edward live on a sheep farm. My class ____ them this week.
    ○ has visits   ○ has visited

24. Their family has just purchased a new dog. The dog ____ with the sheep.
    ○ help   ○ will help

Journal

Think of a writer whose work you enjoy or admire. What can you tell about the writer's personality based on his or her writing?

_____

_____

_____

_____

_____

_____

_____

_____

_____

_____

Cumulative Review

Put parentheses around each prepositional phrase.

1. The book of Exodus begins a couple hundred years after Joseph.

2. Under new leadership Jacob's descendants have increased greatly in number.

3. Our teacher told us the story of Moses from the Bible.

Write *S* if the group of words is a sentence. Write *F* if the group of words is a fragment.

_____ 4. In an attempt to destroy the Israelites.

_____ 5. Pharoah forced them into slavery.

_____ 6. Commanded all Hebrew boys to be killed.

_____ 7. Jochebed defied Pharoah's command.

_____ 8. Hid her baby in a basket in the bulrushes.

Choose a fragment from the previous exercise and rewrite it as a complete sentence.

9. _____

_____

Write the plural form of the singular noun.

10. chimney _____ 14. echo _____

11. piano _____ 15. mailbox _____

12. calf _____ 16. sheep _____

13. berry _____ 17. monkey _____

Use ▤ to mark letters that should be capitalized.

18. The fifth-grade class at liberty academy studied astronomy.

19. Our science teacher, mr. adams, read the book *the stars speak*.

20. We learned that the milky way has a constellation known as the little dipper.

Underline the simple subject once. Write the correct past-tense verb to complete the sentence.

21. Near Sinai Moses _____ a priest named Jethro.
    meet

22. God _____ to Moses out of the burning bush.
    speak

23. In obedience to God's command, Moses and Aaron _____ to Egypt.
    return

24. Pharaoh _____ he could catch up with the Israelites.
    think

25. He _____ his chariot into the sea and drowned.
    ride

Mark the correct verb form to complete the sentence.

26. When Moses asks God what His name is, God ____, "I AM THAT I AM."
    ○ replies   ○ replied

27. Moses confronted Pharoah in the royal palace. He ____ the release of the Israelites.
    ○ demands   ○ demanded

Underline the simple subject once and the correct helping verb twice.

28. Pharoah (is, are) not impressed with Moses' miracle, turning his staff into a snake.

29. Ten plagues (was, were) sent to punish Pharaoh.

30. Pharoah (do, does) give in and release the Israelites.

31. God (has, have) given Moses and the Israelites the victory.

Label the underlined verb *present perfect, past perfect,* or *future perfect.*

_____ 32. Moses <u>had doubted</u> his ability to confront Pharoah.

_____ 33. God <u>has continued</u> to test Moses' obedience.

Write a sentence about a lesson Moses learned using a perfect-tense verb.

34. _____

    _____

5

Writing a Book Review

Why might an opinion be wrong?

Mentor Text

**Excerpt from *The Wheel on the School*
by Meindert DeJong**

"Janus, did you read what it said in the paper?" Lina asked at last. Her voice quavered.

Then Janus blew up. "Read it? Sure, I read it—read it so many times I know it by heart. But don't you kids stand there and tell me that you took that silly scribbling to heart! There he sits, that inky printer in a cellar somewhere in Amsterdam; buildings all around so high he can't even see as much as a square foot of sky. He and his inky fingers in his cellar!"

Janus drew indignant breath. "Why, I'll bet you he couldn't even tell a stork from a rooster. Storks don't settle in cities. But he knows! Even knows that all the storks drowned in the sea. Was he out in a boat in the storm? Did he see them fall in the sea? Did he see stork bodies wash up against the dike?

"No, he didn't!" Janus fiercely answered himself. "He had a pailful of ink to get rid of, and he had to fill his paper with words. There was a little blank spot he still had to fill, so he put something about storks in that left-over space. Anything he could think up. 'It is thought. It is feared. It is estimated!'" he quoted derisively from the newspaper.

"Who thinks it? Who fears it? The printer! Words! All fancy words to worry kids in Shora with!" . . .

"Look, those storks make that trip twice a year. Look, if that printer came out of his cellar and went to sea in a boat in a storm, he'd go down before he got ten feet from the dike. But your fathers don't go down, do they? They bring a boat through—they know about storms. Well, so do storks! Sure, a few may go down, but those storks just don't fold their wings and let themselves be dumped in the sea to become fish bait. They're too smart to let themselves be caught over water in a storm. They knew in their bones, long before the storm fell, that a storm was coming. And they didn't have to read about it in any printer's silly newspaper!"

Persuasive Writing

Persuasive writing convinces the audience to do something or to agree with the writer's opinion.

| The **opinion** should be supported by reasons.

| The reasons should be supported by facts and examples.

Opinion: *I think the school principal should allow us to have a pep rally on the day of our soccer game.*

Reason: *It would promote school spirit.*

Fact or Example: *More students wear the school colors on days that we have pep rallies.*

Reason: *It would encourage the soccer team.*

Fact or Example: *The soccer coach said that his team played better after last year's pep rally.*

Read each of the following reasons for asking Uncle Jim to build a fence around your family's yard. Choose the fact or example that best supports each reason.

1. Uncle Jim builds tall, sturdy fences.

   Fact or Example: _____

2. Uncle Jim's prices are reasonable.

   Fact or Example: _____

Facts and Examples

A Uncle Jim charges the lowest price for the same job of any builder in town.

B Grandma's German shepherd has not escaped from her yard since Uncle Jim built her new fence.

Read each of the following reasons for voting for Kaitlyn in the school election. Choose the fact or example that best supports each reason.

3. Kaitlyn is a good student.

   Fact or Example:_____

4. Kaitlyn cares about our class.

   Fact or Example: _____

5. Kaitlyn is a hard worker.

   Fact or Example: _____

6. Kaitlyn has good speaking skills.

   Fact or Example: _____

7. Kaitlyn is a Christlike example.

   Fact or Example: _____

Facts and Examples

A She has participated in every class fundraiser since first grade.

B She works with her father on weekends cleaning the school buildings, and she also helps with the housework at home.

C She is kind to the other students, obedient to the teachers, and honest in her work.

D She has had speaking parts in plays, and she was chosen to recite a poem at the spring program.

E She diligently does her best in her schoolwork.

Choose an opinion and write two reasons that support it.

Our neighborhood should have a safety program.
You should participate in the church Christmas program.

8. _____

   _____

   _____

   _____

   _____

   _____

Parts of a Book Review

The writer of a **book review** describes a book and tries to persuade the audience to agree with his opinion about it.

In the **introduction**, the writer engages the reader and gives the title and author of the book.

The writer provides a **summary** of the book's main events without giving away the ending.

The writer states his **opinion** about the book, gives **reasons** for the opinion, and includes **details** from the book that support the reasons.

In the **conclusion**, the writer gives a recommendation to the reader.

Wonder, Water, and Wheels

Why would someone put a wheel on a school? You can find the answer to this question in *The Wheel on the School* by Meindert DeJong.

After Lina writes a story about storks, the schoolchildren begin to wonder why no storks live in their fishing village. With encouragement from their teacher, they form a plan to bring storks to Shora. The children scatter in all directions to search for a wagon wheel, and soon their dream seems possible. But then a great storm threatens to make it impossible again. You will have to read the book to find out if storks come to Shora.

Although I felt upset that Janus seemed so mean at first, this book has become one of my favorites. One reason is the fascinating setting. The story takes place by the sea in Holland, and the people ride in wagons and wear wooden shoes. Another reason is that the exciting plot gripped my attention. In one part of the story, Lina and Douwa race against time as the tide rushes toward them. Most important, I like the way that characters of all ages help solve problems in the book. The older characters Grandmother Sibble, Janus, and Douwa work with the children, share wisdom and laughter with them, and become their friends.

I would highly recommend this book to anyone who likes nature, interesting personalities, or lots of action. Reading this book will make you think about how each person is important.

Transitional words and phrases connect a writer's ideas. They can be used to show where one reason ends and another reason begins.

Transitional Words and Phrases

1. First of all, . . .
2. One thing I like is that . . .
3. One thing that bothers me is that . . .
4. One reason is that . . .
5. I also think . . .
6. Second, . . .
7. Another reason is that . . .
8. Another problem is that . . .
9. Finally, . . .
10. Most important, . . .

Underline the topic sentence of the following opinion paragraph twice and the detail sentences (reasons and supporting details) once. Choose appropriate transitional words or phrases for the paragraph from the box above. Insert their numbers in the paragraph where you feel they are needed.

Although *The Path to Pine Lake* by Harriet Isaac had a good message at the end, I found many problems with this book. The characters are too concerned about money. They are always getting into arguments over how they should raise the money for a week of camp at Pine Lake. The author does not tell the story in an interesting way. There is a lot of conversation between characters but not much action. Adding more action to the story would make it move faster. The ending left me disappointed. I wanted to read about the week at camp, but the book ends right before the characters go to camp.

Where does one reason end and the next reason begin?

Evaluating a Book

A book review may be a mixture of positive and negative opinions. To help form an overall opinion of a book, ask yourself whether you would recommend the book to others.

Check off the questions that help you evaluate the book you have chosen to review.

Characters

- ☐ Do they seem like real people?
- ☐ Is there one who does something heroic?
- ☐ Is there one who makes a good decision?
- ☐ Did you feel sorry for any of the characters?

Setting

- ☐ Did you like the time period of the book?
- ☐ Did the place where the events happened interest you?
- ☐ When you read the book, did you feel as if you were there, in that place and time?

Plot

- ☐ Does the plot have some exciting parts?
- ☐ Does the plot have some funny parts?
- ☐ Does the plot have some sad parts?
- ☐ Does the plot have some happy parts?
- ☐ Does the plot have enough action?
- ☐ Have you ever had a problem like the one in the story?
- ☐ Do you think the characters solve their problem in a good way?
- ☐ Do you like the way the book ends?

Think about It

- ☐ Did the book teach you anything new about God?
- ☐ Did the book teach you anything new about yourself?
- ☐ Did the book remind you of an important truth from God's Word?
- ☐ Did the book help you think of something you could do to please God?
- ☐ Does the book make something false look true?

Would you recommend the book to someone else?

Complete the T-Chart to help you form an overall opinion of the book you have chosen. Write your opinion at the bottom of the chart.

Title of the Book: _____

What I Liked	**What I Didn't Like**

My Opinion: _____

_____

Book Review: Plan

Organize ideas for the book review in a planning chart.

Title of the Book: _The Wheel on the School_

Author of the Book: _Meindert DeJong_

Introduction

Question: Why would you put a wheel on a school?

Main Events (Summary)

Children wonder why storks don't live in their village

Make a plan to bring storks to Shora, teacher encourages

Many land and water adventures as they look for a wagon wheel

Climax—_A great storm might keep the storks away_

My Opinion of the Book

This book is one of my favorites.

Reasons	Supporting Details
Interesting setting	Holland by the sea, wagons, and wooden shoes
Exciting plot	Lina, Douwa race against time as tide comes in
Characters of all ages help solve problems	Older characters share wisdom with kids, become friends

Conclusion (Recommendation)

I would recommend this book to anyone who likes nature, interesting personalities, or lots of action.

Use the chart to plan a review of the book you have read. Be sure to include at least three reasons for your opinion and support each reason with a detail from the book.

Introduction

Main Events (Summary)

Climax—

My Opinion of the Book

Reasons	Supporting Details

Conclusion (Recommendation)

Book Review: Draft

A good beginning can capture the reader's attention.

| Ask a question to stir up the reader's curiosity.

> *Why would a dog be given a medal of honor at a special ceremony in a small town? The exciting story is found in the book* A Dog Named Watson *by Terri Bledsoe.*

| Make an intriguing statement to raise the reader's interest.

> *When Phoebe Chipp agrees to help her cousin hold a bake sale in their neighborhood, she has no idea what she is getting into!* Cookie Crumbs *by Ginger S. Napp will keep you laughing from cover to cover.*

A writer who likes a book ends by giving a recommendation to the reader. Sometimes the writer of a review may not encourage others to read the book.

> *Although the book has some good points, it is not very well written, and the characters do not solve their problem in an honest way. In my opinion, the book is not worth spending the time to read.*

Use the ideas from your planning chart to draft your book review. Follow the drafting guide, checking off the parts of the book review as you write.

Drafting Guide			
Introduction	Begin the review in an interesting way.		
	Give the title and author of the book.		
	State or hint at your opinion near the beginning of the review.		
Summary Paragraph	Summarize the main events of the book up to the climax (the most exciting part of the story).		
	Do not give away the ending.		
Opinion Paragraph	Opinion	Write a sentence stating your opinion about the book.	
	Reasons	Include at least three reasons for your opinion. Use transitional words and phrases to keep the reasons separate from one another.	
	Supporting details	Include details from the book to support each reason.	
Conclusion	Would you recommend the book to the reader?		

Book Review: Revise

Revise your book review. Use your writing tools and skills to make improvements.

Wonder, Water and Wheels

Why would someone put a wheel on a school? You can find the answer to this question in The Wheel on the School by Meindert DeJong.

After Lina writes a story about storks, the schoolchildren begin to wonder why no storks live in With encouragement from their teacher, *their fishing village. They form a plan to bring storks to Shora. The children scatters in all directions to search for a wagon wheel.* ,and *Soon their dream seems possible. But then a great storm threatens to make it impossible again. You will have to read the book to find out if storks come to shora.*

Although I felt upset that Janus seemed so mean at first, this book has become one of my favorites. One fascinating *reason is the ~~interesting~~ setting. The story takes place by the sea in Holland, and the people ride in wagons and* Another reason is that *wear wooden shoes.* gripped *The exciting plot ~~held~~ my attention. In one part of the story, Lina and Douwa race against*

> An added detail makes the summary clearer.

> Some sentences can be combined.

> The writer looked in a thesaurus for the best words to express his ideas.

> This transitional phrase separates the second reason from the first one.

Continued

time as the tide rushes toward them. Most important, I like the way that characters of all ages help solve problems in the book. The older characters grandmother Sibble, Janus, and Douwa work with the children. They share wisdom and and *laughter with them. They become their friends.*

I would highly recomend this book to anyone who likes nature, interesting personalities, or lots of action. You will learn whether a shark actually bit off Janus's legs. Reading this book will make you think about how each person is important.

> This sentence does not belong.

Use the following checklist as you revise your book review.

Revising Checklist	
My book review begins in an interesting way.	
My book review summarizes the main events of the plot up to the climax, or most exciting part.	
I included details about the characters and setting.	
I stated my opinion clearly.	
I gave three good reasons for my opinion.	
I included details from the book to support each reason.	
I used interesting words and included transitional words and phrases.	
My book review closes with a recommendation to the reader.	

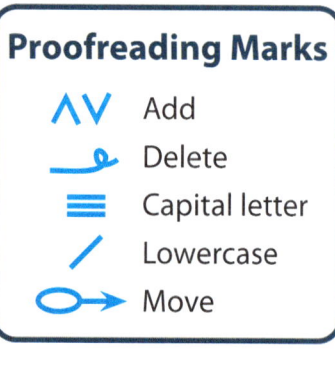

Proofreading Marks

∧∨ Add
⟶ℯ Delete
≡ Capital letter
/ Lowercase
⟶ Move

Book Review: Proofread

Proofread your book review.

Read it through several times, looking for only one or two types of mistakes each time.

Correct the mistakes you find.

Wonder, Water and Wheels

Why would someone put a wheel on a school? You can find the answer to this question in The Wheel on the School *by Meindert DeJong.*

After Lina writes a story about storks, the schoolchildren begin to wonder why no storks live in their fishing village. With encouragement from their teacher, they form a plan to bring storks to Shora. The children scatter *~~scatters~~ in all directions to search for a wagon wheel, and soon their dream seems possible. But then a great storm threatens to make it impossible again. You will have to read the book to find out if storks come to shora.*

Although I felt upset that Janus seemed so mean at first, this book has become one of my favorites. One reason is the fascinating setting. The story takes place by the sea in Holland, and the people ride in wagons and wear wooden shoes. Another reason is that the exciting plot gripped my attention. In one part of the story, Lina and Douwa race

Continued

against time as the tide rushes toward them. Most important,

I like the way that characters of all ages help solve problems

in the book. The older characters grandmother Sibble, Janus,

and Douwa work with the children share wisdom and laughter

with them and become their friends.

recommend
I would highly ~~recomend~~ this book to anyone who likes

nature, interesting personalities, or lots of action. Reading this

book will make you think about how each person is important.

Use the following checklist as you proofread your book review.

Proofreading Checklist

I wrote the title of my book review correctly.
I indented the first line of each paragraph.
I began each sentence with a capital letter and ended it with a punctuation mark.
I used correct punctuation within sentences.
I used correct verb forms.
I wrote proper nouns correctly.
I corrected misspelled words.

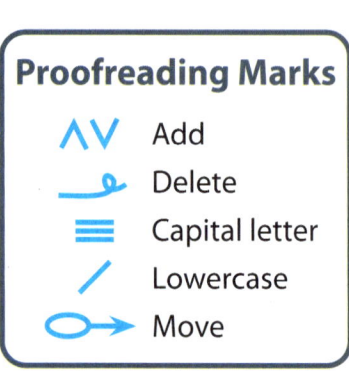

Proofreading Marks

∧∨ Add
 ↄ Delete
 ≡ Capital letter
 / Lowercase
⟿ Move

Speaking: Presenting Your Book Review

A **visual aid** is anything a speaker shows during a presentation that helps the audience understand or picture what he is saying.

book bag containing objects related to the presentation

picture, chart, or diagram

digital slideshow

Many people find it easier to listen to and concentrate on a speaker's words when they have something to look at while he speaks.

Tips for Using Visual Aids
Make sure each member of your audience can see your visual aid.
Most visual aids should be large enough for the audience to see comfortably from their seats.
If you are holding the visual aid, hold it at a height that makes it visible to everyone.
If your visual aid is small, you may need to pass it around the room.
Explain how the visual aid relates to your topic.
Displaying a visual aid without referring to it in your presentation causes confusion for your listeners.
Be sure to point out specific features of your visual aid as you discuss them.
Display the visual aid only when you are actually talking about it.
Put your visual aid away when you are finished discussing it. Continuing to display the visual aid while you talk about something else distracts your audience.

Reread the tips for using visual aids, thinking about your own book review. Make some notes about how and when you plan to display your visual aid during your presentation.

_____

_____

_____

_____

Good speaking is a skill that takes practice. Follow these tips to help make your presentation a success.

Tips for Good Speaking	
Prepare well.	Plan ahead what you will say and how you will say it. Good preparation will help you stay calm and speak better.
Use expression.	Use your voice, face, hands, and body movements to capture and hold the interest of your audience.
Look at your audience.	Do not stare at one person, but try to look each person in the eye at least once or twice while you speak.
Speak clearly.	Enunciate your words clearly so that everyone can understand you.
Speak with good volume.	You do not need to shout, but make sure that you speak loudly enough for everyone to hear.
Speak at a good pace.	Do not speak too slowly, and do not rush to get through.
Speak confidently.	Trust God to help you. You have prepared something important to share, and your listeners will appreciate it.

Present your book review to an audience. When you finish, mark the checklist for each thing you remembered to do while speaking.

My Speaking Self-Check	
I used expression with my voice, face, hands, or body movements.	
I looked at each person in my audience while I spoke.	
I spoke clearly.	
I spoke with good volume.	
I spoke at a good pace.	
I spoke confidently.	

Reflection

The following opinion paragraph includes a statement of the writer's opinion, reasons for the opinion, and details to support the reasons.

Parents should let their children decide how much allowance they receive. First of all, my parents do not pay enough attention to what my brother and I want or realize how much money we need to buy those things. My brother wants an electronic watch, so he checks the price every day. Second, children should have the opportunity to save their money as fast as their friends. Since my friend's allowance is twice as much as mine, it took him only half as long as it took me to save up for a remote-control airplane. Finally, children need to control their own lives. Children usually have a better idea than their parents of what will bring them true happiness.

Read the opinion paragraph and answer the question.

Are the reasons for the opinion supported by biblical truth or only by the writer's feelings? Explain your answer.

_____

_____

_____

_____

_____

_____

Cumulative Review

Add a prepositional phrase to expand the sentence.

1. God helps me. _____

2. God will provide. _____

3. I trusted God. _____

Write an imperative sentence encouraging a friend to do what's right.

4. _____

Write a sentence about how you can obey God. Use a helping verb in the sentence.

5. _____

Underline each simple subject once and each simple predicate twice.

6. The Israelites produced crops, but the Midianites stole them.

7. The Israelites confessed their sins and called to God for help.

Write a compound sentence using a comma and a conjunction.

8. Gideon was afraid of the Midianites. He became one of the greatest judges of Israel.

_____

_____

9. Gideon asked God for a sign. God answered Gideon's prayer.

_____

_____

Use ⌃ to add commas where they are needed.

10. Gideon met an angel tore down the altar to Baal and led an army into battle.

11. Still Gideon remained unsure about leading the Israelites into battle.

Rewrite the phrase using a possessive noun.

12. the fleece of Gideon _____

13. the threat of the enemies _____

Underline the simple subject once and the verb twice. Write *present*, *past*, or *future* to identify the verb tense.

_____ 14. I will make you victorious.

_____ 15. Gideon struggled to believe God's promise of victory.

_____ 16. Gideon asks God for a sign.

_____ 17. God caused dew to fall only on the fleece, not on the ground.

_____ 18. God demonstrates grace to Gideon.

Write a sentence about something God has done. Use a past-tense verb.

19. _____

_____

Write a sentence about something God tells us He will do. Use a future-tense verb.

20. _____

_____

Mark the sentence that is written correctly.

21. ○ An army prepare for the battle.
    ○ An army prepares for the battle.

22. ○ I want you to make your army smaller.
    ○ I wants you to make your army smaller.

23. ○ Gideon and three hundred men surround the Midianite camp.
    ○ Gideon and three hundred men surrounds the Midianite camp.

Underline the simple subject once. Write the correct past-tense verb to complete the sentence.

24. After they surrounded the camp, the Israelite armies _____ their trumpets.
    blow

25. The Midianites _____ they were outnumbered when they heard the trumpets.
    think

26. They _____ the trumpets and fled.
    hear

27. Gideon _____ God gave the victory.
    know

6

Adjectives and Adverbs

How can precise language help people?

Mentor Text

Excerpt from *You Wouldn't Want to Live Without Extreme Weather!* by Roger Canavan

"Can Electrical Storms Help Us?"

The rolling boom of thunder and the bright flash of lightning often occur during a powerful storm. A thunderstorm is sometimes called an electrical storm, because the lightning is an incredibly powerful electric charge. (American scientist and statesman Benjamin Franklin proved this in 1752, in a very dangerous experiment involving a key tied to a kite string.) A lightning bolt carves a tunnel through the air as it rushes down from a cloud. Hot air around the lightning expands quickly, producing vibrations that create the sound of thunder. Light travels much, much faster than sound. That's why we often see the lightning first, then a few seconds later we hear the thunder.

A THUNDERSTORM in a big city is a dramatic sight, with lighting striking the tops of skyscrapers. All tall buildings are fitted with a lightning rod, a metal strip that leads the electricity safely to the ground, avoiding damage to the building.

PLANTS depend on nitrogen in the soil to grow and to produce their own food. There is nitrogen in the air all around us. The powerful jolt of electricity from lightning can change some of the nitrogen in air into forms that plants can use. Rain carries the usable forms of nitrogen to the ground.

How It Works

People often say they feel better, and even happier, after a thunderstorm. Part of this feeling is caused by the rain and wind clearing and cooling the air. But your mood can also be lifted by some of the electric charge remaining in the air.

Special Adjectives

The words *a*, *an*, and *the* are special adjectives called **articles**.

Special
Adjectives

a column of air	*a heavy rainstorm*
an hour later	*an air column*
the storms	*the air pocket*

A **proper adjective** is an adjective formed from a proper noun. Proper adjectives are always capitalized.

A German meteorologist gave a report on the flooding.

The **demonstratives** *this*, *that*, *these*, and *those* are pronouns that can be used as adjectives. They answer the question **which one?**

This heavy wind is blowing these curtains.

Those birds are flying away quickly.

Demonstrative Adjectives	Near	Far
Singular	this	that
Plural	these	those

Underline all the adjectives, including articles, demonstratives, and proper adjectives. Draw an arrow from each adjective to the noun it describes.

1. A Canadian cold front pushes cold air south.

2. Those wild thunderstorms can form these destructive tornadoes.

Use ▤ to mark each capitalization mistake.

3. The Fujita scale was named after the japanese american scientist Ted Fujita.

4. American and canadian meteorologists use an updated version of this scale.

5. Tornadoes also happen in european, south american, african, and asian countries.

**Write one or two sentences describing the loudest storm you have heard.
Use articles and demonstratives in your sentences.**

6. _____

_____

_____

_____

Underline all the adjectives, including articles, demonstratives, and proper adjectives. Draw an arrow from each adjective to the noun it describes.

7. That hurricane caused this tornado.

8. Strong winds bend trees.

9. Flying objects can be dangerous.

10. Some scientists study the damaged city.

11. Those towns have warning sirens.

12. A big tornado can be two miles in width.

13. That city had many tornadoes this year.

Use 🔲 to mark each capitalization mistake.

Tornado in Campo, Colorado

14. American and european scientists keep track of tornado data.

15. Tornado Alley is the place in north america that has the most tornadoes.

16. Scientists have also traced the pathways of tornadoes through south american countries.

17. Tornadoes on the african continent are most common in the southern and western countries.

Adverbs

AfterSchoolHelp

Adverbs

Adverbs describe verbs and answer the question **how**, **when**, or **where**. Adverbs often end in *-ly*.

Adverbs may come before or after the verb. Some adverbs come between a helping verb and a main verb.

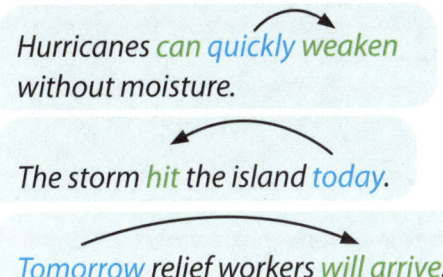

Hurricanes can quickly weaken without moisture.

The storm hit the island today.

Tomorrow relief workers will arrive.

Adverbs that mean *no* are negative. Common negative adverbs include *not, never, nowhere,* and *rarely*. *Not* can be part of a contraction with the verb.

Rainbows are never found in the sky after a snowstorm.

Double rainbows aren't common.

Underline the adverb in the sentence. Draw an arrow from the adverb to the verb it describes.

1. Today scientists can predict hurricanes.

2. Hurricane researchers nervously gathered storm data.

3. That hurricane moved rapidly.

4. Without modern technology, people would not receive hurricane warnings.

Add at least one adverb to expand the sentence.

5. The city prepared for the storm.

Write two sentences about this week's weather. Use at least one adverb in each sentence and circle it.

6. _____

_____

_____

_____

Underline each adverb in the sentence. Draw an arrow from the adverb to the verb it describes. One sentence has two adverbs.

7. The plane did not leave the ground before the winds increased.

8. The pilot gathers weather information daily.

9. Hurricane winds always exceed 74 miles per hour.

10. The storms sometimes cause flooding.

11. Hurricanes commonly happen from August to October.

12. That hurricane destroyed the crop completely.

13. Yesterday the fierce winds headed westward.

Add at least one adverb to expand the sentence.

14. The airplane taxied down the runway.

_____

15. The pilot spoke to the passengers.

_____

16. His copilot checked the instruments.

_____

Preposition or Adverb?

Some words may be used as either adverbs or as prepositions in a sentence.

An **adverb** describes a verb, an adjective, or another verb. Adverbs do not have objects.

> *A turtle ambled by.*

A **preposition** shows the relationship between a noun or a pronoun and another word in the sentence. Prepositions are used as part of a phrase that ends with the object of the preposition.

> *Two more turtles sat by the creek.*

Common Words Used as Prepositions or Adverbs

above	around	down	near	out	through
across	below	in	off	outside	under
along	by	inside	on	over	up

AfterSchoolHelp

Preposition or Adverb?

Mark *adverb* or *preposition* for the underlined word.

1. Arianna is looking for a topic to write <u>about</u>.
   - ○ adverb   ○ preposition

2. Here is a book <u>about</u> turtles and other reptiles.
   - ○ adverb   ○ preposition

3. Arianna found some interesting photographs <u>on</u> page twenty.
   - ○ adverb   ○ preposition

4. She carefully wrote <u>down</u> some facts for her science report.
   - ○ adverb   ○ preposition

Choose a word from the chart. Write one expanded sentence using the word as an adverb and one expanded sentence using the word as a preposition.

The squirrel ran.

5. Adverb: _____

6. Preposition: _____

Mark *adverb* or *preposition* for the underlined word.

7. The Blanding's turtle lives <u>in</u> the American Northeast.
   ○ adverb   ○ preposition

8. Every year, these turtles travel to new habitats <u>through</u> populated areas.
   ○ adverb   ○ preposition

9. Scientists follow <u>along</u> and place turtle crossing signs by the highways on the migration routes.
   ○ adverb   ○ preposition

10. The roads are dangerous, but the signs allow the turtles to move safely <u>across</u>.
    ○ adverb   ○ preposition

11. Drivers who see the signs will watch <u>out</u> for the turtles.
    ○ adverb   ○ preposition

12. People can recognize a Blanding's turtle <u>by</u> the yellow skin on its neck.
    ○ adverb   ○ preposition

Blanding's turtle

Add an adverb from the word bank to expand the sentence.

along	around	below	by	outside

13. The big black tires spun. _____

14. Huge trucks rumbled. _____

15. A horn blared. _____

16. The traffic moved. _____

Add a prepositional phrase to expand the sentence.

17. Cold rain splashed. _____

18. The icy wind whipped. _____

19. My puppy snuggled. _____

20. The door suddenly opened. _____

21. My brother trudged slowly. _____

Practice

Underline the adjective in the sentence. Draw an arrow from the adjective to the noun it describes.

1. There are thousands of miles of underground caves across the United States.

2. Mammoth Cave National Park boasts the largest system of caves and passageways.

Add at least one adjective to expand the sentence.

3. Timothy visited the state park and hiked the trails.

_____

Write two sentences using adjectives to describe a local or state park you have visited.

4. _____

_____

_____

Underline all the adjectives, including articles, demonstratives, and proper adjectives. Draw an arrow from each adjective to the noun it describes.

5. Mammoth Cave is an American national park located in western Kentucky.

6. This name refers to the immense size of many underground rooms.

Use 🔲 to mark each capitalization mistake.

7. Audubon Avenue, a 60-feet-wide and 30-feet-high passageway, is named after a famous north american painter, John James Audubon.

Write two sentences describing the biggest place you have ever been. Use articles and demonstratives in your sentences.

8. _____

_____

_____

_____

Underline the adverb in the sentence. Draw an arrow from the adverb to the verb it describes.

9. This map accurately shows two popular passageways: Fat Man's Misery and Tall Man's Misery.

10. Hikers cautiously squeezed through a keyhole-shaped corridor called Fat Man's Misery.

Mark *adverb* or *preposition* for the underlined word.

11. Timothy looked <u>around</u> at the large underground room nicknamed the Methodist Church.

    ○ adverb   ○ preposition

12. <u>Around</u> 1830 Reverend George Slaughter Gatewood preached to his congregation from a 15-foot ledge in this room.

    ○ adverb   ○ preposition

Choose a word from the word bank. Write one expanded sentence using the word as an adverb and one expanded sentence using the word as a preposition.

across	down	off	under	up

Timothy and his friends slowly trudged.

13. Adverb: _____

14. Preposition: _____

Add an adverb from the word bank to expand the sentence.

above	around	below	by	over

15. The trail wound. _____

16. A winding stream could be seen._____

Using prepositions from the word bank, add a prepositional phrase to expand the sentence.

after	at	down	near	over

17. The boys reached the overlook. _____

18. They started back. _____

Adjectives and Adverbs

Adverbs describe verbs and answer the question *how*, *when*, or *where*. An adverb may come before or after the verb it describes.

> *Tsunamis are usually caused by volcanoes, earthquakes, or landslides.*

Adverbs can also describe **adjectives** and **other adverbs**. An adverb that describes an adjective or adverb comes before the word it describes.

> *A tsunami is an extremely high wave.*

> *The floodwaters swirled very quickly up the street.*

AfterSchoolHelp

Adjectives & Adverbs

Write *Adj* for *adjective* or *Adv* for *adverb* to label the underlined word. Draw an arrow from the underlined word to the word it describes.

_____ 1. Tsunamis <u>very</u> often hit islands.

_____ 2. These <u>destructive</u> waves usually happen along the shore.

_____ 3. Forecasters <u>quickly</u> warned the coastal people.

Write a sentence about the ocean. Use at least one adjective and one adverb in your sentence.

4. _____

_____

Tsunami

Write *Adj* for *adjective* or *Adv* for *adverb* to label the underlined word. Draw an arrow from the underlined word to the word it describes.

_____ 5. <u>Powerful</u> tsunamis are very dangerous.

_____ 6. That scientist <u>cautiously</u> watched the sea.

_____ 7. In 1835, a tsunami almost <u>completely</u> destroyed Concepción, Chile.

_____ 8. The waves along the <u>Japanese</u> coast reached one hundred feet.

_____ 9. "The Ring of Fire" is a <u>very</u> common

area for earthquakes and active

volcanoes.

_____ 10. This active area reaches from the

<u>west</u> coasts of North and South

America to the east coast of Asia.

Ring of Fire

_____ 11. Tsunamis occur when coastal waters

rise extremely <u>quickly</u>.

_____ 12. Extremely strong floodwaters <u>easily</u> lift cars.

Write a sentence about a volcano. Use at least one adjective and one adverb in your sentence.

13. _____

_____

Sakurajima Volcano, Japan

Comparing with -er and -est

Adjectives can be used to compare two or more nouns or pronouns. **Adverbs** can be used to compare two or more actions.

Short adjectives and short adverbs not ending in *-ly* add *-er* or *-est* to compare two or more things.

The sky was redder today than yesterday.

This sandstorm moved the fastest of all the storms during the month of May.

The whirlwind was dustier today than the one on Monday.

The tornado siren sounds loudest on a quiet day.

We saw a whirlwind on the hottest day of the week.

AfterSchoolHelp

Comparing with -er & -est

Mark the sentence that is written correctly.

1. ○ Winds can spin faster in a landspout than they can in a gustnado.
   ○ Winds can spin fastest in a landspout than they can in a gustnado.

2. ○ The redder skies of the week happened on Friday.
   ○ The reddest skies of the week happened on Friday.

3. ○ The air was clearer today than it was yesterday.
   ○ The air was clearest today than it was yesterday.

Write the correct form of the word to complete the sentence.

4. Whirlwinds throw sand _____ than normal winds.
   <u>high</u>

5. The whirlwinds came _____ than the storm.
   <u>early</u>

Write a sentence about rain, comparing two things or actions.

6. _____

_____

Mark the sentence that is written correctly.

7. ○ Waterspouts are damper than sandy whirlwinds.
   ○ Waterspouts are dampest than sandy whirlwinds.

8. ○ The higher waterspout of all was several thousand feet high.
   ○ The highest waterspout of all was several thousand feet high.

9. ○ The greater wind speed of a landspout was recorded at 175 miles per hour.
   ○ The greatest wind speed of a landspout was recorded at 175 miles per hour.

10. ○ Wind howls the loudest inside a large tornado.
    ○ Wind howls the louder inside a large tornado.

11. ○ Landspouts last longer than gustnadoes.
    ○ Landspouts last longest than gustnadoes.

12. ○ Sandstorms have drier winds than gustnadoes.
    ○ Sandstorms have driest winds than gustnadoes.

Waterspout

Write the correct form of the word to complete the sentence.

13. The _____, _____ region in all of the United States is in the
    flat   dry
    West.

14. It is _____ indoors than outdoors during a sandstorm.
    safe

15. The wind over the desert is _____ than the wind over the sea.
    dry

16. The cloudy desert air is _____ than city air.
    dense

17. The _____ dust wall ever recorded was more than a mile high.
    high

Write a sentence about snow, comparing more than two things or actions.

18. _____

_____

Comparing with *More, Most, Less,* and *Least*

An **adjective** can compare nouns or pronouns. Short adjectives add *-er* or *-est*, while long adjectives use ***more/most*** or ***less/least*** to compare.

> *Snowstorms are less forceful than blizzards.*

> *Blizzards are the most dangerous winter storms.*

An **adverb** can be used to compare actions. Short adverbs not ending in *-ly* add *-er* or *-est*. Long adverbs use ***more/most*** or ***less/least*** to compare actions.

> *Snowstorms occur less frequently in Alabama than in Vermont.*

> *Snow was cleared more quickly on the main roads than on the secondary roads in Merrimac County.*

Do not add *-er* or *-est* at the end of an adjective or adverb when ***more/most*** or ***less/least*** is used.

> **Correct:** *The strongest winds blew across the lake.*

> **Incorrect:** *The most strongest winds blew across the lake.*

> **Correct:** *The chilliest weather happens in January.*

> **Incorrect:** *The most chilliest weather happens in January.*

Mark the sentence that is written correctly.

1. ○ The biting winds during the storm were the harmfulest.
   ○ The biting winds during the storm were the most harmful.

2. ○ Frostbite is less common in Georgia than in Minnesota.
   ○ Frostbite is least common in Georgia than in Minnesota.

AfterSchoolHelp

Comparing with More, Most, Less & Least

Write the correct form of the word to complete the sentence.

3. The blizzard of 1866 was one of the _____ storms ever.

tough

4. The first snowfall was _____ than the last.

beautiful

5. January is the _____ month of all in Jackson, Wyoming.

snowy

Write a sentence with the adjective or adverb given.

6. More modern: _____

   _____

7. More quickly: _____

   _____

Mark the sentence that is written correctly.

8. ○ The snowstorm was more forceful during the night.
   ○ The snowstorm was forcefuler during the night.

9. ○ As nightfall approached, the temperatures became more low.
   ○ As nightfall approached, the temperatures became lower.

10. ○ Blizzards must have winds more greater than thirty-five miles per hour.
    ○ Blizzards must have winds greater than thirty-five miles per hour.

11. ○ South Dakota is often called the Blizzard State.
    ○ South Dakota is more often called the Blizzard State.

Write the correct form of the word to complete the sentence.

12. _____ winds are expected with a blizzard warning than a winter storm
        high
    warning.

13. Four-wheel-drive vehicles are _____ to travel over snow-packed roads
                                          able
    than front-wheel-drive cars are.

14. Snowmobiles are the _____ rescue vehicles to people stranded in the
                              helpful
    woods.

15. The highway was _____ than the country road.
                          slippery

16. Travelers were _____ delayed on Tuesday than on Monday.
                       drastically

17. Driving on a snow-packed road is _____ than driving when the roads
                                          difficult
    are dry.

18. A driver must be _____ on snow-packed roads than on dry pavement.
                         careful

19. They rode the snowmobile for an hour on the _____ day of the whole week.
                                                     stormy

Special Forms of *Good* and *Bad*

Good and *well* are often confused when used in sentences.

> *Good* is an adjective that describes a noun or pronoun.
>
> > *Arctic air is a good source of moisture-producing cold air.*

> *Well* is an adverb that describes a verb. *Well* is used as an adjective only to describe someone's health.
>
> > *Solar radiation reflects well from the dry winter snow.*
> >
> > *After being ill for two days, I finally felt well.*

AfterSchoolHelp

Special Forms for
Good & Bad

The adjectives *good* and *bad* and the adverbs *well* and *badly* are irregular. The spelling of these words changes when they are used to compare two or more things.

Special Forms of Good and Bad That Compare			
		Comparing Two	Comparing Three or More
Adjective	good	better	best
Adverb	well	better	best
Adjective	bad	worse	worst
Adverb	badly	worse	worst

Underline the correct word to complete the sentence.

1. (Good, Well) weather in the Arctic inland reaches highs of 70°F to 100°F.

2. The ice fisherman did not feel (good, well) after being on the ice for several hours.

3. People can be injured (bad, badly) by an avalanche.

4. Because Siberia's temperatures are so cold, people have to bundle up (good, well).

Write a form of *good*, *well*, *bad*, or *badly* to complete the sentence.

5. W. A. Bentley is a _____ photographer of snow scenes than of wild animals.

6. Inland Arctic temperatures are _____ than those along the coast.

7. Last night was the _____ snowstorm in January.

Write a sentence comparing summer weather to winter weather. Use one of the following adjectives or adverbs: *better*, *best*, *worse*, or *worst*.

8. _____

_____

Underline the correct word to complete the sentence.

9. Tropical rainforests do a (good, well) job of controlling the jungle climate.

10. The tropics are watered (good, well) with their abundant rainfall.

11. The shallow tropical tree roots take in a (good, well) collection of nutrients.

12. These trees would be (bad, badly) harmed by a drought.

13. A (bad, badly) snakebite made the jungle explorer sick.

Write a form of *good*, *well*, *bad*, or *badly* to complete the sentence.

14. Wet ground soaks up water _____ than dry, snow-covered ground.

15. Desert plants adapted _____ to the hot, dry climate.

16. Thorns are the _____ protection from hungry desert animals.

17. _____ winds blew across the desert.

18. A camel can survive dehydration _____ than a tiger can.

19. One of the desert's _____ problems is its limited water supply.

20. The _____ problem of all is the loss of underground water supplies.

21. An empty desert well is _____ than empty wells in other places.

22. The Nile and Niger Rivers provide the _____ water source for the Sahara Desert.

23. That book is a _____ place to learn more about deserts and rainforests.

Practice

Write *Adj* for adjective or *Adv* for adverb to label the underlined word. Draw an arrow from the underlined word to the word it describes.

_____ 1. Moaning Caverns in California was <u>first</u> explored by gold miners in the 1840s and 1850s.

_____ 2. J. B. Trask wrote an <u>exciting</u> story of an exploration of this cave.

Accounts vary as to how Moaning Caverns got its name. Write a sentence imagining how the cave got its name. Use at least one adjective and one adverb in your sentence.

3. _____

_____

Mark the sentence that is written correctly.

4. ○ Moaning Caverns is the larger cave open to the public in California.

   ○ Moaning Caverns is the largest cave open to the public in California.

5. ○ The braver gold miners used to swing into the cave on ropes.

   ○ The bravest gold miners used to swing into the cave on ropes.

6. ○ This metal staircase is a safer way to enter the cave than a rope would be.

   ○ This metal staircase is a safest way to enter the cave than a rope would be.

Write the correct form of the word to complete the sentence.

7. The passageway is _____ than the massive 180-foot cave opening.

narrow

8. The huge opening is _____ than the Statue of Liberty.

tall

9. One of the _____ of all the tours through Moaning Caverns requires crawling

hard
   through tight spaces.

Imagine you have discovered an unexplored cave. Write a sentence describing your exploration comparing two things or actions.

10. _____

_____

Mark the sentence that is written correctly.

11. ○ Caves are more frequently found in the state of Tennessee.

○ Caves are most frequently found in the state of Tennessee.

12. ○ Caves are less common in Georgia than in Tennessee.

○ Caves are least common in Georgia than in Tennessee.

Write the correct form of the word to complete the sentence.

13. Ruby Falls houses one of the _____ underground waterfalls.
                                        tall

14. Visitors notice that some stalactites are hanging _____ than others.
                                                            loosely

15. Of all the features of the cave, visitors are _____ by the waterfalls.
                                                        astonished

Write a sentence with the adjective or adverb given.

16. Most amazing: _____

_____

17. More often: _____

_____

Write a form of *good*, *well*, *bad*, or *badly* to complete the sentence.

18. Visitors are able to see _____ because of the lights installed in the cave.

19. Many signs along the highways provide the _____ advertising for this

popular attraction.

**Write a sentence comparing two tourist spots you have visited or would like to visit.
Use one of the following adjectives or adverbs: *better*, *best*, *worse*, or *worst*.**

20. _____

_____

Chapter 6 Review

Match the underlined word with the correct term.

| **A** adjective | **C** article | **E** preposition |
| **B** adverb | **D** demonstrative | **F** proper adjective |

_____ 1. Scientists send helium balloons <u>through</u> atmospheric layers to monitor the weather.

_____ 2. Meteorologists <u>constantly</u> record the temperatures.

_____ 3. <u>This</u> instrument is called an anemometer.

_____ 4. <u>The</u> anemometer measures wind speed.

_____ 5. <u>Special</u> buoys measure ocean conditions.

_____ 6. Typhoons in the <u>Pacific</u> Ocean can threaten the <u>Chinese</u> coastline.

Add at least one adjective to expand the sentence.

7. My brothers and sisters enjoy games.

_____

Add at least one adverb to expand the sentence.

8. My older brother wins.

_____

Use ▤ to mark each capitalization mistake.

9. Bright lights can be seen across canadian skies at night.

10. These beautiful colors also show up in the alaskan wilderness.

11. Many north american tribes had legends about those amazing sights.

12. The greek scientist Galileo gave these lights their scientific name.

Mark the sentence that is written correctly.

13. ○ A breeze from the north often results in cooler temperatures than a breeze from the south.
    ○ A breeze from the north often results in coolest temperatures than a breeze from the south.

14. ○ Our local weather station has the more accurate forecasts in all of our state.
    ○ Our local weather station has the most accurate forecasts in all of our state.

15. ○ That small dog stays calmer in a storm than this big dog does.
    ○ That small dog stays calmest in a storm than this big dog does.

16. ○ On rainy days, Marie likes to lie on the couch under her fluffiest blanket.
    ○ On rainy days, Marie likes to lie on the couch under her most fluffiest blanket.

17. ○ The beautifulest sunsets can happen before a storm.
    ○ The most beautiful sunsets can happen before a storm.

Write a form of *good*, *well*, *bad*, or *badly* to complete the sentence.

18. Farmers, sailors, and fishermen are often the _____ weather forecasters.

19. The weather close to the coast was _____ than the weather was farther inland.

20. The new weather forecaster did a _____ job on his first television broadcast.

21. The weather computer performed _____ on Friday.

22. The weathervane worked _____ during the heavy winds on Saturday.

Write a sentence comparing two or more animals.

23. _____

_____

Write a sentence comparing three or more animals.

24. _____

_____

Journal

Write a sentence describing one type of extreme weather that interests you.

1. _____

_____

Research the type of weather you have chosen. Write a list of safety tips for surviving this kind of weather. Use precise words.

2. _____

_____

_____

_____

_____

_____

_____

_____

Cumulative Review

Underline each simple subject once and each simple predicate twice.

1. Elimelech and his family moved to Moab after a famine in Judah.

2. Elimelech died, and his wife Naomi was left with her two sons.

Make a compound subject or predicate by combining the sentences.

3. Mahlon married a Moabite woman. Chilion married a Moabite woman.

_____

The following paragraph should be written in past tense. Circle the three incorrect verbs in the paragraph. Write the correct verb form to improve the paragraph.

Naomi heard that the famine was ended in Judah. She makes plans to leave Moab. She encouraged her daughters-in-law to remain in Moab and remarry. Orpah kisses her mother-in-law and went back to her home. Ruth held on to her and insisted on returning with her. She vows that Naomi's people would be her people and Naomi's God, her God.

4. _____

5. _____

6. _____

Underline the simple subject once and the correct helping verb twice.

7. When Naomi arrived in Bethlehem, all the townspeople (was, were) excited to see her.

8. "I (has, have) returned with nothing," Naomi told the people.

Underline the simple subject once. Write the correct past-tense verb to complete the sentence.

9. "When I _____ to Moab, I had plenty," Naomi said.
   go

10. Naomi _____ that God had dealt bitterly with her.
    say

Underline all the adjectives, including articles, demonstratives, and proper adjectives. Draw an arrow from each adjective to the noun it describes.

11. Naomi returned that spring when barley was beginning to be harvested.

12. The wealthy farmers knew that God cares about poor people.

13. They left grain in the corners of the field to provide food for hungry people.

Write *Adj* for adjective or *Adv* for adverb to label the underlined word. Draw an arrow from the underlined word to the word it describes.

_____ 14. Ruth and Naomi were very <u>poor</u>.

_____ 15. Boaz was a <u>particularly</u> rich kinsman or relative of Ruth.

_____ 16. "Do <u>not</u> harvest the edges of the field," Boaz instructed his workers.

Mark *adverb* or *preposition* for the underlined word.

17. Ruth asked Naomi if she could gather the grain left <u>behind</u>.
    ○ adverb   ○ preposition

18. Boaz asked his workers, "Who is the young woman following <u>behind</u> the reapers?"
    ○ adverb   ○ preposition

Choose a word from the word bank. Write one expanded sentence using the word as an adverb and one expanded sentence using the word as a preposition.

around   down   inside   outside

The workers sat together.

19. Adverb: _____

20. Preposition: _____

Mark the sentence that is written correctly.

21. ○ Ruth proved to be more loyal to Naomi than Orpah.
    ○ Ruth proved to be most loyal to Naomi than Orpah

22. ○ God had bigger plans for Ruth and Naomi than they ever dreamed.
    ○ God had the most biggest plans for Ruth and Naomi than they ever dreamed.

Write a form of *good*, *well*, *bad*, or *badly* to complete the sentence.

23. Boaz redeemed Ruth and became a _____ husband to her.

24. _____ of all, Ruth and Naomi became great-grandmothers of Christ.

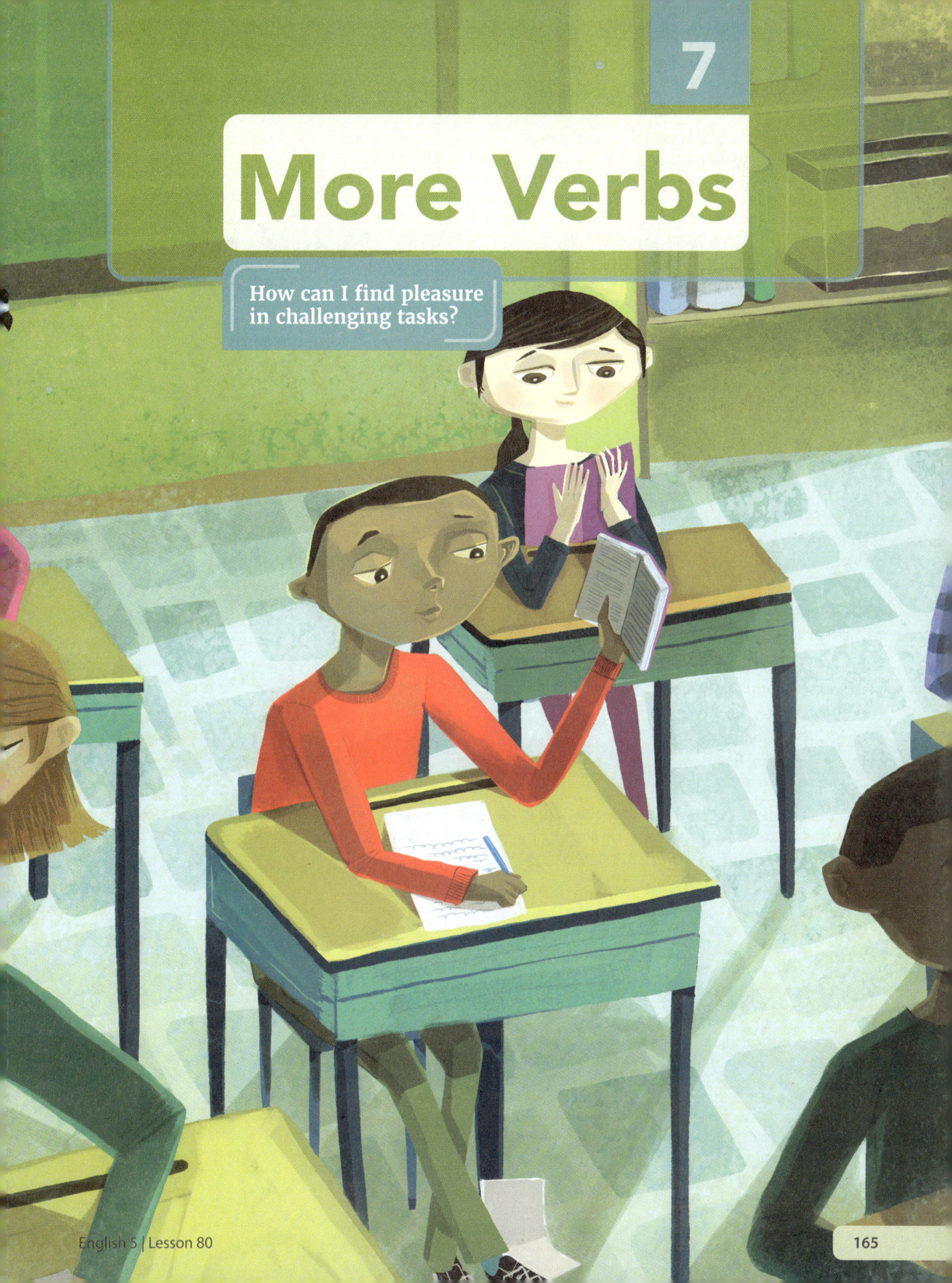

7

More Verbs

How can I find pleasure in challenging tasks?

Mentor Text

Excerpt from "Queen of the Slopes: An Interview with Sarah Will"
by Emily Cambias

Sarah Will has loved skiing since she was a kid. She skied competitively through elementary school, high school, and college. In 1988, she had an accident that paralyzed her from the waist down. Within a year, however, she was back on slopes—on a monoski. The monoski is a piece of adaptive equipment. Monoskiers rely on upper-body strength and control to ride. Within a few years, Will was competing again, joining the U.S. Adaptive Ski Team. Over four Paralympic Games, she won a record 13 medals (12 gold and 1 silver). Today, she advocates for accessibility. *COBBLESTONE* talked with Will about her life. . . .

How did you find out about adaptive skiing? . . .

The next year, I planned a trip to Winter Park with Brian, my father, and some friends. When I first saw the monoski, it looked quite unbalanced. It also came with two instructors, and I wasn't used to anyone being with me. I was fearful of some things and that was a feeling I wasn't used to, either. But I knew that

Sarah Will

I had to listen to the people who knew how to use the monoski, and to check my ego. The concepts, though, were exactly the same. A ski is still a ski! . . .

Could you tell us about your first Paralympics?

My first Paralympics were in Albertville, France, in 1992. The French Alps are spectacular—it snowed for days before we got there. It was just beautiful. My hotel was right at the finish line, so I could see races from the window. We were racing on the same hill the Olympians had used. There was a lot of pride and wanting to do well because the U.S. Olympic team had just won gold there.

I had a good downhill race. That was the event I really wanted to excel in. It was wide open, and it was fast. I reached 63 miles an hour. My heart was pumping—I had never gone that fast before.

Winter Park, Colorado

Action and Linking Verbs

An **action verb** tells what the subject does.

The hockey player glided toward the goal.

A **linking verb** tells what the subject is by connecting the simple subject to a noun or an adjective in the predicate.

Forms of the verb *be* are often used as linking verbs.

Linking Verbs				
am	is	are	was	were

The fans are enthusiastic.

Sensory verbs can be action verbs or linking verbs.

Sensory Verbs				
feel	look	smell	sound	taste

Action verb: The players look at the referee.
Linking verb: The coaches look excited.

The verbs *seem* and *appear* can also be used as linking verbs.

Each team appears ready for the competition.
The rules seem simple.

Underline the simple subject once and the verb twice. Mark *action verb* or *linking verb*.

1. The fans appear nervous.
   ○ action verb   ○ linking verb

2. The referee blew the whistle.
   ○ action verb   ○ linking verb

3. The coach is my uncle.
   ○ action verb   ○ linking verb

4. Justin shot the puck toward the goal.
   ○ action verb   ○ linking verb

5. The red team was victorious!
   ○ action verb   ○ linking verb

AfterSchoolHelp

Action Verbs and Linking Verbs

Choose one of the sensory verbs. Write one sentence using the verb as an action verb and one sentence using it as a linking verb.

feel   look   smell   sound   taste

6. Action: _____

_____

7. Linking: _____

_____

Underline the simple subject once and the verb twice. Mark *action verb* or *linking verb*.

8. The players are excellent skaters.
   ○ action verb   ○ linking verb

9. We watch our hockey team every Saturday.
   ○ action verb   ○ linking verb

10. My brother plays hockey on our neighborhood team.
    ○ action verb   ○ linking verb

11. The rink feels cold to the fans.
    ○ action verb   ○ linking verb

12. The puck sailed into the goal cage.
    ○ action verb   ○ linking verb

13. Each team sends six players to the ice.
    ○ action verb   ○ linking verb

14. The hot chocolate smells delicious!
    ○ action verb   ○ linking verb

15. Any foul causes a penalty for that team.
    ○ action verb   ○ linking verb

16. The Blazers were the champions last year.
    ○ action verb   ○ linking verb

Action Verbs

An **action verb** tells what the **simple subject** does.

Many sentences with action verbs have **direct objects**.

> A direct object is usually a noun. It receives the action of the verb and answers the question *who or what?* after the verb.

The hockey player hit the puck (into the goal.)

The simple subject, action verb, and direct object will not be part of a prepositional phrase. Mark the prepositional phrases in the sentence first, and then identify the other words.

AfterSchoolHelp

Direct Objects

Put parentheses around each prepositional phrase. Label the parts of the sentence with the correct abbreviation.

1. The players slice the ice with their skates during the game.

2. The Zamboni machine smoothes the ice after the game.

3. These machines also clean the surface of the ice.

4. The ice freezes again smoothly.

S	simple subject
V	action verb
DO	direct object

Write two sentences about how to score points in a sport of your choice. Use an action verb and a direct object in each sentence.

5. _____

_____

_____

_____

Put parentheses around each prepositional phrase. Label the parts of the sentence with the correct abbreviation.

6. Frank Zamboni's parents came from Italy.

S	simple subject
V	action verb
DO	direct object

7. Frank invented the famous ice-cleaning machine.

8. Today, the Zamboni machine cleans hockey rinks around the world.

9. The goalie blocks with special pads and with a stick.

10. The sideboards keep the puck in the rink.

11. The roster lists the players on each team.

12. Players receive penalties for violations of the rules.

13. No player can pass the puck with his hand during a play.

14. The facemask protects the goalie from the puck.

15. The center line divides the rink in half.

16. The player sent a pass to his teammate across the rink.

Zamboni machine

Linking Verbs

A **linking verb** tells what the subject is by connecting the **simple subject** to a noun or an adjective in the predicate.

| A **predicate noun** renames the subject.

The man (with the red hair) is Colton's hockey coach.

| A **predicate adjective** describes the subject.

The referee was tired (after the game.)

The simple subject, linking verb, and predicate noun or predicate adjective will not be part of a prepositional phrase. Mark the prepositional phrases in the sentence first, and then identify the other words.

AfterSchoolHelp

Linking Verbs

Put parentheses around each prepositional phrase. Label the parts of the sentence with the correct abbreviation.

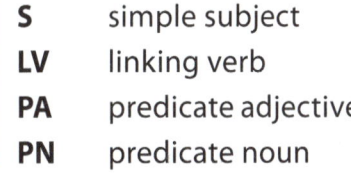

S	simple subject
LV	linking verb
PA	predicate adjective
PN	predicate noun

1. My sister was excited about the game.

2. The players are students at Christian Heritage Academy.

3. Her team is ready for the game.

4. The students were noisy on the bus.

5. That team's uniforms are new.

Use the sentence patterns *S-LV-PN* and *S-LV-PA* to write two sentences about your favorite food.

6. S-LV-PN: _____

_____

7. S-LV-PA: _____

_____

Put parentheses around each prepositional phrase. Label the parts of the sentence with the correct abbreviation.

8. Hockey is a popular sport.

9. The stick is very hard.

10. In this game, the puck is a small disk.

11. Hockey was a new sport around 1918 in Nova Scotia.

12. The first game of hockey was thrilling!

13. Lorne Chabot is famous in hockey history.

14. He was a legendary goalkeeper for the Rangers.

15. Helmets are important equipment for hockey players.

S	simple subject
LV	linking verb
PA	predicate adjective
PN	predicate noun

Practice

Put parentheses around each prepositional phrase. Label the parts of the sentence with the correct abbreviation.

1. Louisa May Alcott's family lived in many places over a thirty-year period.

2. In 1857 her father moved his family to Concord, Massachusetts.

3. The Alcott family included four daughters.

S	simple subject
V	action verb
DO	direct object

4. The Alcotts bought Orchard House.

5. The house sat on twelve acres with a large apple orchard.

Put parentheses around each prepositional phrase. Label the parts of the sentence with the correct abbreviation.

6. Orchard House is close to the home of Nathaniel Hawthorne.

7. Orchard House was the family home from 1858 to 1877.

S	simple subject
LV	linking verb
PA	predicate adjective
PN	predicate noun

8. The farmhouse was old.

9. Mr. Alcott's handyman skills were a necessity.

10. Many structural changes to the house were necessary.

Write two sentences about the house where you live. Use an action verb and a direct object in each sentence.

11. _____

_____

_____

Use the sentence patterns *S-LV-PN* and *S-LV-PA* to write two sentences about this house.

12. S-LV-PN: _____

_____

13. S-LV-PA: _____

_____

Underline the simple subject once and the verb twice. Mark *action verb* or *linking verb*.

14. Orchard House seemed quite rickety.
    ○ action verb   ○ linking verb

15. The floors in the old house sounded squeaky.
    ○ action verb   ○ linking verb

16. Mr. Alcott looked at his finished handiwork with pride.
    ○ action verb   ○ linking verb

17. The Alcotts felt proud of their newly remodeled home.
    ○ action verb   ○ linking verb

18. Mrs. Alcott smelled her scrumptious apple pies.
    ○ action verb   ○ linking verb

19. Mrs. Alcott appeared very pleased with her finished dessert.
    ○ action verb   ○ linking verb

20. The family tasted the mouthwatering pie.
    ○ action verb   ○ linking verb

21. The Orchard House is open for tours today.
    ○ action verb   ○ linking verb

22. The rooms look similar to their original appearance.
    ○ action verb   ○ linking verb

23. The antique furniture in the house belonged to the Alcott family.
    ○ action verb   ○ linking verb

Choose one of the sensory verbs. Write one sentence using the verb as an action verb and one sentence using it as a linking verb.

| feel   look   smell   sound   taste |

24. Action: _____

   _____

25. Linking: _____

   _____

Sentence Patterns

A **sentence pattern** is the way words are put together to form complete thoughts.

Sentence Pattern Key			
simple subject	**S**	direct object	**DO**
action verb	**V**	predicate adjective	**PA**
linking verb	**LV**	predicate noun	**PN**

AfterSchoolHelp

Sentence Patterns

Sentences with **action verbs** may have the following sentence patterns.

S-V
S   V
The Bobcats won.

S-V-DO
S   V   DO
Paul shot the puck.

Sentences with **linking verbs** may have the following sentence patterns.

S-LV-PN
S   LV   PN
My dad is a coach.

S-LV-PA
S   LV   PA
The coach looks excited.

Put parentheses around each prepositional phrase. Label the sentence pattern. Write the sentence pattern on the line.

_____ 1. My aunt cheers for her team.

_____ 2. The fans are enthusiastic about this game.

_____ 3. Some people wave signs over their heads.

_____ 4. We dress in our team's colors.

_____ 5. The fans are great supporters for their team.

Write a paragraph about an organized sport you have watched being played. Use each sentence pattern at least one time.

6. _____

_____

_____

_____

_____

_____

Put parentheses around each prepositional phrase. Label the sentence pattern. Write the sentence pattern on the line.

_____ 7. Bobby Orr's good sportsmanship is legendary.

_____ 8. He was a defenseman for the Boston Bruins.

_____ 9. Bobby Orr retired in 1978.

_____ 10. His team won the Stanley Cup twice.

_____ 11. Wayne Gretzky won a significant award in 1999.

Bobby Orr

Wayne Gretzky

Contractions and Double Negatives

A **contraction** is a shortened form of two words.

she + will = she'll	*are + not = aren't*	*dog + is = dog's*
they + are = they're	*does + not = doesn't*	

Won't and *can't* are exceptions. *Won't* is formed from the words *will* and *not*. *Can't* is formed from one word, *cannot*.

A **double negative** is the use of two negative words in the same sentence. A good writer will avoid using a double negative in a sentence.

Incorrect: *I don't have no homework.*   *There isn't no one at home.*
Correct: *I don't have homework.*   *There is no one at home.*
I don't have any homework.   *There isn't anyone at home.*

Underline the words that can form a contraction. Write them as a contraction.

1. I am going to the game tonight with my brother. _____

2. We are hoping our team wins! _____

3. The Eagles cannot come to the tournament next week. _____

4. They have won four times this week. _____

Rewrite the sentence to correct the underlined double negative.

5. There <u>wasn't no</u> milk left.

   _____

6. Josiah <u>doesn't never</u> like to eat green beans.

   _____

Write a sentence about something you do not like to do. Use a contraction. Be careful not to use a double negative.

7. _____

   _____

Underline the words that can form a contraction. Write them as a contraction.

8. You are looking at the Stanley Cup. _____

9. The Stanley Cup is a famous hockey trophy. _____

10. I have seen a replica of the Stanley Cup. _____

11. It is an amazing trophy! _____

12. Many teams have not reached their goal yet. _____

13. They will not quit trying to win. _____

Stanley Cup

Rewrite the sentence to correct the underlined double negative.

14. There <u>isn't no</u> more time left in the game.

_____

15. We <u>don't</u> have <u>no</u> tickets to the championship.

_____

16. Ellie <u>doesn't</u> know <u>nobody</u> in the room.

_____

17. It <u>doesn't never</u> take Ellie long to make new friends.

_____

**Write several sentences about a championship. Use at least one contraction.
Be careful not to use any double negatives.**

18. _____

_____

_____

_____

_____

Confusing Verbs

Some pairs of verbs can be confusing because they have similar meanings.

Verb	Definition	Past Tense	Past Participle	Example
teach	to give instruction	taught	taught	My aunt teaches fifth grade.
learn	to gain knowledge	learned	learned	I learned something new.
rise	to get up	rose	risen	The sun rises every morning.
raise	to bring up	raised	raised	We raise the flag at 8:00 a.m.
sit	to rest	sat	sat	I sit in the back row.
set	to put	set	set	I set the book on the table.
let	to allow	let	let	I let my dog into the house.
leave	to allow to remain	left	left	I will leave my dog outside.
lie	to recline	lay	lain	She will lie down to take a nap.
lay	to put something down	laid	laid	I will lay the keys on the counter.

The helping verbs *may* and *can* are also commonly misused.

can	to be able to do something	Jacob can run a mile.
may	to be allowed or permitted to do something	You may borrow my eraser.

Write *C* if the confusing verb is used correctly or *I* if the verb is used incorrectly.

_____ 1. We may rejoice over the story of Easter.

_____ 2. Mary saw the angel setting on the rock.

Write the correct form of the verb to complete the sentence.

3. Jesus _____ from the grave.

rise

4. God _____ Him from the grave.

raise

Choose a pair of confusing verbs from the chart. Write a sentence using each verb that demonstrates the correct meaning.

5. Verb 1: _____

   _____

6. Verb 2: _____

AfterSchoolHelp

Confusing Verbs

Write *C* if the confusing verb is used correctly or *I* if the verb is used incorrectly.

_____ 7. Mr. Perez will learn us about astronauts.

_____ 8. Students learn about many interesting things at my school.

_____ 9. We rise to our feet when the flag goes by in the parade.

_____ 10. Please rise the blinds to let in more light.

_____ 11. The teacher set the cookies on the table for the class.

_____ 12. The open windows leave the beautiful sunshine flow into the room.

_____ 13. The puppy lets muddy paw prints all over the floor.

_____ 14. The baby lays down for a nap at 2:00 p.m.

_____ 15. She carefully laid out her clothes for the party.

_____ 16. Gianna can draw very well.

Write the correct form of the verb to complete the sentence.

17. Please _____ your wet boots outside.
        set

18. Andrew _____ his tickets on the table.
        lay

19. My brother _____ me how to shoot a basket.
        teach

20. Dad _____ the hoop higher when I grew taller.
        raise

Practice

Put parentheses around each prepositional phrase. Label the sentence pattern. Write the sentence pattern on the line.

_____ 1. Louisa May Alcott wrote *Little Women* at a desk in her room.

_____ 2. Like Jo March, Louisa was a tomboy with a rich imagination.

_____ 3. Louisa wrote her own plays.

_____ 4. She and her sisters performed the plays.

_____ 5. In her early twenties, she published *Flower Fables*.

_____ 6. Louisa also served as a Civil War nurse.

_____ 7. May, Louisa's youngest sister, was very talented as an artist in real life.

_____ 8. May studied under several famous artists.

_____ 9. The designer of the Lincoln Memorial was actually a student of May's.

_____ 10. May died shortly after her baby's birth.

_____ 11. Louisa raised May's child as her own.

Write a paragraph about the characters in *Little Women* or another favorite book of yours. Use each sentence pattern at least one time.

12. _____

_____

_____

_____

_____

Underline the words that can form a contraction. Write them as a contraction.

13. Beth's name was not changed in the novel. _____

14. She will always be remembered as a homebody. _____

15. Beth did not like anything better than sewing and playing her piano. _____

Rewrite the sentence to correct the underlined double negative.

16. Louisa's oldest sister Anna <u>wasn't never</u> called that in the novel.

_____

17. Anna's husband John <u>doesn't</u> live <u>no</u> longer than ten years after their marriage.

_____

Write a sentence about one of your siblings or a special friend. Use a contraction. Be careful not to use a double negative.

18. _____

_____

Write *C* if the confusing verb is used correctly or *I* if the verb is used incorrectly.

_____ 19. Mr. Alcott did not serve in the Union Army. In reality he learned students in schools he established.

_____ 20. He rose to the position of superintendent of schools in Concord, Massachusetts.

Write the correct form of the verb to complete the sentence.

21. Mrs. Alcott was caring, strong, and loving. She _____ her girls develop
    their individual talents.
                                                            let

22. The Alcotts' home was a safe house on the Underground Railroad. The fugitive slaves

    _____ there for the night on their journey to freedom.
         lie

Choose a pair of confusing verbs from the word bank. Write a sentence using each verb that demonstrates the correct meaning.

| lay   lie   raise   rise   set   sit |

23. Verb 1: _____

_____

24. Verb 2: _____

_____

Chapter 7 Review

Match the underlined word with the correct term.

_____ 1. The Winter Olympics <u>happen</u> every four years.

_____ 2. Skiing is a popular Olympic <u>sport</u>.

_____ 3. Olympic skiers race <u>down</u> the hill.

_____ 4. Lincoln takes skiing lessons with his <u>brother</u>.

_____ 5. The <u>boys</u> live in Colorado.

_____ 6. Many people in Colorado <u>are</u> interested in skiing.

_____ 7. Experts label the ski <u>slopes</u> with different colors to show their difficulty levels.

_____ 8. Black diamond slopes are extremely <u>difficult</u>.

> **A** simple subject
> **B** action verb
> **C** linking verb
> **D** direct object
> **E** predicate adjective
> **F** predicate noun
> **G** preposition
> **H** object of the preposition

Write a sentence about a winter sport. Use an action verb.

9. _____

_____

Write a sentence about an athlete. Use a linking verb.

10. _____

_____

Match the sentence with the correct sentence pattern.

_____ 11. Addison takes lessons in figure skating.

_____ 12. She practices daily.

_____ 13. Last year Addison was the state figure skating champion.

_____ 14. She seems ready for next week's competition.

_____ 15. The judges look carefully at each jump.

_____ 16. The skaters earn points for jumps and spins.

_____ 17. This trophy is the top prize.

_____ 18. Friends and family watch the competition from the stands.

> **A** S-V
> **B** S-V-DO
> **C** S-LV-PA
> **D** S-LV-PN

Rewrite the sentence to correct the underlined double negative.

19. Amelia <u>hasn't never</u> been skating.

_____

20. There <u>aren't no</u> skating rinks in her town.

_____

21. The weather <u>doesn't never</u> get very cold where she lives.

_____

Write *C* if the confusing verb is used correctly or *I* if the verb is used incorrectly.

_____ 22. A ski instructor can learn you how to ski.

_____ 23. Most people learn the basics very quickly.

_____ 24. Dad said I may choose new ski pants.

_____ 25. The ski lift rises people up to the top of the hill.

_____ 26. Set still until the ski lift stops moving.

_____ 27. Don't leave your ski poles behind!

_____ 28. All four of my cousins have learned to ski very well.

_____ 29. People can buy food and hot chocolate at the ski lodge.

_____ 30. Lie your dirty dishes on the counter when you are finished.

Journal

Think about the ways that writing can be difficult and the ways that writing can be enjoyable. Write down some helpful advice for a person who is struggling to find pleasure in the writing process.

Cumulative Review

Use ⌃ to add commas where they are needed.

1. The Israelites disobeyed God's commands and God used the Philistines to oppress them.

2. The Philistines sent their armies to rob them of their swords spears and crops.

Mark the sentence that is written correctly.

3. ○ The Israelites cries out to God.

   ○ The Israelites cry out to God.

4. ○ One day an angel appears to Manoah's wife and tells her that her son will be a Nazirite, separated unto God.

   ○ One day an angel appear to Manoah's wife and tells her that her son will be a Nazirite, separated unto God.

5. ○ Wine and strong drink is two things her son should not consume.

   ○ Wine and strong drink are two things her son should not consume.

Underline the simple subject once. Write the correct past-tense verb to complete the sentence.

6. As a Nazirite Samson _____ he should never cut his hair or come into contact

   (know)

   with a dead body.

7. Samson _____ up to be the strongest person in the Bible.

   (grow)

Mark the correct verb to complete the sentence.

8. Samson was a judge over Israel, and he ____ vengeance on the Philistines in his own strength.

   ○ takes   ○ took

9. Samson's downfall began when he ____ a Philistine wife against his parents' wishes.

   ○ will marry   ○ married

Mark *adverb* or *preposition* for the underlined word.

10. The Philistines came <u>down</u> to Delilah's house to find out the secret to Samson's strength.

    ○ adverb   ○ preposition

11. Samson revealed that cutting his hair <u>off</u> would take away his strength.

    ○ adverb   ○ preposition

Put parentheses around each prepositional phrase. Label the sentence pattern. Write the sentence pattern on the line.

_____ 12. Delilah cut off his hair during Samson's nap.

_____ 13. Delilah called the Philistines into her house.

_____ 14. Samson was now the Philistines' captive.

_____ 15. The Philistines brought Samson before a crowd.

_____ 16. Samson was repentant about his sin.

_____ 17. God gave strength to Samson

_____ 18. Samson brought down the temple on the enemy.

_____ 19. The Israelites were free from Philistine rule.

_____ 20. Samson could have done many more things with God's strength.

Write *C* if the confusing verb is used correctly or *I* if the verb is used incorrectly.

_____ 21. God <u>teached</u> Samson a very important lesson.

_____ 22. <u>Let</u> God be your source of strength.

Write several sentences about a life lesson God has taught you. Use at least one contraction. Be careful not to use any double negatives.

23. _____

_____

_____

_____

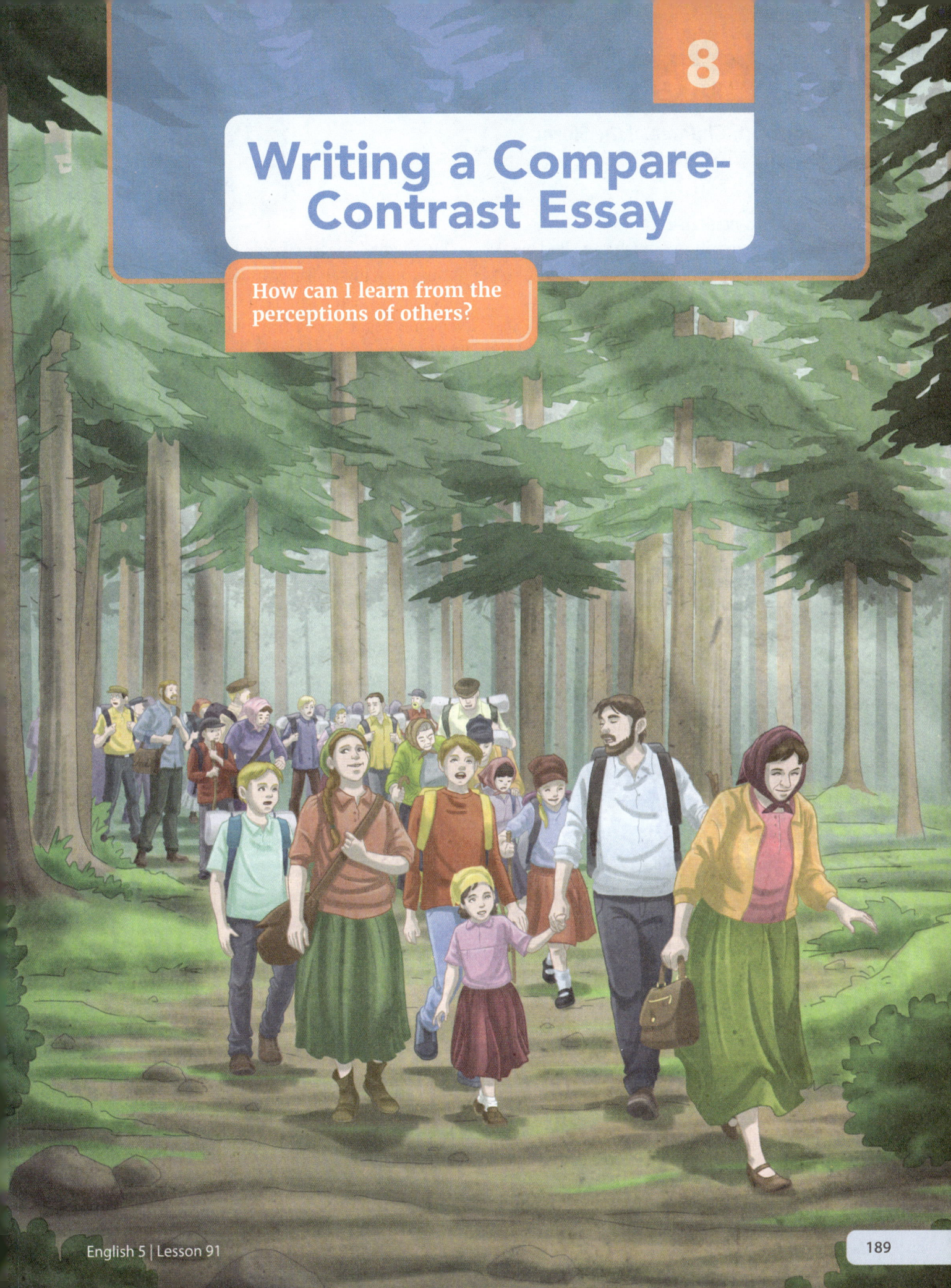

8

Writing a Compare-Contrast Essay

How can I learn from the perceptions of others?

Mentor Text

**Excerpt from *Children of the Storm*
by Natasha Vins**

One summer evening, Babushka called Peter and me away from our play and told us to wash up and get ready for bed. Her words drew a storm of protests. "Why must we go to bed so early? It is not even dark yet!"

But Babushka said, "Tomorrow, early in the morning, we are all going to a church service."

Peter and I could not believe what we heard. "But children aren't allowed at the services! Did you forget, Babushka?"

"No, I did not forget. But things have changed, and now you can come to church with us. So, hurry up and get ready for bed."

The next day we awoke to a bright Sunday morning, had breakfast, and set out for church. We traveled for two hours by bus, tram, and lastly commuter train. At last the train stopped at a small station in the woods. About thirty other people got off with us, and we all started down a pathway into the woods.

As we walked I tugged at Babushka's hand. "Where are we going? This is not the way to church!"

"Just wait." she answered without stopping. "Soon you will see for yourself."

At last we reached a large meadow. Everyone began spreading blankets on the grass and taking a seat. I still did not understand what was happening. "Babushka, is the service going to be right here? But where is the church building? Where is the pulpit?"

Babushka smiled, "This is our new place for Sunday services. Don't you like it? Look, the trees surround us like walls, and the sky is our ceiling. The sun is shining, birds are singing—don't you like it?"

I looked around. "Yes, it's nice, . . . but is this really a church?"

Just then one of the men standing in the middle asked everyone to bow his head for prayer. From that moment on the familiar atmosphere of Sunday worship surrounded me—hymns, sermons, prayers. One of the preachers was my papa.

Paragraph Structure

A paragraph is a group of sentences that tell about one main idea. The paragraph's topic sentence gives the main idea, and detail sentences support the topic sentence.

In a paragraph of **comparison**, the detail sentences support the topic sentence by telling how two things are alike.

> _My friend Sara and I have many things in common._ We are both in the fifth grade at Lifeway Christian School. Also, we are both from large families. I have four brothers and one sister, and Sara has three brothers and three sisters. We enjoy reading to our younger brothers and sisters. Another similarity is our hair color. Our red hair has led many people to think we are sisters when they see us together. It is fun to have a friend who is like me because that helps us understand each other very well.

In a paragraph of **contrast**, the detail sentences support the topic sentence by telling how two things are different.

> _I found two shells on the beach last week, but they are very different from each other._ One of them is a large, flat shell. It is pink, and it is shaped like a fan. The other shell is a small shell in a spiral shape. It is dark brown with light brown rings on it. I think the pink shell belonged to a clam or a scallop. However, the brown shell probably belonged to a snail.

Underline the topic sentence of the paragraph. Delete the two sentences that do not fit with the topic.

1.

> A bagel and a doughnut are alike in several ways. First of all, they have the same shape. Both a bagel and a doughnut are round, and most have a small hole in the middle. I ate a jelly-filled doughnut one time, and it didn't have a hole. Both a bagel and a doughnut are about three or four inches in diameter and about an inch thick. Bagels and doughnuts are also similar in popularity. Many people buy bagels or doughnuts for a special snack. One time my dad bought doughnuts for my birthday. Both bagel shops and doughnut shops are popular places for families and friends to enjoy together.

Proofreading Marks

   🖉 Delete

2.

> Although they look alike, bagels and doughnuts are different in many ways. Bagels have chewy insides, while doughnuts are soft inside like a cake. Bagels are boiled and then baked in the oven, but most doughnuts are fried. My favorite kind of doughnut is blueberry. Many people slice their bagels and eat them as sandwiches with meat on them. However, most people like to eat doughnuts plain or frosted. Bagels are usually not sweet, and they could be eaten for breakfast, lunch, or dinner. In contrast, doughnuts are sweet, and people usually eat them for breakfast or as a dessert. I usually have cereal for breakfast.

Mark the correct answer.

3. The first paragraph compares two _____.
   - ○ shops
   - ○ foods
   - ○ people

4. The second paragraph is an example of a paragraph that _____.
   - ○ compares
   - ○ contrasts

5. A good paragraph tells about _____.
   - ○ one main idea
   - ○ many different ideas

Compare-Contrast Essay

A **compare-contrast essay** explains the similarities and differences between two different people, places, or things.

The first paragraph, the introduction, tells what the essay is going to be about.

The second paragraph begins the main part of the essay. It is a comparison of the two states, telling how they are alike.

The third paragraph is a contrast of the two states. It tells how they are different.

The fourth paragraph, the conclusion, sums up how the writer feels about both states.

Southerners Go North

Most people have many adjustments to make when they move to a new place. My family moved from South Carolina to Nebraska last year. We enjoyed living in South Carolina, but we like Nebraska too. We have noticed many similarities and also a few differences between the two states.

Many things about Nebraska and South Carolina are similar. My school in Nebraska is a lot like my old school in South Carolina. We study all the same subjects, and we even use the same kind of textbooks. Similarly, our neighborhood here in Nebraska reminds me of our neighborhood in South Carolina. Our house there was on a cul-de-sac, and our house here is too. Like the neighbors in South Carolina, the neighbors here in Nebraska are friendly, and there are some kids my own age. South Carolina had a good church for us to attend, and Nebraska does also.

On the other hand, some things about Nebraska are different from South Carolina. For example, the winter weather is much different here in Nebraska. In South Carolina, we got a large amount of rain in the winter, but we hardly ever got snow. In contrast, Nebraska winters are frigid, and we get a lot of snow. Another difference is that we do not have the same kind of soil here. The South Carolina soil has a red color to it, but the Nebraska soil is dark brown. Nebraska has more farms than South Carolina does. We also see many more cows here than we saw in South Carolina.

We like our new home in Nebraska. Although people here like to tease us about being southerners, we enjoy seeing more snow and more farmland. We sometimes miss South Carolina, but we are glad God brought our family here.

Continued

Comparing and contrasting words can help make the details in an essay clearer and more connected.

Comparing Words	Contrasting Words
also	but
both	however
like	in contrast
similarly	even though
in the same way	on the other hand

Using proofreading marks, add comparing or contrasting words to make the paragraph clearer.

Winters in the North are quite different from winters in the South. Northern winters are very cold. In the South, the temperatures do not drop as low in winter. Many northern states lie under heavy layers of snow for weeks or months at a time. Snow in the southern states usually melts quickly. Roads are usually cleared and salted quickly after a snowfall in the North. Southern roads may remain snowy for longer periods of time.

Proofreading Marks

∧∨   Add

／   Lowercase

Compare-Contrast Essay: Shared Writing

Descriptive words used in a compare-contrast essay can help readers see the two subjects in their minds. Look for words or phrases that appeal to one or more of the five senses.

> *Our family's two cars have some differences. Our Subaru station wagon is an old car, but our Honda sedan is only two years old.*

> *Our family's two cars have some differences. Our red Subaru station wagon is an old car with some rust spots and a loud rumbly engine. However, our sleek silver Honda sedan is only two years old.*

Draft a compare-contrast essay with your teacher using the information from the Venn diagram you completed together. Follow the drafting guide, checking off the parts of the essay as you write.

Drafting Guide	
Introduction	Tell about the two subjects you will be comparing and contrasting in the main part of the essay.
Comparison	Tell how the two subjects are alike.
Contrast	Tell how the two subjects are different.
Conclusion	End by summing up the main part of the essay.

Check the class essay for one item on the revising checklist at a time. After you have completed the checklist, work on the items you were unable to check off.

Revising Checklist	
I compared and contrasted two things in my essay.	
My introduction leads into the main part of the essay.	
I included a good number of details in the comparing paragraph.	
I included a good number of details in the contrasting paragraph.	
I used comparing and contrasting words.	
I used descriptive words.	
My conclusion sums up the main part of the essay.	

Use the following checklist as you proofread the class essay.

Proofreading Checklist	
I indented the first line of each paragraph.	
I began each sentence with a capital letter and ended it with a punctuation mark.	
I used correct punctuation within sentences.	
I used correct verb forms.	
I wrote proper nouns correctly.	
I corrected misspelled words.	

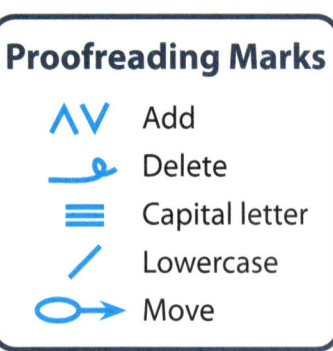

Proofreading Marks
∧∨ Add
Delete
Capital letter
Lowercase
Move

Compare-Contrast Essay: Plan

Begin planning your essay by listing details about both subjects on a T-Chart. Circle similar items and connect them with lines.

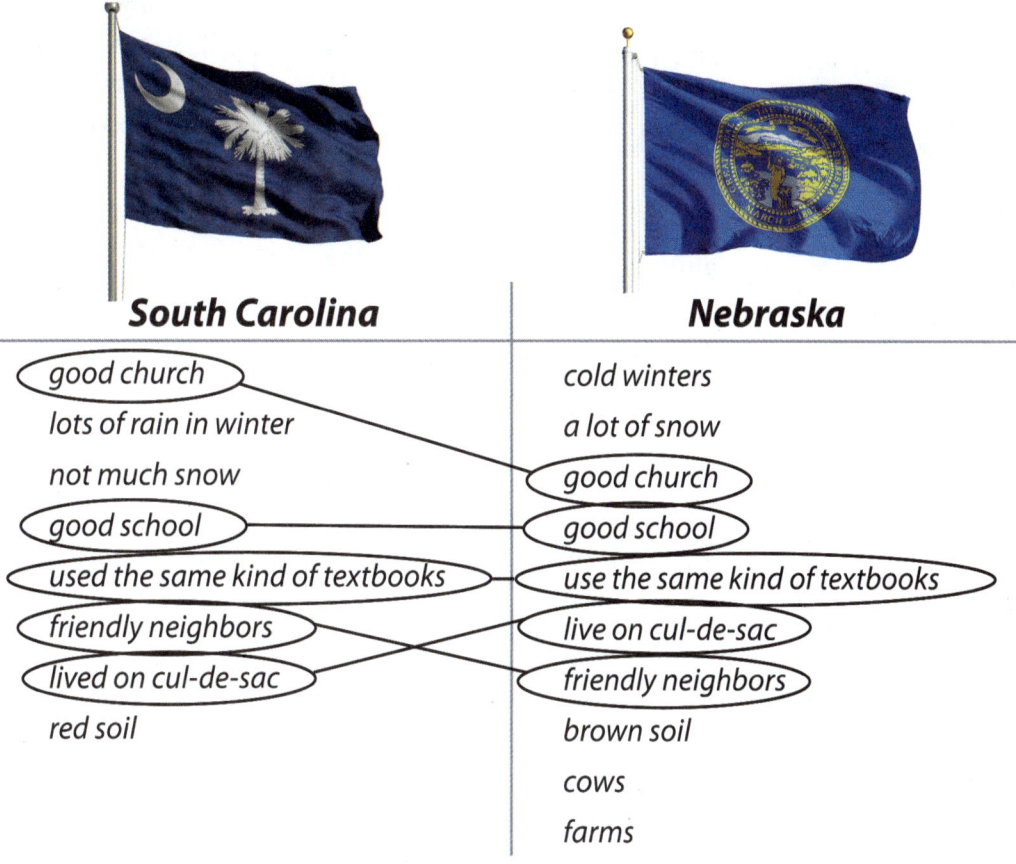

South Carolina	Nebraska
good church	cold winters
lots of rain in winter	a lot of snow
not much snow	good church
good school	good school
used the same kind of textbooks	use the same kind of textbooks
friendly neighbors	live on cul-de-sac
lived on cul-de-sac	friendly neighbors
red soil	brown soil
	cows
	farms

Then organize the similarities and differences in a Venn diagram.

South Carolina
lots of rain in winter
not much snow
red soil

good church
good school
use same kind of textbooks
live on cul-de-sac
friendly neighbors

Nebraska
cold winters
a lot of snow
brown soil
farms
cows

Possible Subjects

two places you have lived	fourth grade and fifth grade
two kinds of cars	walking and riding a bike
two friends	you and your brother or sister
two neighbors	summer and fall weather
two kinds of candy	two Bible characters
two kinds of birds	two kinds of meat

Remember to choose two subjects that are different but have some things in common.

Write your two subjects as the headings for the T-Chart. List details about each subject in the chart. Remember to include both likenesses and differences.

Circle the items that are similar on each side of the T-Chart and connect them with lines. Complete the Venn diagram your teacher provides, using the information from the chart.

Compare-Contrast Essay: Draft

Draft your essay using the details from your Venn diagram. The essay should have four paragraphs: an introduction, a paragraph of comparison, a paragraph of contrast, and a conclusion.

Nebraska and South Carolina

Most people have many adjustments to make when they move to a new place. My family moved from South Carolina to Nebraska last year. We like it here.

Many things about Nebraska and South Carolina are similer. My school in Nebraska is a lot like my old school in South carolina. We study all the same subjects, and we even use the same kind of textbooks. My favorite subject is math, but I like science too. Also our neighborhood here in Nebraska reminds me of our neighborhood in South Carolina. Our house there was on a culdasak, and our house here is too. Also the neighbors here in Nebraska are friendly, and there are some kids my own age. Also South Carolina had a good church for us to attend, and Nebraska does also.

On the other hand, some things about Nebraska is different from South Carolina. The winter weather is much different

Continued

here in Nebraska. In South Carolina, we got tons of rain in the winter, but we hardly ever got snow. In contrast, Nebraska winters are cold, and we get a lot of snow. We do not have the same kind of soil here. The South Carolina soil has a red color to it, but the nebraska soil is dark brown. Nebraska has more farms than South Carolina does. We also see tons more cows here than we saw in South Carolina.

We like our new home in Nebraska. Although people here like to tease us about being southerners. We enjoy seeing more snow and more farmland. We sometimes miss South Carolina but we are glad God brought our family here.

Use the details from your Venn diagram to draft your compare-contrast essay. Follow the drafting guide, checking off the parts of the essay as you write. Remember to use comparing and contrasting words to connect details.

Drafting Guide		
Introduction	Tell about the two subjects you will be comparing and contrasting in the main part of the essay.	
Comparison	Tell how the two subjects are alike.	
Contrast	Tell how the two subjects are different.	
Conclusion	End by summing up the main part of the essay.	

Compare-Contrast Essay: Revise

Listening to another person's perceptions about your essay can help you improve your writing. Think carefully about each peer conference comment as you revise.

> The writer revised the title to engage the reader's attention.

Southerners Go North
Nebraska and South Carolina

Most people have many adjustments to make when

they move to a new place. My family moved from South
We enjoyed living in South Carolina, but we like Nebraska too. We have
Carolina to Nebraska last year. We like it here.
noticed many similarties and also a few differences between the two States.
Many things about Nebraska and South Carolina are

> Added sentences lead into the main part of the essay.

similer. My school in Nebraska is a lot like my old school

in South carolina. We study all the same subjects, and we

even use the same kind of textbooks. My favorite subject

> This sentence does not belong in the paragraph.

Similarly,
is math, but I like science too. Also our neighborhood here

in Nebraska reminds me of our neighborhood in South

> The writer added different comparing words for variety.

Carolina. Our house there was on a culdasak, and our
Like the neighbors in South Carolina,
house here is too. Also the neighbors here in Nebraska are

friendly, and there are some kids my own age. Also South

> A transitional phrase connects the points more smoothly.

Carolina had a good church for us to attend, and Nebraska

does also.

On the other hand, some things about Nebraska is different
For example,
from South Carolina. The winter weather is much different

— Continued —

> *here in Nebraska. In South Carolina, we got ~~tons~~ a large amount of rain in the winter, but we hardly ever got snow. In contrast, Nebraska winters are ~~cold~~ frigid, and we get a lot of snow. Another difference is that We do not have the same kind of soil here. The South Carolina soil has a red color to it, but the nebraska soil is dark brown. Nebraska has more farms than South Carolina does. We also see ~~tons~~ many more cows here than we saw in South Carolina.*
>
> *We like our new home in Nebraska. Although people here like to tease us about being southerners. We enjoy seeing more snow and more farmland. We sometimes miss South Carolina but we are glad God brought our family here.*

The writer found places to use more exact and more descriptive words.

Use the following checklist as you revise your essay.

Revising Checklist
I compared and contrasted two things in my essay.
My introduction leads into the main part of the essay.
I included a good number of details in the comparing paragraph.
I included a good number of details in the contrasting paragraph.
I used comparing and contrasting words.
I used descriptive words.
My conclusion sums up the main part of the essay.

Proofreading Marks

∧∨ Add
Delete
≡ Capital letter
/ Lowercase
Move

Compare-Contrast Essay: Proofread

Proofread your essay to find and correct mistakes.

Southerners Go North

Most people have many adjustments to make when they move to a new place. My family moved from South Carolina to Nebraska last year. We enjoyed living in South Carolina, but we like Nebraska too. We have noticed many *similarities* ~~similarties~~ and also a few differences between the two ~~s~~States.

Many things about Nebraska and South Carolina are *similar* ~~similer~~. My school in Nebraska is a lot like my old school in South ~~c~~arolina. We study all the same subjects, and we even use the same kind of textbooks. Similarly, our neighborhood here in Nebraska reminds me of our neighborhood in South Carolina. Our house there was on a *cul-de-sac* ~~culdesak~~, and our house here is too. Like the neighbors in South Carolina, the neighbors here in Nebraska are friendly, and there are some kids my own age. South Carolina had a good church for us to attend, and Nebraska does also.

On the other hand, some things about Nebraska *are* ~~is~~ different from South Carolina. For example, the winter weather is

Continued

much different here in Nebraska. In South Carolina, we got a large amount of rain in the winter, but we hardly ever got snow. In contrast, Nebraska winters are frigid, and we get a lot of snow. Another difference is that we do not have the same kind of soil here. The South Carolina soil has a red color to it, but the nebraska soil is dark brown. Nebraska has more farms than South Carolina does. We also see many more cows here than we saw in South Carolina.

We like our new home in Nebraska. Although people here like to tease us about being southerners, We enjoy seeing more snow and more farmland. We sometimes miss South Carolina but we are glad God brought our family here.

Use the following checklist as you proofread your essay.

Proofreading Checklist	
I indented the first line of each paragraph.	
I began each sentence with a capital letter and ended it with a punctuation mark.	
I used correct punctuation within sentences.	
I used correct verb forms.	
I wrote proper nouns correctly.	
I corrected misspelled words.	

Proofreading Marks

∧∨   Add

 ✎   Delete

≡   Capital letter

╱   Lowercase

⊶→   Move

Reflection

Think of something you understand better now than in the past. Complete the T-Chart with details about how you thought then and how you think now. Then write several sentences about why your perception changed.

How I Thought Then	How I Think Now

Why my perception changed:

_____

_____

_____

_____

_____

_____

Cumulative Review

Use ∧ to add commas where they are needed.

1. Hannah a godly woman prayed to the Lord for a child.

2. In thanks to God for a baby boy Hannah presented Samuel to Eli to serve in the temple.

Change the underlined words to phrases with possessive nouns and combine the sentences to make a sentence with a compound subject.

3. The ways of God were taught to Samuel by Eli, the priest.
   The practices of the temple were taught to Samuel by Eli, the priest.

   _____

   _____

The following paragraph should be written in present tense. Circle the three incorrect verbs in the paragraph. Write the correct verb form to improve the paragraph.

One night Samuel lies down to sleep. He heard a voice calling his name. Three times he ran to Eli's room. The final time Eli tells Samuel that God is speaking. God spoke again, and Samuel responds, "Speak, Lord, for your servant is listening." Samuel learns to trust and obey God.

4. _____

5. _____

6. _____

Underline the topic sentence of the following opinion paragraph twice and the detail sentences (reasons and supporting details) once. Choose appropriate transitional words or phrases for the paragraph from the word bank. Insert their numbers in the paragraph where you feel they are needed.

7.   Samuel was one of the most important leaders in Israel. After Eli's death, he served as the chief priest in the tabernacle making sacrifices for the people. He was a prophet, delivering God's messages to the people. He was Israel's last judge before Israel was led by kings.

1. First of all,
2. One reason is that
3. One thing I like is that
4. Second,
5. I also think
6. Another reason is that
7. Finally,

Write the correct adjective or adverb form to complete the sentence.

8. What the Israelites desired the _____was to have an earthly king
   greatly

   like other nations.

9. The king's faith was _____ to God than his strength as a warrior.
   important

10. It is _____ to obey God than to disobey Him.
    wise

Write the correct form of *good*, *well*, *bad*, or *badly* to complete the sentence.

11. The Israelites thought Saul would be a _____ king than other men.

12. Saul's reign began _____ because he did not fully obey God.

13. At God's command Samuel anointed God's _____ choice, David.

Underline the words that can form a contraction. Write them as a contraction.

14. David <u>was not</u> perfect, but he asked for forgiveness with a repentant heart. _____

15. <u>I am</u> going to try to keep a pure heart before God. _____

Rewrite the sentence to correct the underlined double negative.

16. It <u>isn't never</u> right to disobey God's commands.

_____

Read the excerpt from an essay. Mark the correct answer.

> Although my frogs have some similarities, they are definitely very different. MacDuff is green, but Harvey is dark brown with tan stripes down his back. MacDuff likes to climb up on the branches in his cage but Harvey likes to burrow under the leaves. Harvey is also a little smaller than MacDuff. Harvey comes from Asia, but MacDuff comes from Australia.

17. The paragraph ____ the two pet frogs.
    ○ compares   ○ contrasts

18. What kind of mistake does the paragraph contain?
    ○ spelling   ○ punctuation

9

Pronouns

What makes you like or dislike a particular place?

SYDNEY BOARDING

Mentor Text

"Hide and Reef" by Elizabeth Preston

The world's largest coral reef is the Great Barrier Reef. It stretches for 1,400 miles (2,300 km) off the coast of Australia. Hundreds of divers and scientists visit it every year. You'd think we'd know all about it. But recently scientists found a surprise—another, unknown reef, right next door. The newly noticed reef is big and pointy. It stands about 1,640 feet (500 m) tall. That's bigger than the Empire State Building.

SuBastian

Researchers came across the pointy reef while they were working on a 3D map of the ocean floor. They sent a robot down to investigate. The diving robot, named SuBastian, sent back video of the reef. It's the first new coral reef anyone has discovered in more than 120 years.

The Great Barrier Reef

Singular and Plural Pronouns

A **pronoun** takes the place of a **noun**.

Singular pronouns replace singular nouns. Plural pronouns replace plural nouns or more than one noun or pronoun.

Max enjoys reading. He recommends many books to the other students. We often borrow books from him.

The teachers organized a reading contest. They will give prizes to the winning class.

The pronoun **you** can be singular or plural.

Did you remember to fill out your reading form?
You two have the top reading scores.

Pronouns				
Singular			Plural	
I	he	him	we	they
me	she	her	us	them
you	it		you	

Underline each pronoun in the sentence.

1. They are missionaries to New Zealand.

2. It is made up of several islands.

3. They asked us to come on a short-term mission trip.

4. Mom and Dad told us how we would be helping them.

5. The Baileys met us at the airport, and they took us with them for supper.

Write the correct pronoun to complete the sentence.

6. _____ told us about the Maori people.
      Mr. Bailey

7. _____ lived in New Zealand before the European explorers came.
      The Maoris

AfterSchoolHelp

Singular & Plural Pronouns

Write a sentence about one person. Use a singular pronoun.

8. _____

_____

Write a sentence about a group of people. Use a plural pronoun.

9. _____

_____

Underline each pronoun in the sentence.

10. There is one country that is also a continent, and it is Australia.

11. He told us that missionaries in Australia also need help.

12. I hope we can go on a mission trip to Australia someday.

13. Mr. Bailey told me that New Zealand has two main islands.

14. They are the North Island and the South Island.

15. You may look at these pictures from the trip.

Write the correct pronoun to complete the sentence.

16. _____ talked about Christ to people who had never heard.
    My family and I

17. _____ have no religion.
    Many New Zealanders

18. I invited _____ to the service.
    Lila and Kai

19. _____ played our violins.
    Beau and I

20. _____ played the piano.
    Mom

21. "Thank you for helping _____," Mr. Bailey said.
    Mr. Bailey and me

Practice

Underline each subject pronoun in the sentences.

1. Boston is one of the most historic towns in Massachusetts. It is known as the "birthplace of the American Revolution."

2. The early colonists settled in Boston in 1630. They named the town after their hometown in England.

3. John Cotton was a Puritan preacher in England. After coming to Boston, he became the pastor of the biggest church in the colony, First Church of Boston.

4. He is often given credit for writing an early version of the *New England Primer* used for schooling children.

Write the correct pronoun to complete the sentence.

5. By the mid-1700s _____ had become the main port for trade with a growing population.

Boston

6. Many of Boston's most famous buildings were built in the 1700s. _____ included buildings such as the Old State House and the Old North Church.

These buildings

Write a sentence about a building in your hometown. Use a singular pronoun.

7. _____

_____

Old State House

Old North Church

Underline each subject pronoun in the sentences.

8. The British soldiers were based in Boston, and they were attacked by a mob of angry colonists.

9. The conflict between the British and the colonists developed into a bigger conflict. It is referred to as the Boston Massacre.

Write the correct pronoun to complete the sentence.

10. The news about the Massacre was spread by _____.

Hancock and Adams

11. Historians give _____ credit for stirring up the colonists' desire for

the Massacre
    independence from the British.

Write a sentence about a military hero. Use at least one subject pronoun.

12. _____

    _____

Write a sentence about a military hero. Use at least one object pronoun.

13. _____

    _____

Underline each object pronoun in the sentences.

14. The colonists rebelled against the British Tea Act. They disagreed with it because the Act set limits on free trade.

15. The colonists met in the Old South Meeting House to make a request of the governor. They asked him to send the ships of tea back to England, but he refused.

16. The Sons of Liberty rowed out to the British ships full of tea. No one stopped them from dumping pounds of tea into Boston Harbor.

Write the correct pronoun to complete the sentence.

17. The British decided to stop the growing rebellion with force. This decision led

    _____ into the Revolutionary War.

the British

18. The siege of Boston by the British soldiers marks the first phase of the Revolutionary War. Bos-

    ton was occupied by _____ for eight years.

the British

Pronouns and Prepositions

An object pronoun can be used as a **direct object** or as an **object of a preposition**.

The missionary made a video about his time in Australia and showed it to our church.

Their church needs a new building, and our church took a special offering to help with it.

Object Pronouns	
Singular	**Plural**
me	us
you	you
him	them
her	
it	

Write *S* if the underlined pronoun is singular. Write *P* if the underlined pronoun is plural.

_____ 1. Our gym teacher taught <u>us</u> how to play tennis.

_____ 2. Leo, I brought this tennis racket for <u>you</u>.

_____ 3. I told <u>him</u> that the Australian Open is a famous tennis competition.

Write *DO* if the underlined pronoun is a direct object. Write *OP* if the underlined pronoun is an object of a preposition.

_____ 4. Dad practices with <u>me</u> after school.

_____ 5. He helps <u>me</u> use correct tennis technique.

_____ 6. Our dogs think the tennis balls are toys for <u>them</u>.

Write a sentence about a sport. Use a prepositional phrase with an object pronoun in your sentence.

7. _____

_____

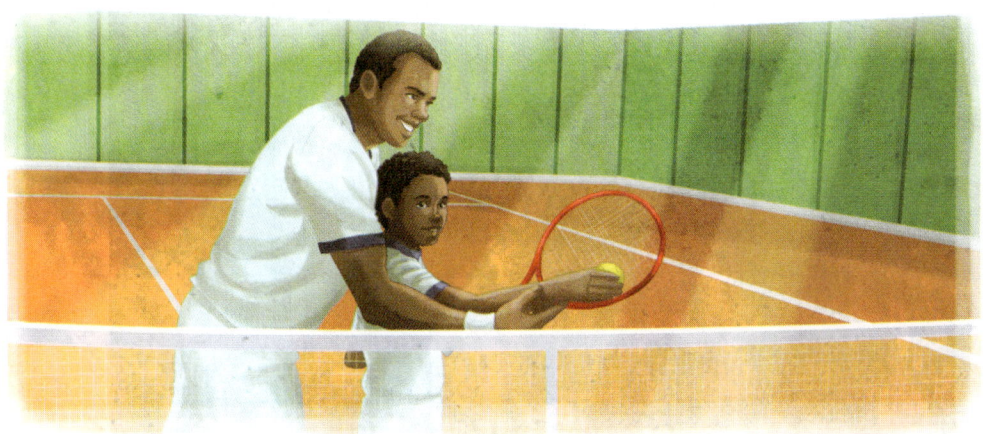

AfterSchoolHelp

Object Pronouns in Prepositional Phrases

Write *S* if the underlined pronoun is singular. Write *P* if the underlined pronoun is plural.

_____ 8. Students, let me tell <u>you</u> about the history of tennis shoes.

_____ 9. The name has an interesting story behind <u>it</u>.

_____ 10. She told <u>me</u> that the shoes have had many names.

_____ 11. Shoes with rubber soles were invented for British sailors who used <u>them</u> to walk across slippery decks.

Write *DO* if the underlined pronoun is a direct object. Write *OP* if the underlined pronoun is an object of a preposition.

_____ 12. She explained to <u>us</u> why the the shoes were called sneakers.

_____ 13. The rubber sole made <u>it</u> a very quiet shoe.

_____ 14. You might surprise someone if you sneaked up behind <u>him</u> in these shoes.

_____ 15. Soon, rich people used <u>them</u> to play sports like tennis.

_____ 16. Tennis was a popular game, and the shoes became associated with <u>it</u>.

_____ 17. Have you heard of Charles Goodyear? We can thank <u>him</u> for a new kind of rubber that improved the shoes.

_____ 18. Today many brands of tennis shoes are available to <u>us</u>.

_____ 19. How many of <u>you</u> are wearing tennis shoes today?

Write a sentence about shoes. Use a prepositional phrase with an object pronoun in your sentence.

20. _____

_____

Write a sentence about another piece of sports equipment. Use a pronoun as a direct object in your sentence.

21. _____

_____

Compound Subjects and Compound Objects

Two sentences may be joined by combining subjects or objects to form a **compound subject** or **compound object**.

Remember to use subject pronouns in a compound subject and object pronouns in a compound object.

Subject Pronouns		Object Pronouns	
Singular	**Plural**	**Singular**	**Plural**
I	we	me	us
you	you	you	you
he	they	him	them
she		her	
it		it	

Name yourself last when you write or speak about another person and yourself.

Jeremy and I went hiking.

Mom made cookies for Jeremy and me.

One plural pronoun can take the place of a compound subject or compound object.

We went hiking. Mom made cookies for us.

AfterSchoolHelp

Compound Subjects & Compound Objects

Mark the sentence that is written correctly.

1. ○ I and Theodore like to ride our bikes.
   ○ Theodore and I like to ride our bikes.

2. ○ Someone roller blades past Theodore and me.
   ○ Someone roller blades past Theodore and I.

Write the correct pronoun to complete the sentence.

3. Uncle Tim bought boomerangs for _____ and his brother.
   <u>Theodore</u>

4. _____ and Aunt Kathy explained that boomerangs come from Australia.
   <u>Uncle Tim</u>

Rewrite the sentence using a pronoun to replace the underlined words.

5. <u>Miles and I</u> wanted to throw the boomerangs.

_____

6. Theodore showed <u>Miles and me</u> what to do.

_____

Mark the sentence that is written correctly.

7. ◯ Mom helped Amaya and me with a missionary project.
   ◯ Mom helped Amaya and I with a missionary project.

8. ◯ I and Amaya wanted to include things for the children.
   ◯ Amaya and I wanted to include things for the children.

9. ◯ We asked her and Mrs. Nelson what snacks the children like.
   ◯ We asked she and Mrs. Nelson what snacks the children like.

10. ◯ You and I can finish packing the box.
    ◯ You and me can finish packing the box.

Write the correct pronoun to complete the sentence.

11. Mrs. Scott cooked a traditional Maori meal for _____ and me.
    _{Amy}

12. _____ and I were surprised to find sweet potatoes on the menu.
    _{Amy}

13. Mr. Scott explained to _____ that South Americans brought them many
    _{Amy and me}
    years ago.

14. _____ and the church people enjoy the sweet potatoes with roast pork.
    _{Mr. Scott}

15. We thanked _____ and Mr. Scott for the delicious meal.
    _{Mrs. Scott}

Rewrite the sentence using a pronoun to replace the underlined words.

16. Mom read to <u>Greg, Amos, and Owen</u>.

_____

17. <u>Greg, Amos, and Owen</u> enjoyed hearing about western Australia.

_____

18. <u>The boys and I</u> would like to visit someday.

_____

Pronoun-Antecedent Agreement

An **antecedent** is the noun or nouns that a **pronoun** renames. The antecedent usually comes before the pronoun.

The pronoun must be singular if the antecedent is singular and plural if the antecedent is plural.

A singular pronoun must match its antecedent in gender.

The girls have been practicing hard because they want to win the game.

Mrs. Oliver coaches the girls' team, and she brings snacks to every game.

Joe and Cora promised that they would save us seats.

The ball missed the goal, and then it went out of bounds.

Although Rowan likes soccer, he enjoys basketball the most.

Jasmine plans to come to the game, but she may be late.

correct   correct   incorrect

Underline the pronoun and its antecedent. Draw an arrow from the pronoun to its antecedent.

1. Adrian said he wondered what a typical week was like for the missionary family.

2. Mr. Young teaches Sunday school, and he gives the morning message.

3. Mrs. Young runs the nursery, and she leads a ladies' Bible study.

4. The children help set up refreshments after they finish Sunday school.

Write the pronoun that correctly renames the underlined antecedent.

5. Mrs. Young was surprised when _____ saw a parrot!

6. Mr. Young said _____ had never seen such a colorful bird.

7. The parrot came close to me but flew away before I could touch _____ .

AfterSchoolHelp

Pronoun/ Antecedent Agreement

Write sentences using the following antecedents and pronouns.

8. Abigail/she: _____

_____

9. Henry and I/we: _____

_____

Underline the pronoun and its antecedent. Draw an arrow from the pronoun to its antecedent.

10. Many Australians live in cities, and they work in offices.

11. My pen pal Ryan lives on a sheep farm, and he is homeschooled.

12. This sweater was a present from Ryan. It is made of pure wool.

Write the pronoun that correctly renames the underlined antecedent.

13. Mrs. Hayes asked us to find a fact about Australia that _____ could write on the board.

14. Sam and I looked online, and _____ found some interesting facts.

15. The capital city is called Canberra. _____ is one of several large cities in Australia.

16. Although Australians are far from England, _____ have many British traditions.

17. The Queen of England is also the Queen of Australia, and _____ appoints an Australian governor-general.

18. We read about a popular sport in Australia. _____ is a British game called cricket.

Possessive Pronouns

A **possessive pronoun** shows ownership. Possessive pronouns replace **possessive nouns**. The pronoun must be singular if its antecedent is singular and plural if its antecedent is plural.

Rachel's dog was barking.   That dog is Andrew and Santiago's.

Her dog was barking.   That dog is theirs.

Some possessive pronouns are used before nouns.

This is his dog.   The dog chased its tail.

Some possessive pronouns can stand alone.

That bike is his.   Three of the kittens are ours.

Possessive Pronouns			
Used before Nouns		**Used Alone**	
my	his	mine	his
our	her	ours	hers
your	its	yours	theirs
their			

Underline the possessive pronoun in the sentence.

1. Dad helps me with my homework.

2. This textbook used to be his.

3. Its cover is all worn out.

4. We have our study sessions at the kitchen table.

Write the correct possessive pronoun to complete the sentence.

5. Dad told me about one of _____ teachers.

Dad's

6. _____ name was Mrs. Flores.

The teacher's

7. This large collection of missionary biographies was _____.

Mrs. Flores's

8. She encouraged the students to read about _____ Christian heritage.

the students'

AfterSchoolHelp

Possessive Pronouns

Write a sentence about something that belongs to you. Use a possessive pronoun that can stand alone in your sentence.

9. _____

_____

Write a sentence about something that belongs to one of your friends. Use a possessive pronoun before a noun in your sentence.

10. _____

_____

Underline the possessive pronoun in the sentence.

11. Our school is raising money for a special project.

12. The idea for the fundraiser was mine.

13. The project will help a missionary and his church.

14. Their goal is to give away one hundred Bibles.

15. The money we raise will be added to theirs.

16. Your contribution will be very helpful.

Write the correct possessive pronoun to complete the sentence.

17. The red sweater is _____.
   my sweater

18. The striped sweaters are _____.
   Julie's and Kyle's

19. Hunter, are the brown shoes _____?
   Hunter's

20. _____ sisters are the same age.
   Derrick's and my

21. I handed Eric _____ coat.
   Eric's

22. Do you know if this book is _____?
   Jasmine's

23. Mom's cooking is better than _____.
   my cooking

Reflexive Pronouns

A **reflexive pronoun** reflects or renames the subject of a sentence.

Reflexive pronouns are used as direct objects or objects of prepositions.

My brother drove himself home.   *I choose a snack for myself.*

A reflexive pronoun is never used as a subject.

Correct: *She volunteered herself to help.*
Incorrect: *Herself volunteered to help.*

Reflexive Pronouns	
Singular	**Plural**
myself	ourselves
yourself	yourselves
himself	themselves
herself	
itself	

Underline the reflexive pronoun and its antecedent. Draw an arrow from the reflexive pronoun to its antecedent.

1. I addressed and mailed the letter by myself.

2. The cat licked itself.

3. Mom wrote herself a reminder.

Write *DO* if the underlined pronoun is a direct object. Write *OP* if the underlined pronoun is an object of a preposition.

_____ 4. The dog shook <u>itself</u>.

_____ 5. My brother changed the tire by <u>himself</u>.

Mark the sentence that is written correctly.

6. ○ They sat by theirselves.
   ○ They sat by themselves.

7. ○ Herself sang a solo.
   ○ She sang a solo.

8. ○ He congratulated himself.
   ○ He congratulated hisself.

AfterSchoolHelp

Reflexive Pronouns

Write two sentences about a game you have participated in. Use at least one reflexive pronoun.

9. _____

_____

_____

_____

Underline the reflexive pronoun and its antecedent. Draw an arrow from the reflexive pronoun to its antecedent.

10. We decided to start a prayer group among ourselves.

11. Did you go by yourself?

12. I enjoyed myself very much.

Write *DO* if the underlined pronoun is a direct object. Write *OP* if the underlined pronoun is an object of a preposition.

_____ 13. We cooked dinner for ourselves.

_____ 14. The toddler fed herself.

_____ 15. Elias and Matthew introduced themselves to me.

_____ 16. Nova keeps a journal for herself.

Mark the sentence that is written correctly.

17. ○ Our sin problem cannot fix himself.
    ○ Our sin problem cannot fix itself.

18. ○ We cannot help others by ourself.
    ○ We cannot help others by ourselves.

19. ○ We must pray that God will make Himself known to them.
    ○ We must pray that God will make Hisself known to them.

Prefixes and Suffixes

A **prefix** is a group of letters added to the beginning of a base word to make a new word.

Prefix	Meaning	Example	Meaning
bi-	having two of; twice	bicycle	having two wheels
dis-, un-	not; opposite of	distrust	to not trust
im-, in-, non-	not	imperfect	not perfect
mis-	wrong; incorrectly	misunderstood	understand incorrectly
out-	greater; better	outdo	to do better than
pre-	before	preview	to view before
re-	again or back	reprint	to print again

A **suffix** is a group of letters added to the end of a base word to make a new word.

Suffix	Meaning	Example	Meaning
-able, -ible	capable or worthy of	likeable	worthy to be liked
-en	to make	brighten	to make bright
-er, -or, -ist	one who ...es	painter	one who paints
-ful	full of	truthful	full of truth
-ish	like; some...	girlish	like a girl
-less	without; not hav...	penniless	without money
-ly	like in nature or manner		in a glad manner
-ment	the act, state, quality, or result...		the act of adjusting
-ness	state, condition, or quality of	n...	...ate of being neat

Write a new word by adding a prefix or a suffix to the base word to fit the mean... of the sentence.

1. Wallace Carothers invented the _____ fabric called nylon.

wonder

2. Nylon is _____ because it is man-made.

usual

Mark the correct meaning of the underlined word.

3. Today, many nylon products are <u>inexpensive</u>.
   - ○ not expensive
   - ○ in an expensive manner

4. Nylon is well-known for its <u>toughness</u> and its variety of uses.
   - ○ one who is tough
   - ○ quality of being tough

Choose two of the following words: *babyish, impossible, operator, restless,* and *return.* Write a sentence using each word correctly.

5. Word 1: _____

_____

6. Word 2: _____

_____

Write a new word by adding a prefix or a suffix to the base word to fit the meaning of the sentence.

7. Carothers's _____ was the first of many synthetic materials.

accomplish

8. Carothers was a _____ at the University of South Dakota.

teach

9. His _____ in the Chemistry Department helped him with his research.

appoint

10. By 1924, he was _____ his ideas about polymers at Harvard University.

testing

11. Four years later Carothers was _____ involved in research at the DuPont

active
Company.

12. His team of scientists spent _____ hours conducting their experiments.

end

13. The scientists hoped to develop a fabric to _____ Japanese silk.

place

Mark the correct meaning of the underlined word.

14. DuPont's team searched <u>diligently</u> for a way to create the first synthetic fiber in 1934.
   ○ not diligent   ○ in a diligent way

15. Carothers's <u>adjustment</u> of the process made the fiber better.
   ○ one who adjusts   ○ act of adjusting

16. The new method would <u>strengthen</u> the fibers.
   ○ without strength   ○ to make stronger

17. <u>Confidently</u>, the DuPont Company introduced nylon to the American public in 1938.
   ○ in a confident manner ○ not confident

Practice

Write *S* if the underlined pronoun is singular. Write *P* if the underlined pronoun is plural.

_____ 1. "Students, do <u>you</u> know where the Freedom Trail is?" inquired Mrs. Thompson.

_____ 2. Many tourists visit Boston every year. <u>They</u> are interested in exploring the Revolutionary sites.

_____ 3. Mayor John Hynes opened the Freedom Trail. <u>It</u> is a walking tour through downtown Boston.

Write *DO* if the underlined pronoun is a direct object. Write *OP* if the underlined pronoun is an object of a preposition.

_____ 4. Mayor Hynes marked the path between the sixteen historic landmarks with a red line for <u>us</u> to follow.

_____ 5. The landmarks helped <u>me</u> to learn about the Revolutionary War events.

_____ 6. Mrs. Thompson told <u>us</u> about the landmarks along the Trail.

Write a sentence about a historical character you would like to meet. Use a prepositional phrase with an object pronoun in your sentence.

7. _____

_____

Write the correct pronoun to complete the sentence.

8. "Colton and _____ felt like we were traveling back in time!" Mrs.
Mrs. Thompson
Thompson said.

9. "First, the tour guide took _____ to the Boston Common, which was
Colton and me
occupied at different times by both the colonial militia and the British Redcoats."

Underline the pronoun and its antecedent. Draw an arrow from the pronoun to its antecedent.

10. Next, tourists see the Massachusetts State House. It sits on land once owned by John Hancock.

11. Paul Revere laid the State House's cornerstone, and he covered the dome with copper.

Write the pronoun that correctly renames the underlined antecedent.

12. <u>The men</u> who died in the Boston Massacre are considered heroes. _____ are buried in Granary Graveyard with Paul Revere and Samuel Adams.

13. <u>King's Chapel</u> hosted many famous people and notable events during this time period. _____ houses the oldest pipe organ in regular use in the United States.

Write the correct possessive pronoun to complete the sentence.

14. The Old Corner Bookstore was a publishing company. _____ fame came by
    The bookstore's
    publishing well-known titles, such as "The Midnight Ride of Paul Revere."

15. The Old South Meeting House was where the tea tax was debated and Samuel Adams gave
    _____ signal to start the Boston Tea Party.
    Adams's

Write *DO* if the underlined pronoun is a direct object. Write *OP* if the underlined pronoun is an object of a preposition.

_____ 16. Colonists gathered <u>themselves</u> together at Faneuil Hall during the British occupation.

_____ 17. Faneuil Hall identifies <u>itself</u> by the grasshopper weathervane on top.

_____ 18. Shem Drowne crafted the weathervane by <u>himself</u>.

Mark the homophone that correctly completes the sentence.

19. Paul Revere's house is the only home on the Freedom Trail. It is a ____ wooden structure many visitors like to tour.
    ○ plane   ○ plain

20. Paul Revere is famous for riding his ____ to Lexington to warn John Hancock and Samuel Adams that the British were coming.
    ○ horse   ○ hoarse

21. The church sexton looked out from the top of the Old North Church. He would hold up one lantern if the British were coming by land or two if they were coming by ____.
    ○ see   ○ sea

Chapter 9 Review

Write the correct pronoun to complete the sentence.

1. Jake showed _____ some pictures of a kauri tree.

Callie

2. _____ is one of the largest, oldest trees in the world.

The tree

3. _____ grow in forests on New Zealand's North Island.

Kauri trees

4. Callie would like to see a kauri tree for _____.

Callie

5. She enjoyed hearing about _____ travels.

Jake's

Write two sentences about a plant. Use at least one pronoun.

6. _____

_____

_____

Write *DO* if the underlined pronoun is a direct object. Write *OP* if the underlined pronoun is an object of a preposition.

_____ 7. The beauty of New Zealand reminds <u>us</u> of our Creator's power.

_____ 8. We praise <u>Him</u> for all the beautiful things in our world.

_____ 9. He created all of <u>them</u>.

Mark the sentence that is written correctly.

10. ○ Jake told Steven and me about the Southern Alps on the South Island.

○ Jake told Steven and I about the Southern Alps on the South Island.

11. ○ He showed us a picture of hisself on a hike.

○ He showed us a picture of himself on a hike.

12. ○ I and Steven found more information about these mountains in this library book.

○ Steven and I found more information about these mountains in this library book.

13. ○ He and me want to go there ourselves.

○ He and I want to go there ourselves.

Rewrite the sentence using a pronoun to replace the underlined words.

14. <u>Elizabeth and her dad</u> went fly fishing in New Zealand.

_____

15. She told <u>my sister and me</u> about the beautiful lake.

_____

Write the pronoun that correctly renames the underlined antecedent.

16. That island is called <u>Stewart Island</u>. _____ is an excellent place to view the southern lights.

17. The island was named for <u>William W. Stewart</u>. _____ helped establish a settlement there.

18. Around five hundred <u>people</u> live on the island. _____ make their money from fishing and tourism.

Mark the homophone that correctly completes the sentence.

19. Christopher spent one _____ at the island.
    ○ week   ○ weak

20. His family enjoys spending time near the _____.
    ○ see   ○ sea

21. _____ you enjoy an island vacation?
    ○ Wood   ○ Would

22. I enjoy visiting the seashore _____.
    ○ too   ○ two

Mark the correct meaning of the underlined word.

23. Titus <u>misunderstood</u> the directions.
    ○ understood incorrectly   ○ understood very well

24. He was <u>discouraged</u> by his quiz grade.
    ○ to feel the opposite of courage   ○ to feel very courageous

25. Our school has a <u>bimonthly</u> newsletter.
    ○ twice a month   ○ once a month

Journal

Imagine that you are writing a travel brochure about one of your favorite places. Explain what you like about this place and why someone else would enjoy visiting it. Circle any pronouns that you use.

_____

_____

_____

_____

_____

_____

_____

_____

Cumulative Review

Write *S* if the group of words is a sentence. Write *F* if the group of words is a fragment.

_____ 1. Created the sea and the dry land.

_____ 2. God's plans are perfect.

_____ 3. The God of mercy.

Choose a fragment from numbers 1–3 and rewrite it as a complete sentence.

4. _____

_____

Use ▤ to mark the letters that should be capitalized.

5. jonah is an old testament book written during the reign of king jeroboam II of israel.

Make a compound subject or predicate by combining the sentences. Use the conjunction *and* or *or*.

6. God instructed Jonah to go to Nineveh. God told him to call on its people to repent.

_____

_____

Write a compound sentence using a comma and a conjunction.

7. Jonah could choose to obey God's command. Jonah could choose to disobey it.

_____

_____

The following paragraph should be written in present tense. Circle the three incorrect verbs in the paragraph. Write the correct verb form to improve the paragraph.

Instead of obeying, Jonah rebels and flees in the opposite direction. He boarded a ship that is bound for the city of Tarshish. God sends a great storm. Jonah knew the storm is punishment for his rebellion, so he tells the crew to throw him overboard. The storm stops. God sent a big fish to rescue Jonah.

8. _____

9. _____

10. _____

Write the correct pronoun to complete the sentence.

11. _____ spit Jonah out on dry land.
       The big fish

12. God's command was given to _____ once again.
                                              Jonah

13. This time _____ obeyed God by going to Nineveh.
                          Jonah

Write the pronoun that correctly renames the underlined antecedent.

14. The <u>Ninevites</u> listened to Jonah's message, and _____ repented.

15. Because the <u>Ninevites</u> repented, God abandoned His plan to destroy _____.

Write the correct possessive pronoun to complete the sentence.

16. Jonah was disappointed by _____ change of heart.
                                          the Ninevite's

17. Perhaps Jonah believed the Ninevites would remain a threat to _____
                                                                                      Jonah's

    homeland.

Write *DO* if the underlined pronoun is a direct object. Write *OP* if the underlined pronoun is an object of a preposition.

_____ 18. God showed <u>Himself</u> merciful to even the most wicked.

_____ 19. Christians should look for opportunities for <u>themselves</u> to share God's message of

    salvation.

10

Writing a Persuasive Letter

How can persuasion be deceitful?

Mentor Text

Excerpt from *The Mysterious Benedict Society*
by Trenton Lee Stewart

"It sounds like there are no rules here at all," Sticky said.

"That's true, George," said Jillson. "Virtually none, in fact. You can wear whatever you want, just so long as you have on trousers, shoes, and a shirt. You can bathe as often as you like or not at all, provided you're clean every day in class. You can eat whatever and whenever you want, so long as it's during meal hours in the cafeteria. You're allowed to keep the lights on in your rooms as late as you wish until ten o'clock each night. And you can go wherever you want around the Institute, so long as you keep to the paths and yellow-tiled corridors."

"Actually," Reynie observed, "those all sound like rules."

Jackson rolled his icy blue eyes. "This is your first day, so I don't expect you to know much, Reynard. But this is one of the rules of life you'll learn at the Institute: Many things that sound like rules aren't actually rules, and it always sounds as if there are more rules than there really are."

"That sounds like *two* rules I'll learn," Reynie said.

Dishonest Tactics

Most people read or listen to persuasive words every day. Advertisements in magazines and newspapers or on television, radio, and the internet are examples of persuasive writing.

BRIGHT BITES

Today's kids are **bright, energetic,** and **ready for action!**

That's why today's kids are tired of eating those boring cereals with no taste and no color.

All over the country, **kids just like you are choosing Bright Bites.**

Bright Bites, a truly tasty cereal, is **sparkling with color and packed with vitamins.**

Don't settle for boring cereal.

Join today's bright kids who go for the **big fruity taste of Bright Bites!**

Dishonest tactics of persuasion are often used in advertising. Writers appeal to people's feelings to get them to buy or do something.

Examples of Dishonest Tactics	
Bandwagon "Do it so you'll be part of the group."	Everyone else is eating Bright Bites. If you want to fit in with the group, you need to eat them too.
Name-calling "People who don't do it are losers."	People who don't eat Bright Bites are behind the times. You don't want to be old-fashioned and unpopular like they are.
Promises "Do it, and wonderful things will happen."	If you eat Bright Bites, you will be viewed as intelligent, and you will be liked and respected.
Testimonial "Do it because this famous person does."	President Coleman sits down to a bowl of Bright Bites every morning. That's how he got where he is.

When you write to persuade, avoid using dishonest tactics. If you cannot think of an honest way to persuade someone, it is probably not worth persuading the person at all.

Identify the dishonest tactic being used in the example. Match the example with the letter of the tactic.

_____ 1. If you wear Spede tennis shoes, you will become a star basketball player.

_____ 2. More students use Pearly Whites toothpaste than any other brand. Won't you join the thousands of other students who are showing off their pearly white grins?

A bandwagon
B name-calling
C promises
D testimonial

_____ 3. Channel 5 news anchor Millie Turnquist wears dresses with the Favorites label. Look for that brand when you shop—and make headlines.

_____ 4. Those who do not give to our cause are robbing the world's children of a better life. Don't be one of the robbers. Call today to support the Relief Fund.

Rewrite the following ad to be honest in its persuasion.

Try **ONE** of our SEVENTY-TWO flavors of ice cream. ✕✕✕✕✕✕✕

DREAM CONES **ice cream will make** **ALL YOUR DREAMS** COME TRUE.

5. _____

_____

_____

_____

Formal and Informal Letters

219 Ellis Dr.
Apple Creek, KS 66100
July 24, 2023

Dear Adam,

You'll never guess what I did with Dad last week! We went for a hot-air balloon ride at the fair. The ground slipped away as we floated up over the treetops. I took lots of pictures, but my favorite one shows our balloon's reflection in a lake below us. It was amazingly quiet up high above the world—the only noise was the gas burner. We got to see three different states!

Will you be coming to Apple Creek next summer? If so, I think you should take a balloon ride with us. Write soon and tell us about your summer. We miss you!

Your friend,
Toby

> An **informal letter** may be written to express thanks, to offer congratulations, to give advice, or to share news. It is usually written to someone the writer knows.

219 Ellis Dr.
Apple Creek, KS 66100
July 29, 2023

Fuller Farms
15302 Orchard Rd.
Apple Creek, KS 66100

Dear Sir or Madam:

The Fuller Farms Fall Festival is one of my family's favorite places to go each year. I would like to suggest that you make it even better by offering hot-air balloon rides. Balloon rides are very popular. Recently my dad and I went for a hot-air balloon ride at the Tri-County Fair, and there was a waiting list for those who wanted to ride. Many of my friends here in Apple Creek are very interested in taking a balloon ride as well.

Thank you for considering my suggestion. I appreciate all you do to make the festival such a wonderful event.

Yours truly,
Toby Graham
Toby Graham

> A **formal letter** may be written to make a request, to give information, or to express an opinion. It is usually written to someone the writer does not know or does not know very well.

Continued

Good formal letters have four characteristics:

1. **Precise wording**:

   The writer avoids including unnecessary details. Each detail has a purpose.

2. **Polite tone**:

   The greeting and closing are more formal than those of an informal letter. The writer uses *please* and *thank you*.

Dear Sir or Madam:	*Sincerely,*
Dear Dr. Garber:	*Yours truly,*

3. **Plain facts**:

   Necessary facts are included.

4. **Proper form**:

   The letter follows the correct form.

Compare the two letters on the previous Worktext page. Mark the correct answer.

1. Which letter includes more details about balloon rides?
   ○ the informal letter   ○ the formal letter

2. Which letter contains only necessary details?
   ○ the informal letter   ○ the formal letter

3. Which letter is more conversational in tone?
   ○ the informal letter   ○ the formal letter

4. Which letter has two addresses?
   ○ the informal letter   ○ the formal letter

5. Which letter's greeting is usually written to someone the writer does not know?
   ○ the informal letter   ○ the formal letter

Parts of a Formal Letter

A formal letter has six parts.

Heading

91 Riverview Dr.
Blue Valley, AR 71688
December 1, 2023

Capt. Kenneth Jones
Blue Valley Police Department
7 South Sparrow St.
Blue Valley, AR 71688

Inside Address

Greeting

Dear Captain Jones:

Body

My fifth-grade class at Crossroads Academy has been learning about law enforcement. Would you be willing to come speak to us about your work as a police captain? You could tell us about your training, explain what you do each day, and perhaps show us your police car and equipment.

The class would benefit from meeting an officer in person. Many of my classmates have never met an officer or seen a police car up close. Hearing you speak about your duties and experiences would help all of us understand our police officers' work better.

Your visit would also help the police department and the people of Blue Valley. As we understand more about the officers, our appreciation for their work will grow. Maybe some of us will even decide to work in law enforcement in the future.

A possible time for you to speak to us would be at 10:00 a.m. on January 9, National Law Enforcement Day. My teacher, Mr. Dominic Cannelloni, said he could work to find a different day or time if needed. If you would like to come, please contact him at (861) 423-4231 or dcannello@bluevalleycrossroads.net. Thank you for considering this invitation.

Closing

Sincerely,
Eliana Zander
Eliana Zander

Signature

Continued

The address in the **heading** of the formal letter tells the person who receives the letter where to send his reply. The heading also includes the date.

The **inside address** shows who should receive the letter.

In the **greeting**, write *Sir or Madam* if you do not know the name of the person who should receive the letter. Use a colon after the greeting.

Choose a formal **closing** such as *Sincerely* or *Yours truly* and put a comma after it.

Include your first and last name in your **signature**. In a typed letter, the signature is written by hand and then typed on the line beneath it.

Read the following formal letter and answer the questions.

> Mrs. Leah Mace
> Mansfield Laboratories
> 700 E. Beech Drive
> Chattanooga, TN 37404
>
>
> Dear Mrs. Mace:
>
> I want you to come and speak to our class about your work. We are studying chemicals in science. We would all love to have you come. Please let me know whether you can.
>
> Sincerely,
> *Aaron McNeil*
> Aaron McNeil

1. What fact does the writer leave out of his letter?
   ○ his name   ○ how Mrs. Mace can get in touch with him

2. What mistake has the writer made in his form?
   ○ He has left out the heading.   ○ He has placed a colon after the greeting.

3. Write a more polite wording for the first sentence of the letter.

_____

_____

Email Form and Etiquette

An email is similar to a printed letter, but it has some important differences in form.

The email address of the sender replaces the heading. The date will appear automatically in the email.

The email address of the person receiving the letter replaces the inside address.

The subject line tells the topic or purpose of the email.

The greeting, paragraphs, closing, and signature are not indented.

Following good email etiquette is a way to show courtesy. It communicates thoughtfulness and consideration for others.

Do not use all capital letters for words or sentences. This is called SHOUTING and is considered impolite.

In a formal email, avoid using a texting abbreviation or an emoji.

Why do I need to email a registered nurse?

What does LMK mean?

New message

To: mfox973@chs.edu

Subject: Judging talent show

Dear Dr. Fox:
The three fifth-grade classes here at Crossroads Academy are holding a talent show on March 10, 2023, at 10:00 a.m. Would you be willing to serve as a judge? Your experience as a band director would make you an excellent judge for this event since many students will be performing musical numbers. Please reply to let me know if you can help. Thank you for considering this opportunity.
Sincerely,
Shawn Ryan

Send

New message

To: mfox973@chs.edu

Subject: Question

Hey Mr.:
We're having a fifth-grade talent show. Can U judge it? I've already asked FIVE PEOPLE and they all said no, so I decided to check with you. 😉 I hope you can do it because I'm really tired of writing emails. Email RN to LMK.
So long,
Skipp

Send

Continued

Like a formal letter, a formal email should use precise wording, have a polite tone, and give plain facts.

Skipp's Letter:

Wasted Words

"I've already asked five people . . ."

". . . I'm tired of writing emails."

Impolite Tone

"Hey Mr. :"

"FIVE PEOPLE"

"Email RN to LMK."

"So long,"

Not Enough Facts

Does not give time and place

Shawn's Letter:

Precise Wording

Makes request without giving unnecessary details

Polite Tone

"Dear Dr. Fox:"

"Please reply to let me know . . ."

"Thank you for considering . . ."

"Sincerely,"

Plain Facts

Gives the time and place

The writer of this email does not know the name of the person at the classic car dealership who will receive the request. Rewrite the greeting, body, and closing of the email using precise wording, a polite tone, and plain facts.

New message

To: support@classicauto.com

Subject: Car for July 3 parade

Dear Car Guys:
Next week is the Independence Day parade. It will be on July 3, and my grandpa's birthday is July 4. Could you have someone drive a classic car from your store in the parade? Tell me TODAY. THX.
Bye for now,
Cameron

Send

_____

_____

_____

_____

_____

_____

_____

_____

_____

Persuasive Letter: Plan

Organize ideas for your letter in a persuasion chart.

Audience

Capt. Kenneth Jones

Blue Valley Police Department

7 South Sparrow St.

Blue Valley, AR 71688

Purpose

to persuade the police officer to come speak to our class

Explanation of Purpose

class learning about people who serve our community

tell about your training, explain what you do

show your car, other equipment

Reason 1	Reason 2
The students would benefit from meeting an officer in person.	It would help the police department and our community.

Facts and Examples	Facts and Examples
first time for many to meet an officer, see equipment up close	appreciation for the officers' work will grow
would understand better what a police officer does	some of us may decide to work in law enforcement

Plan a persuasive letter. After choosing your purpose, complete the chart.

Audience

Purpose

Explanation of Purpose

Reason 1	Reason 2

Facts and Examples	Facts and Examples

Persuasive Letter: Draft

The inside address of a formal letter can help direct the letter to the correct person.

At a business, where someone else may open the letter, the envelope may be lost or thrown away. When known, the recipient's name can be included in the inside address.

Mr. James Radcliffe
Beacon Book and Gift Company
9600 East Bearcreek Lane
Cheyenne, WY 82009

Some large organizations are divided into many different departments. When known, the specific department name can be given after the company name in the address.

American Wildlife
Human Resource Department
1412 16th Street
Washington, DC 20036

Use the ideas from your persuasion chart to draft your letter. Follow the drafting guide, checking off each part of the persuasive letter as you write. Remember the four *P*s of writing good formal letters.

Precise wording   Polite tone   Plain facts   Proper form

Drafting Guide			
Heading	Write your address followed by the date.		
Inside Address	Write the name and address of the person who should receive the letter.		
Greeting	Write an appropriate greeting.		
Body	Purpose	State the purpose of your letter.	
	Reason 1	Give your first reason.	
	Facts and Examples	Support your first reason with at least two facts or examples.	
	Reason 2	Give your second reason.	
	Facts and Examples	Support your second reason with at least two facts or examples.	
Closing	Write a formal closing.		
Signature	Sign the letter with your first and last name.		

Persuasive Letter: Revise

Revise your letter. Think about how you can use suggestions from your peer conference to improve your writing.

91 Riverview Dr.

Blue Valley, AR 71688

December 1 2023

Capt. Kenneth Jones

Blue Valley Police Department

7 South Sparrow St.

Blue Valley, AR, 71688

Dear Captain Jones:

An added sentence helps explain the purpose of the letter.

My fifth-grade class at Crossroads Academy has been learning

Would you be willing to come speak to us about your work about law enforcement.

as a police captain? You could tell us about your training, explain

what you do each day, and perhaps show us your police car and

The writer removed the "bandwagon" sentence.

equipment. ~~Every other person we have invited to speak this year~~

~~has come.~~

The class would benifit from meeting an officer in person.

Many of my classmates have never met an officer or seen a

This fact is unnecessary to the letter.

police car up close. ~~My uncle has a brand-new patrol car.~~ Hearing

you speak about your duties and experiences would help all of us

understand our police officers' work better.

Your visit would also help the police department and the

people of Blue valley. As we understand more about the

Continued

This sentence repeats information already given.

More precise wording tells how the teacher can help with scheduling.

Adding "please" gives a more polite tone.

officers, our appreciation for their work will grow. Some

of us may even decide to work in law enforcement in the

future. ~~Your coming would help the police and the whole town.~~

A possible time for you to speak to us would be at 10:00 am

on January 9, National Law Enforcement Day. My teacher, Mr.

Dominic Cannelloni said he could work ~~with you.~~ *to find a different day or time if needed*

If you would like to come, contact him. Thank you for *please*   *at (861) 423-4231 or*

considering this invitation. *dcannello@bluevalleycrossroads.net*

Sincerly,

Eliana Zander

The recipient of the letter will need this information.

Use the following checklist as you revise your persuasive letter.

Revising Checklist
My letter uses precise wording. It does not waste words.
My letter has a polite tone. It uses *please* and *thank you*.
My letter gives plain facts. It tells what the recipient needs to know and includes no unnecessary details.
The purpose of my letter is stated at the beginning and clearly explained.
Each reason is well supported.
I did not use dishonest tactics of persuasion.

Proofreading Marks

∧∨ Add

⌐ Delete

≡ Capital letter

/ Lowercase

⟼ Move

Persuasive Letter: Proofread

Proofread your letter carefully to find and correct mistakes.

91 Riverview Dr.

Blue Valley, AR 71688

December 1⌃ 2023

Capt. Kenneth Jones

Blue Valley Police Department

7 South Sparrow St.

Blue Valley, AR 71688

Dear Captain Jones:

My fifth-grade class at Crossroads Academy has been

learning about law enforcement. Would you be willing to

come speak to us about your work as a police captain? You

could tell us about your training, explain what you do each

day, and perhaps show us your police car and equipment.

benefit
The class would ~~benift~~ from meeting an officer in person.

Many of my classmates have never met an officer or seen a

police car up close. Hearing you speak about your duties and

experiences would help all of us understand our police officers'

work better.

Your visit would also help the police department and the

people of Blue valley. As we understand more about the officers,

Continued

our appreciation for their work will grow. Some of us may even

decide to work in law enforcement in the future.

    A possible time for you to speak to us would be at

10:00 a̶m̶ on January 9, National Law Enforcement Day. (a.m.)

My teacher, Mr. Dominic Cannelloni said he could work to

find a different day or time if needed. If you would like to

come, please contact him at (861) 423-4231 or dcannello@

bluevalleycrossroads.net. Thank you for considering this

invitation.

        Sincerely
        S̶i̶n̶c̶e̶r̶l̶y̶,̶

        Eliana Zander

Use the following checklist as you proofread your persuasive letter.

Proofreading Checklist	
I used correct letter form.	
I indented each paragraph.	
I began each sentence with a capital letter and ended it with a punctuation mark.	
I used correct punctuation within sentences.	
I wrote proper nouns correctly.	
I used commas and colons correctly in the heading, inside address, greeting, and closing.	
I corrected misspelled words.	

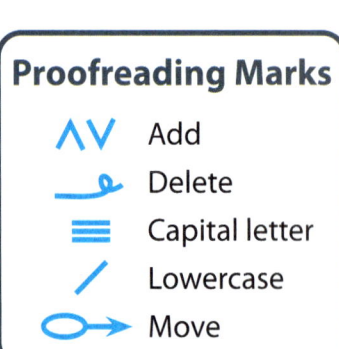

Proofreading Marks

∧∨   Add

    Delete

≡   Capital letter

/   Lowercase

    Move

Reflection

PETS POINT ACADEMY

Does your dog misbehave in the house?

Are you afraid to take it out in public?

Does your dog . . .

pull on the leash?   dig in the backyard?

chew up slippers?   jump on guests?

growl at other dogs?

GOOD NEWS!

We can train your dog to behave perfectly

WE OFFER . . .

puppy basics   obedience training   advanced training

General Jack Russell: ⭐⭐⭐⭐⭐

"Every dog needs the structure and discipline of Pets Point Academy. Enroll your pet today!"

Don't be a deadbeat dog owner.

Join the most caring owners from miles around who are turning to the only pet trainers you can trust—

PETS POINT ACADEMY.

**EVERY CUSTOMER A SATISFIED CUSTOMER.
EVERY DOG A GOOD DOG.**

Read the advertisement and answer the question.

Will this advertisement help the reader make a good decision? Explain your answer.

_____

_____

_____

_____

_____

_____

Cumulative Review

Underline each simple subject once and each simple predicate twice.

1. Elijah and Elisha lived in the times of the kings in the Old Testament.

2. Elisha was a pupil of Elijah's and took his place.

Mark the sentence that uses the correct form of *have*.

3. ○ God has told Elijah to anoint Elisha in his place.
   ○ God have told Elijah to anoint Elisha in his place.

4. ○ Seven thousand faithful men have not bowed the knee to Baal.
   ○ Seven thousand faithful men has not bowed the knee to Baal.

Underline the adverb in the sentence. Draw an arrow from the adverb to the verb it describes.

5. Elijah completely obeyed God's command to anoint Elisha.

6. Elisha left his plowing and immediately followed Elijah.

Write *Adj* for adjective or *Adv* for adverb to label the underlined word. Draw an arrow from the underlined word to the word it describes.

_____ 7. <u>Soon</u> Elisha watched Elijah be taken to heaven in a fiery chariot.

_____ 8. Elisha picked <u>up</u> Elijah's fallen cloak.

_____ 9. Elisha traveled <u>widely</u> and counseled many kings.

Put parentheses around each prepositional phrase. Label the sentence patterns. Write the sentence pattern on the line.

_____ 10. Elisha warned Israel's king of an attack by the enemy.

_____ 11. Gehazi, Elisha's servant, looked afraid.

_____ 12. Elisha prayed for his servant.

_____ 13. The servant looked at God's chariots of fire around Elisha.

_____ 14. Elisha's servant felt comforted.

Write the pronoun that correctly renames the underlined antecedent.

15. Elisha commanded the <u>woman</u> to borrow all the empty pots that _____ could find.

16. She obeyed Elisha's command to pour the oil into the <u>pots</u>, and _____ were all filled.

17. The widow made <u>money</u> by selling the oil and used _____ to pay off her debts.

18. <u>God</u> did a miracle for the widow when she believed and obeyed _____.

Read the letter. Then mark the correct answer.

733 Canterbury Drive
Charleroi, PA 15022

Mrs. Harriet Feldman
Feldman's Cookie Company
165 Castleview Rd.
Harrisburg, PA 17111

Dear Mrs. Feldman:

Our school is publishing a newspaper, and we hope you will consider advertising your company on one of our pages. We have a one-eighth page ad available for $20, or you could purchase a one-fourth page ad for $30.

We believe advertising in our paper would be good for your business. Many of the students at our school enjoy your cookies. Seeing your ad in the paper would remind them of a great place to get a snack.

We also feel that your company is the kind of place we want to promote in our paper.

Please contact me at (724) 829-7604 to purchase an ad. We hope to hear from you soon.

Sincerely,
Kia Blakemore
Kia Blakemore

19. Kia clearly explained her purpose for writing in the _____ paragraph.

   ○ first   ○ third

20. Which of Kia's two reasons why Mrs. Feldman should buy an ad needs more support?

   ○ first   ○ second

21. Kia has left out an important part of the _____.

   ○ heading   ○ inside address

11

More Sentences

What makes a person, place, or event worthy of being remembered?

Mentor Text

Excerpt from *Where Is Stonehenge?*
by True Kelley

Circles of Stones

In the south of England, about ninety miles west of London, sits the Salisbury Plain. It is a lonely-looking area. There are few trees. Not much grows except grass. Few creatures live there except sheep. Yet the Salisbury Plain is famous. Well over a million people travel there every year. They come from all over the world to visit one of the great monuments of the ancient world—the stone circle called Stonehenge.

Stonehenge sits at the top of a slight slope. Because the Salisbury Plain is so bare, Stonehenge can be seen from miles away. Lichen-covered stones seven feet wide and fourteen feet tall form a huge circle about one hundred feet across. That's as wide as two basketball courts. The stones are a hard brown sandstone called sarsen. The sarsen stones were carved so that they are narrower at the top. This makes them look even taller than they really are. The stones are buried at different depths so that the tops are level with each other. Seventeen of these stones still stand. Many others have fallen and lie about on the ground.

sarsen stone

sarsen stones with lintel

Coordinating Conjunctions

AfterSchoolHelp

Conjunctions

A **coordinating conjunction** is a joining word such as *and*, *but*, or *or* that connects words, phrases, or simple sentences.

> *Sunshine* and *rain* make a rainbow.
> *Clouds appear solid,* but *they are made of water droplets.*

Use **commas** in a series of three or more words joined by a coordinating conjunction.

> *Rainbows are always* red*,* orange*,* yellow*,* green*,* blue*,*
> indigo*,* and *violet*.

Use a **comma** before a coordinating conjunction in a compound sentence.

> *Amber went outside after the storm,* and *she saw a beautiful*
> *double rainbow*.

Circle the conjunction. Underline the words joined by the conjunction.

1. Round or spherical raindrops usually fill a cloud.

2. Rainbows are often seen in the summer, but they are rarely seen in the winter.

3. Joey wants a red and blue bicycle.

Label the underlined words as *sentences, subjects, predicates, direct objects, objects of the preposition, adjectives,* or *adverbs*.

_____ 4. Water and glass bend light differently.

_____ 5. Two rainbows were reflected brightly and clearly.

_____ 6. Megan saw a rainbow and photographed it.

Use △ to add commas where they are needed.

7. Green blue and violet are Megan's favorite colors.

8. Our teacher read the story of Noah and we learned about the history of the rainbow.

Circle the conjunction. Underline the words joined by the conjunction.

9. God loved Noah and his family.

10. God told Noah to build an ark, and He said that the rain would come.

11. Noah heard and followed God's instructions.

Label the underlined words as *sentences, subjects, predicates, direct objects, objects of the preposition, adjectives,* or *adverbs.*

_____ 12. Noah went into the ark, and God shut the door.

_____ 13. God remembered Noah and his family.

_____ 14. Rainbows and clouds remind me of heaven.

_____ 15. Heaven is beautiful and glorious.

_____ 16. God deals with His children lovingly and patiently.

Use ⌃ to add commas where they are needed.

17. Shem Ham and Japheth were saved from the Flood with their parents and their wives.

18. Noah stepped from the ark and he built an altar.

19. God put a rainbow in the sky and He promised that seasons would come as usual.

Christians should be faithful to God to honor Him and develop a closer relationship with Him. Write several sentences telling how you can be faithful and obedient to God. Use at least two conjunctions in your sentences.

20. _____

_____

_____

_____

_____

Correlative Conjunctions

Correlative conjunctions are joining words that work together in pairs. They join two words, phrases, or clauses of the same type.

Both Isabella and Lucas attend Richmond Academy.

At recess the students either walk or run around the field.

Isabella not only plays the piano but also studies the flute.

Lucas neither plays soccer nor enjoys basketball.

Common Correlative Conjunctions	
both . . . and	either . . . or
neither . . . nor	not only . . . but also

Circle the correlative conjunctions.

1. Either Kate or Dominic will help the librarian this week.

2. The helper will not only reshelve the books but also dust the bookshelves.

3. Both Kaylee and Dominic like to read.

4. Neither Kaylee nor Dominic has read the longest book in the library.

5. The librarian not only answers questions but also recommends books.

Write a pair of correlative conjunctions to complete the sentence.

6. _____ Paisley _____ Hudson collect stamps.

7. _____ this stamp _____ that stamp is the oldest one in the collection.

8. Hudson _____ shows me his collection _____ tells me about it.

Choose a pair of correlative conjunctions from the chart and use them in a sentence.

9. _____

_____

Circle the correlative conjunctions.

10. Neither Bella nor Connor had ever been to Washington, DC, before this week.

11. Today they visited not only the Library of Congress but also the National Mall.

12. The Franklin Delano Roosevelt Memorial has statues of both the president and his wife.

Franklin Delano Roosevelt Memorial

13. Bella liked the sculpture that showed both President Roosevelt and his dog.

14. Either Bella or Conner took these pictures.

15. Both the Vietnam Memorial and the Korean War Memorial honor fallen soldiers.

16. Not only the Thomas Jefferson Memorial but also the Lincoln Memorial reminds visitors of influential leaders in American history.

Common Correlative Conjunctions

both . . . and	either . . . or
neither . . . nor	not only . . . but also

Write a pair of correlative conjunctions to complete the sentence.

17. _____ Hazel _____ Nicholas takes swimming lessons.

18. _____ Hazel _____ Nicholas knows how to do the backstroke.

19. _____ Hazel _____ Nicholas enjoy jumping off the diving board.

20. The teacher demonstrates _____ the sidestroke _____ the butterfly.

21. _____ the lifeguard _____ the teacher will blow the whistle to clear the pool at the end of swim time.

Choose a pair of correlative conjunctions from the chart and use them in a sentence.

22. _____

_____

Subordinating Conjunctions

AfterSchoolHelp

Subordinating Conjunctions

A clause is a group of words that has a subject and a verb. An **independent clause** has a complete thought, so it can stand alone as a sentence.

> *We will go outside.*

A **dependent clause** does not have a complete thought, so it cannot stand alone as a sentence.

> *When it is time for recess.*

A **subordinating conjunction** joins a dependent clause to an independent clause to make a complete sentence.

A dependent clause can come at the beginning or the end of a sentence. Use a comma after a dependent clause if it is at the beginning of the sentence.

> *We will go outside **when** it is time for recess.*
>
> ***When** it is time for recess, we will go outside.*

Common Subordinating Conjunctions				
after	because	since	until	where
although	before	though	when	wherever
as	if	unless	whenever	while

Circle the subordinating conjunction in the sentence. Write *I* if the underlined clause is independent. Write *D* if the underlined clause is dependent.

_____ 1. Although the Taj Mahal seems like a palace, it is a great tomb.

_____ 2. When Emperor Shah Jahan's wife died, he built a magnificent building for her tomb.

_____ 3. She was buried in a nearby garden until the tomb was completed twenty-two years later.

Use a subordinating conjunction to combine the sentences. Add commas where they are needed.

4. The tomb was being built. Twenty thousand people worked on it.

_____

_____

Write three sentences about traveling to a specific place. Use a subordinating conjunction in at least two sentences.

5. _____

_____

_____

Circle the subordinating conjunction in the sentence. Write _I_ if the underlined clause is independent. Write _D_ if the underlined clause is dependent.

_____ 6. <u>If you travel overseas</u>, you will need a passport.

_____ 7. <u>You can travel by airplane</u> unless you prefer a long boat trip.

_____ 8. <u>Although traveling is a lot of fun</u>, it can be very tiring.

_____ 9. You should avoid visiting Agra in the hot season <u>because it is sometimes over 100° F.</u>

_____ 10. <u>You can visit other monuments in Agra</u> after you visit the Taj Mahal.

Taj Mahal

Use a subordinating conjunction to combine the sentences. Add commas where they are needed.

11. We drive from Delhi to Agra. We will visit the Taj Mahal.

_____

_____

12. You must take off your shoes. You enter the Taj Mahal.

_____

_____

13. In some pictures the Taj Mahal seems to be floating in the air. It is really sitting on a base of red sandstone.

_____

_____

Sentences: Simple, Compound, and Complex

A **simple sentence** is one independent clause. It can have a compound subject or a compound predicate.

> *The elevator in this building has glass walls.*

A **compound sentence** contains two or more independent clauses joined by a comma and a coordinating conjunction.

> *You can ride the elevator, or you can climb the stairs.*

A **complex sentence** contains an independent clause and one or more dependent clauses. Complex sentences include subordinating conjunctions. Use a comma after a dependent clause if it is at the beginning of a sentence.

> *Because the elevator was broken, Mike climbed the stairs.*

AfterSchoolHelp

Simple, Compound & Complex Sentences

Underline the independent clause or clauses. Circle any coordinating or subordinating conjunctions in the sentence. Mark *simple, compound,* **or** *complex.*

1. As a student Gustave Eiffel studied the science of metals.
   - ○ simple   ○ compound   ○ complex

2. When Eiffel finished school, his first job was designing a metal bridge.
   - ○ simple   ○ compound   ○ complex

3. Eiffel was successful, and he became known as Europe's master metal builder.
   - ○ simple   ○ compound   ○ complex

Eiffel Tower

Combine the simple sentences. Use a coordinating conjunction for a compound sentence or a subordinating conjunction for a complex sentence. Remember to add commas where they are needed.

4. Compound: Such a tall building of wood would collapse. It would break in the wind.

   _____

   _____

5. Complex: They got better pay. Men would not work on such a tall building.

   _____

   _____

Write a compound sentence about a tall building.

6. _____

_____

Write a complex sentence about a construction crew.

7. _____

_____

Underline the independent clause or clauses. Circle any coordinating or subordinating conjunctions in the sentence. Mark *simple, compound,* **or** *complex.*

8. You will have a great view of Paris from the top of the tower.
   ○ simple   ○ compound   ○ complex

9. A spiral staircase was used until it was dismantled in 1983.
   ○ simple   ○ compound   ○ complex

10. When you are on the second platform, you will find the Jules Verne restaurant.
    ○ simple   ○ compound   ○ complex

11. The restaurant is very expensive, and you must make reservations in advance.
    ○ simple   ○ compound   ○ complex

12. Eiffel's office is on the top level.
    ○ simple   ○ compound   ○ complex

Combine the simple sentences. Use a coordinating conjunction for a compound sentence or a subordinating conjunction for a complex sentence. Remember to add commas where they are needed.

13. Compound: The Eiffel Tower was the tallest building in the world for thirty years. Now many buildings are taller.

_____

_____

14. Complex: We visited the tower. We took a tour of the city.

_____

_____

Practice

Circle the conjunction. Underline the words joined by the conjunction.

1. Space Camp in Alabama has provided learning opportunities and STEM experiences for many students.

2. Campers learn a lot, but they also have lots of fun.

Label the underlined words as *sentences, subjects, predicates, direct objects, objects of the preposition, adjectives*, or *adverbs*.

_____ 3. Campers travel from many <u>states</u> and many <u>countries</u> to participate.

_____ 4. Campers learn about <u>space</u> and <u>flight</u> history.

Use ⌃ to add commas where they are needed.

5. Campers work on teams work on simulators and complete pretend space missions just like real astronauts.

6. Instructors teach STEM principles and they encourage campers to think about STEM careers.

Circle the correlative conjunctions.

7. In the Space and Rocket Center, campers can both inspect the powerful Saturn V rocket and observe the Apollo 12 moon rock.

8. Special needs camps include camps for campers who have either hearing loss or vision loss.

Write a pair of correlative conjunctions to complete the sentence.

9. The Center presents _____ exhibits from around the world _____ planetarium showings.

Circle the subordinating conjunction in the sentence. Write *I* if the underlined clause is independent. Write *D* if the underlined clause is dependent.

_____ 10. <u>While they are working in teams</u>, campers use real equipment from NASA's astronaut program.

_____ 11. <u>Campers experience sitting in a gravity chair</u> when they learn about living onboard the International Space Station.

Underline the independent clause or clauses. Circle any coordinating or subordinating conjunctions in the sentence. Mark *simple*, *compound*, or *complex*.

12. Campers build a team rocket, and they launch it.

   ○ simple   ○ compound   ○ complex

13. Since astronauts need to be able to survive on land and in water, campers practice important survival skills.

   ○ simple   ○ compound   ○ complex

Combine the simple sentences. Use a coordinating conjunction for a compound sentence or a subordinating conjunction for a complex sentence. Remember to add commas where they are needed.

14. Compound: Campers learn about future travel to Mars. They plan a modern Martian colony.

   _____

   _____

15. Complex: The Space Camp introduced the Aviation Challenge. They wanted to show campers what it is like to be a fighter pilot.

   _____

   _____

Sentences and Fragments

AfterSchoolHelp

A **fragment** is a group of words that is not a complete thought.

Some fragments are missing a subject or predicate. To correct this type of fragment, add a subject or predicate to make a **simple sentence**.

> **Fragment:** *Prayed and gave offerings to God.*
>
> **Sentence:** *Solomon prayed and gave offerings to God.*

Some fragments are dependent clauses. To correct this type of fragment, combine the dependent clause with an independent clause to make a **complex sentence**, or remove the subordinating conjunction to make a **simple sentence**.

> **Fragment:** *Because David was a man of war.*
>
> **Sentence:** *David was a man of war.*
>
> **Sentence:** *Because David was a man of war, he could not build the temple.*

Simple, Compound & Complex Sentences

Write _S_ if the group of words is a sentence. Write _F_ if the group of words is a fragment.

_____ 1. While Israel was wandering in the wilderness.

_____ 2. God dwelt in the tabernacle.

_____ 3. The tabernacle was a large tent.

_____ 4. Planned to build the temple.

_____ 5. Before Solomon became king.

Choose a fragment from the previous exercise and rewrite it as a complete sentence.

6. _____

_____

Write three sentences about a church building. Use one simple sentence, one compound sentence, and one complex sentence.

7. _____

_____

_____

_____

Write S if the group of words is a sentence. Write F if the group of words is a fragment.

_____ 8. King Hiram sent many trees from Tyre.

_____ 9. The stones were chosen and cut near Jerusalem.

_____ 10. Because the people loved God.

_____ 11. Gave gold and silver for the temple.

_____ 12. Many years later, Jeremiah prophesied about the destruction of the temple.

_____ 13. When Nebuchadnezzar captured Jerusalem.

_____ 14. The temple and city were destroyed.

Wailing Wall

_____ 15. Although the treasures in the temple were taken to Babylon.

_____ 16. When Zerubbabel became king many years later, he rebuilt the temple.

_____ 17. One wall from Herod's temple still stands.

_____ 18. Called the Wailing Wall.

_____ 19. Because Jews from all over the world come to pray at this wall.

Choose two fragments from the previous exercise and rewrite them as complete sentences.

20. _____

_____

21. _____

_____

Commas and Comma Splices

AfterSchoolHelp

Commas and Comma Splices

Run-on sentences are two sentences run together. One type of run-on is a comma splice.

A **comma splice** consists of two independent clauses incorrectly joined by only a comma.

> *People in South Dakota wanted a monument**,** they carved four presidents on Mount Rushmore.*

A comma splice can be corrected in several ways.

1. Make the sentence into two simple sentences.
   People in South Dakota wanted a monument.
   They carved four presidents on Mount Rushmore.

2. Make the sentence a compound sentence. Remember to use a comma before the conjunction.

   People in South Dakota wanted a monument, and they carved four presidents on Mount Rushmore.

3. Make the sentence a complex sentence. Remember to use a comma after a dependent clause if it is at the beginning of a sentence.

   Because people in South Dakota wanted a monument, they carved four presidents on Mount Rushmore.

Write *CS* if the group of words is a comma splice. Write *C* if the sentence is correct.

_____ 1. Mount Rushmore was named for Charles E. Rushmore.

_____ 2. Dynamite blew off portions of rock, workers carved the details by hand.

_____ 3. The work was dangerous, brave men stuck to the task.

Choose one of the comma splices from the previous exercise and rewrite it correctly.

4. _____

_____

Use ⌃ to add commas where they are needed.

5. A historian named Doane Robinson had the idea to carve Mount Rushmore and he planned the project.

6. After the senator from South Dakota supported the project Congress and President Coolidge gave their approval.

Write *CS* if the group of words is a comma splice. Write *C* if the sentence is correct.

_____ 7. Mount Rushmore is a national monument, it is in South Dakota.

_____ 8. Mount Rushmore is a memorial to four great presidents, and it represents different parts of US history.

_____ 9. George Washington was the first president, he is the "Father of Our Country."

_____ 10. Washington was born in 1732, he commanded the Virginia Militia at age twenty-three.

_____ 11. While Washington was the commander of the Continental Army, he helped America gain independence from England.

Choose one of the comma splices from the previous exercise and rewrite it correctly.

12. _____

_____

Use ⌃ to add commas where they are needed.

13. When he was only thirty-three years of age Thomas Jefferson wrote the Declaration of Independence.

14. After he was elected president Abraham Lincoln led the country through the Civil War.

15. Because Lincoln saved the Union and ended slavery he was included on the monument.

16. The sculptor chose to carve Theodore Roosevelt but not everyone agreed.

17. Some thought Roosevelt's presidency was too recent but the others believed Roosevelt had achieved great things.

Which US president do you admire most? Write several sentences explaining why you admire him. Remember to add commas where they are needed.

18. _____

_____

_____

_____

Revising Fused Sentences

Run-on sentences are two sentences run together. One type of run-on is a comma splice. The other type is a fused sentence.

A **fused sentence** consists of two independent clauses incorrectly joined together without a comma or a conjunction.

Low clouds hung in the sky the rain began to fall.

A fused sentence can be corrected in several ways.

1. Make the sentence into two simple sentences.

   Low clouds hung in the sky. The rain began to fall.

2. Make the sentence a compound sentence. Remember to use a comma before the conjunction.

   Low clouds hung in the sky, and the rain began to fall.

3. Make the sentence a complex sentence. Remember to use a comma after a dependent clause if it is at the beginning of a sentence.

   Low clouds hung in the sky before the rain began to fall.

Write *FS* if the group of words is a fused sentence. Write *C* if the sentence is correct.

_____ 1. Carter hit a home run he jogged around the bases.

_____ 2. Charlotte gave me a book, and she made Mia a scarf.

_____ 3. Madison could not come because she had to babysit her little sister.

_____ 4. Mr. Torres gave us homework he wants us to read a news article.

_____ 5. Anthony took the plates he helped with the dishes.

_____ 6. Mom came to the classroom after school she talked to the teacher.

_____ 7. Ezekiel ran as fast as he could, but Jameson won the race.

Choose one of the fused sentences from the previous exercise and rewrite it correctly.

8. _____

_____

Write _FS_ if the group of words is a fused sentence. Write _C_ if the sentence is correct.

_____ 9. My dog is sick we need to take her to the vet.

_____ 10. Raelynn knows how to make fudge, and she made some for the class.

_____ 11. Grandpa will come to our house in November he will stay for the holidays.

_____ 12. I invited Melanie to my house we will study together.

_____ 13. On Sunday Mr. Price led the singing before Pastor Morris preached.

_____ 14. The Diaz family live next door they are from Portugal.

_____ 15. You can wash the windows, or you can clean the bathroom.

_____ 16. Tom and Aaron play baseball their team won the championship.

_____ 17. We were late to school this morning because we got stuck in traffic.

_____ 18. Liliana and Naomi made birthday cards from construction paper.

_____ 19. Easton is in my class this year he was in my class last year too.

_____ 20. Joseph and Joshua are twins they just moved into my neighborhood.

Choose three of the fused sentences from the previous exercise and rewrite them correctly.

21. _____

_____

22. _____

_____

23. _____

_____

Comma Rules

Commas and other punctuation marks can help a reader understand a sentence.

1. **Quotation marks** show the exact words a speaker says. Separate a quotation from dialogue tags with a **comma**, an **exclamation point**, or a **question mark**.

   "I invited the Clarks over for dinner on Friday night," Mom said.
   Dad asked, "Should I grill some hamburgers?"
   "That sounds wonderful!" Mom said.

2. Use commas with **nouns of direct address**.

   *"**Aidan,** please sharpen the pencil."*

   *"Would you pass out the papers, **Hannah**?"*

   *"When we finish, **Carson**, you may collect the quizzes."*

3. Use a comma to separate a **tag question** from the rest of the sentence. A **question mark** should follow a tag question.

   *"The weather is beautiful today, **isn't it**?"*

   *"You aren't going to stay inside all day, **are you**?"*

Mark the sentence that is written correctly.

1. ○ "You have been to the Gateway Arch, haven't you?"
   ○ "You have been to the Gateway Arch haven't you?"

2. ○ "The Gateway Arch is also called the Gateway to the West." our teacher said.
   ○ "The Gateway Arch is also called the Gateway to the West," our teacher said.

Use ⌃ to add commas where they are needed.

3. "Xavier did you know that the Arch is 630 feet tall?"

4. "Watch your step" said the tour guide.

5. "Can we go to the gift shop Mom?" Victoria asked.

Write a sentence with a tag question. Use correct punctuation.

6. _____

_____

Write a sentence with a noun of direct address. Use correct punctuation.

7. _____

_____

Write a sentence with someone's exact words. Use correct punctuation.

8. _____

_____

Mark the sentence that is written correctly.

9. ○ "The special shape of the Arch keeps it safe from high winds, the tour guide explained."

○ "The special shape of the Arch keeps it safe from high winds," the tour guide explained.

10. ○ "When you get to the top, Maya, you might be able to feel the Arch swaying."

○ "When you get to the top Maya, you might be able to feel the Arch swaying."

11. ○ "The Arch was finished in 1965 wasn't it?"

○ "The Arch was finished in 1965, wasn't it?"

The Gateway Arch

Use △ to add commas where they are needed.

12. "Harrison the Museum below the monument tells about the history of the West."

13. "A special tram takes visitors to the top doesn't it?"

14. "I enjoyed my visit" said Hailey.

Practice

Write *S* if the group of words is a sentence. Write *F* if the group of words is a fragment.

_____ 1. The Space Camp Hall of Fame includes biographies of Space Camp graduates.

_____ 2. Whenever they become successful adults.

_____ 3. A hall of fame is similar to a monument.

_____ 4. Because they have been successful.

_____ 5. The Hall of Fame was built to honor these people.

_____ 6. Christians should recognize God-given talent.

_____ 7. We can thank God.

_____ 8. When we recognize scientific progress.

Choose a fragment from the previous exercise and rewrite it as a complete sentence.

9. _____

_____

Write *CS* if the group of words is a comma splice. Write *C* if the sentence is correct.

_____ 10. In 2007 Dottie became the first Space Camp graduate to become an astronaut.

_____ 11. As a child Major John Hecker spent many days at the Space and Rocket Center, he was also a camper at the Space Academy.

_____ 12. At the age of 14, Dottie Lindenburger attended Space Camp, eventually she became a science teacher.

_____ 13. Dottie completed astronaut training, and she became a NASA astronaut.

_____ 14. Though previous crews included women, Dottie was on the first space flight with only women.

Choose one of the comma splices from the previous exercise and rewrite it correctly.

15. _____

_____

Write *FS* if the group of words is a fused sentence. Write *C* if the sentence is correct.

_____ 16. Dr. Serena Auñón was the medical officer of her Space Camp some years later she attended medical school.

_____ 17. Dr. Auñón was a flight surgeon she took care of space shuttle astronauts.

_____ 18. Even though she was a flight surgeon, one of Dr. Auñón's missions was aboard an underwater research station.

Choose one of the fused sentences from the previous exercise and rewrite it correctly.

19. _____

_____

Use ⌃ to add commas where they are needed. One sentence will not require commas.

20. Major Hecker became a pilot in the US Marine Corps at the age of 29 didn't he?

21. "I flew a C-130 four-engine transport plane as part of the Blue Angels squadron" explained Major Hecker.

22. Jason Hopkins remembers creating an imaginary spaceship from his mother's laundry basket.

23. After he attended Space Camp in middle school Jason wanted to pursue a career in space research.

24. Jason has worked on satellite systems for a large company and he has worked on NASA's Orion satellite systems.

Write several sentences about a profession you are interested in. Explain why you are interested. Remember to add commas where they are needed.

25. _____

_____

_____

_____

Chapter 11 Review

Match the underlined word or words with the correct type of conjunction.

> **A** coordinating
> **B** correlative
> **C** subordinating

_____ 1. Thousands of years ago, the First Emperor of the Qin dynasty united China into one country <u>and</u> began to connect the sections of the Great Wall.

_____ 2. <u>Although</u> the wall looks like one long line, it is actually made of many walls put together over time.

_____ 3. This wall has been called <u>both</u> "the Purple Frontier" <u>and</u> "the Earth Dragon."

Write _I_ if the underlined clause is independent. Write _D_ if the clause is dependent.

_____ 4. <u>Workers used sticky rice mixed with lime in the mortar between the bricks.</u>

_____ 5. Many parts of the wall have lasted thousands of years <u>because the mortar was strong and water resistant.</u>

_____ 6. <u>Though the wall goes up and down steep hillsides</u>, thousands of visitors walk on the wall every year.

Match the sentence with the sentence type.

> **A** simple
> **B** compound
> **C** complex

_____ 7. The Great Wall is thousands of miles long, but it has many gaps.

_____ 8. Genghis Khan went around the wall and invaded China.

_____ 9. The Great Wall is famous because it is the longest man-made structure in history.

Combine the simple sentences. Use a coordinating conjunction for a compound sentence or a subordinating conjunction for a complex sentence. Remember to add commas where they are needed.

10. Compound: The wheelbarrow was invented in China. This invention helped the workers with the wall.

_____

_____

11. Complex: Dylan visited the Great Wall last year. He took many pictures.

_____

_____

Write _S_ if the group of words is a sentence. Write _F_ if the group of words is a fragment.

_____ 12. The most famous pyramids in Egypt were built at a place called Giza.

_____ 13. Three pyramids and a large statue called the Sphinx.

_____ 14. Before Khufu built the Great Pyramid around 2560 BC.

Rewrite the fragment as a complete sentence.

15. When a tall lighthouse was built in Alexandria.

_____

16. Visited the Great Pyramids last year.

_____

Write _CS_ if the group of words is a comma splice. Write _C_ if the sentence is correct.

_____ 17. The Sphinx has the head of a man, it has the body of a lion.

_____ 18. This impressive statue was probably built by Khafre, he was an Egyptian pharaoh.

_____ 19. It is 66 feet tall, and it was carved from limestone.

Write _FS_ if the group of words is a fused sentence. Write _C_ if the sentence is correct.

_____ 20. The Egyptians believed in life after death the pharaoh was buried with many treasures.

_____ 21. Centuries later robbers entered the pyramids and took away the treasures.

_____ 22. My teacher showed us a video about the pyramids of Giza I thought it was very interesting.

Mark the sentence that is written correctly.

23. ○ "The Great Pyramid was originally covered with white limestone," the tour guide said.
    ○ "The Great Pyramid was originally covered with white limestone" the tour guide said.

24. ○ "The white stones would have looked dazzling in the sunlight wouldn't they?"
    ○ "The white stones would have looked dazzling in the sunlight, wouldn't they?"

25. ○ "Would you like to learn more about the pyramids Colton?"
    ○ "Would you like to learn more about the pyramids, Colton?"

Journal

Think of something God has done for you or your family that is worthy of being remembered. Write a paragraph about that experience.

Cumulative Review

Underline the simple subject once. Write the correct present-tense verb to complete the sentence.

1. Hezekiah _____ as an example of obedience in the Old Testament.
   serve

2. Hezekiah's name _____ "God has strengthened."
   mean

Mark the correct verb form to complete the sentence.

3. The Bible describes Hezekiah as a king of Judah. People ___ him as a man who walked faithfully with God.
   ○ remember   ○ will remember

4. After Ahaz's wicked reign, Hezekiah boldly ___ the shrines and altars to false gods.
   ○ removed   ○ will remove

Underline the adverb in the sentence. Draw an arrow from the adverb to the verb it describes.

5. The Israelites' worship of the bronze serpent had soon become a great stumbling block.

6. Hezekiah boldly destroyed the bronze serpent Moses made in the wilderness.

Write the correct adjective or adverb form to complete the sentence.

7. Hezekiah opened the temple and paid _____ attention to God's directions for
   close
   worship.

8. God's ways were _____ to Hezekiah than popular forms of worship.
   important

Write about ways you can worship God. Write one sentence for each pattern.

9. S-V-DO: _____

   _____

10. S-LV-PN: _____

   _____

Rewrite the sentence using a pronoun to replace the underlined words.

11. The Assyrians threatened <u>the Israelites</u>.

_____

_____

12. <u>King Hezekiah</u> made the city walls secure, expanded the military, and built a tunnel to supply water.

_____

_____

Circle the conjunction. Use ⌃ to add commas where they are needed.

13. Historians and archeologists have found Hezekiah's tunnel under Jerusalem.

14. Hezekiah tried to satisfy the Assyrians' demands but the Assyrians marched against Jerusalem.

15. Hezekiah went to the temple and he prayed for protection.

16. When God sent an angel to strike down one hundred eighty-five thousand Assyrians the remaining Assyrians fled.

Use a subordinating conjunction to combine the sentences. Add commas where they are needed.

17. Hezekiah prayed. He was faced with an impossible situation.

_____

_____

18. Hezekiah trusted in God. God answered Hezekiah's prayer.

_____

_____

Write a complex sentence about a lesson you have learned from a Bible character.

19. _____

_____

12

Writing a Personal Narrative

How can I use my personality to make my writing interesting?

Mentor Text

Excerpt from *Frances Ridley Havergal: A Poet for the King* by Eileen Berry

"Flora, wait for me!" I race after the spaniel,
    laughing at the way her long ears flap
    like wings when she runs.
Naughty Flo. She knows I can't chase her
    through the hedge.

The white wagging tail disappears
    beneath holly bushes, neatly trimmed.
I groan and sink down on the grass.
    "I'll make up a song about you, naughty dog."

I gaze up past the garden wall to where
    the wooded hills rise,
    wearing their spring dress of golden green.

I love these hills.

For as long as I can remember, my family and I have
    lived here.
The English country air is the air
    I've always breathed.
My first five years were spent in the Astley Rectory;
    then we moved here to Hallow, to Henwick House.

The garden is my favorite place in the world.
From my seat near the hedge, I can see the first
    slender green shoots, daffodils springing up.
I helped Mamma plant them last year.

Now for a song. Hmmm.
What kind of song does one sing to a dog?
I hum a few notes and begin to sing.

    I shall find you, naughty Flo.
    Through the hedge you mustn't go.

Personal Narrative

Narrative writing tells a story. A **personal narrative** is a story about something that has happened to the author.

> The Last Laugh
>
> "Come on out on the ice, Vivian! It's easy!" shouted my cousin Sadie. She glided over to me as though she had wings under her feet instead of thin silver blades.
>
> "I'm too scared," I said. "I've never done this before."
>
> "Take my hand. I'll help you," said Sadie.
>
> I took Sadie's mittened hand and stepped carefully onto the ice of the pond. My feet wobbled under me. But at least I was standing up! I braced my legs, and Sadie started skating. She pulled me slowly around the pond.
>
> "Now start moving your feet," she said.
>
> As soon as I tried to move my feet, my legs started doing the splits! The bad thing about skating on a pond is that there are no walls to grab if you lose your balance. So I grabbed the only thing I could think of—Sadie.
>
> We both screamed as I dragged her down with me. Our feet flew up in the air when we landed, and somehow the blades of our skates got caught on each other. We slid across the ice for several feet after we fell.
>
> At first we were giggling so hard that we couldn't get back up. We finally untangled our feet, and she stood up and held out her hand. I grasped it with both of my hands. But when I tried to stand up, my feet went out from under me. I fell again, jerking her down with me a second time.
>
> We lay there flat on our backs howling with laughter. Then I heard the sound of clapping. We sat up and saw the neighbor boy, Brayden, standing at the edge of the pond. "This is better than the circus!" he yelled. "You should sell tickets!"
>
> Once I got over the embarrassment, I scooped up a handful of snow from the edge of the pond. Maybe I can't skate very well, but I can aim! Brayden got a snowball smack on his left shoulder. Sadie and I will never be able to remember that day without laughing.

Continued

A personal narrative can be about an experience that was unusual, exciting, happy, scary, or humorous. Personal narratives are always told in the **first-person point of view**. This means that you use the pronouns *I* and *me* to refer to yourself as you write the narrative.

Tips for Writing a Personal Narrative

1. Think about your audience, those who will read your personal narrative.

2. Write about something that you remember well.

3. Make the story sound natural so that a reader could imagine your voice telling it aloud.

4. Get the reader's attention with your opening sentence.

5. Tell the events of the narrative in the order they happened.

6. Add details that will help your reader picture each event. Use comparisons and strong verbs to make descriptions vivid.

7. Use **dialogue**, or spoken conversation, to make the people in your narrative come alive. Remember to use quotation marks around someone's spoken words.

8. Make your ending sentence tell what you learned or how you felt about what happened.

What will you write a personal narrative about? List topic ideas. Focus on experiences that you had strong feelings about or that taught you something.

_____

_____

_____

_____

_____

_____

_____

Good Openings and Closings

Be sure to begin your personal narrative with an interesting opening. Consider using one of these ideas to draw your reader in from the very first sentence.

1. Begin with **action**. The reader will feel as if he or she has stepped right into the scene.

Instead of writing . . .	. . . write something like this:
Let me tell you about a really neat experience I had when I was riding my bike to school.	I jumped on my bike and coasted down the driveway for my morning ride to school. I had only gone a few blocks when . . .

2. Begin with **dialogue**. Open with a character's spoken words to make your reader want to keep reading and find out more about that character.

Instead of writing . . .	. . . write something like this:
I was going ice-skating for the first time, and I was really scared.	"Come on out on the ice, Vivian! It's easy!" . . . "I'm too scared," I said. "I've never done this before."

3. Begin by **asking a question** to make your reader think about your topic.

Instead of writing . . .	. . . write something like this:
I really had fun going hiking in the mountains with my grandpa. He knows all the best trails.	What makes a perfect day? Sunshine, a picnic lunch, a mountain, and a grandpa who knows all the best hiking trails make a great day.

Continued

A personal narrative needs a good closing. Consider using one of these ideas for writing a satisfying ending.

1. Tell how you felt about the experience.

2. Tell something you learned.

The closing shows us that the writer is a good sport when teased.

Once I got over the embarrassment, I scooped up a handful of snow from the edge of the pond. Maybe I can't skate, but I can aim! Brayden got a snowball smack on his left shoulder. Sadie and I will never be able to remember that day without laughing.

The last sentence tells us that the writer and Sadie will always view their ice-skating adventure as a happy memory.

Listen to the list of topics that your teacher will read. Imagine that you are writing a personal narrative about one of the topics. Write a good opening and a good closing for the narrative.

1. Opening: _____

_____

_____

_____

_____

2. Closing: _____

_____

_____

_____

_____

Personal Narrative: Plan

Organize ideas for your personal narrative in a planning chart.

| List the events in the order they happened.

| Write additional details about each event. Exact details about what happened will help your readers see the events in their minds.

Topic: _Ice-skating with Sadie_

Opening: _dialogue about being scared to skate_

Events	Details
1. Getting on the ice	cousin Sadie is a good skater offered me her hand feet wobbled under me
2. Falling the first time	legs did splits when I moved feet grabbed Sadie—pulled her down skate blades got caught together
3. Falling the second time	laughing made it hard to get up Sadie got up and offered hand feet slid—pulled her down again
4. Seeing Brayden watching us	heard sound of clapping he said it was better than a circus
5. Throwing snowball at Brayden	embarrassed at first aimed well and hit his left shoulder

Closing: _Sadie and I laughing_

Complete the chart to plan your personal narrative.

Topic: _____

Opening: _____

Events	Details

Closing: _____

Personal Narrative: Draft

A writer can use different kinds of transitional words and phrases to make a narrative clear to the reader.

Time-order words and phrases help make the order of events clear.

> *Just then an ear-splitting screech ripped through the night.*

> *After a while my heart rate returned to normal.*

> *It wasn't until later that I realized what had made the sound.*

Time-Order Words and Phrases			
first	later	now	after a while
then	finally	in the meantime	two years ago
next	when	sometimes	last winter
afterward	as soon as	just then	once

Spatial words and phrases answer questions about space, such as *where*, *how far*, and *which way*. Some spatial words are adverbs. Others are prepositional phrases.

> *I caught a glimpse of the big cat leaping through the treetops.*

> *Jack grabbed my arm and jerked me back into the cabin.*

> *The next morning we found huge paw prints in the dirt outside.*

Decide where transitional words and phrases from the word bank could be added to the paragraph to make the meaning clearer. Insert their numbers in the paragraph.

A Mystery Rider

My mom and I drove under a long avenue of overhanging trees. As the stars sparkled, a small something dropped, brushing my arm. "What was that? Where did it go?" I puzzled. We pulled into our driveway, and I switched the overhead light on. The eyes of a tiny tree frog with shriveled gray skin blinked. I reached to get a plastic bowl from the console and moved it slowly. The frog jumped onto my hand! Carefully, I opened the car door and stepped into the bushes. The frog leaped into the shadows. I have often wondered how our mystery rider liked its new home.

Time-Order Words and Phrases

1. just then
2. one fall night
3. at last
4. since then
5. all of a sudden

Spatial Words and Phrases

6. toward the little creature
7. up at me
8. down through the dark
9. high above the open moon roof
10. off my hand

Use the ideas from your planning chart to draft your personal narrative. Follow the drafting guide, checking off the parts of the personal narrative as you write. Remember to use time-order and spatial words to make the narrative clear to your reader.

Drafting Guide		
Opening	Get your reader's attention with an interesting opening.	
Events and Details	Tell the events of the narrative in the order that they happened.	
	Include details that will help your reader picture each event.	
	Include dialogue in the narrative.	
Closing	Tell what you learned or how you felt about what happened.	

Personal Narrative: Revise

As you revise, look for ways to make your descriptions clearer and more vivid. Think about elements you could add or change.

> *details about characters' actions   comparisons   sensory words   time-order words*
> *strong verbs   adjectives and adverbs   spatial words   personal reaction to the story*

God has designed you with a distinct personality—let it show in the choices you make. Could a reader imagine your voice telling the story aloud?

A comparison makes this description more vivid.

The writer looked for places to add more descriptive words.

Descriptions of the writer's falls add more humor to the story.

The Last Laugh

"Come on out on the ice Vivian! Its easy!" shouted my

glided over to me as though she had wings under her feet instead

cousin Sadie. She ~~skated over to me making it look so easy.~~

of thin silver blades.

"I'm too scared," I said. "I've never done this before."

"Take my hand I'll help you," said Sadie.

mittened   carfully

I took Sadie's hand and stepped onto the ice of the

pond. My feet wobbled under me. But at least I was standing

up! I braced my legs, and sadie started skating. She pulled me

slowly around the pond.

"Now start moving your feet" she said.

As soon as I tried to move my feet, my legs started doing the splits!

~~But then I started to fall.~~ The bad thing about skating on

if you lose your balance

a pond is that there are no walls to grab. So I grabbed the only

thing I could think of—Sadie.

dragged

We both screamed as I ~~pulled~~ her down with me. Our

feet flew up in the air when we landed, and somehow the blads

of our skates got caught on each other. We slid across the ice

for several feet after we fell.

———— Continued ——

At first we were gigling so hard that we couldn't get

back up. We finally untangled our feet, she stood up and

held out her hand. I grasped it with both of my hands. But

my feet went out from under me. I fell again, jerking her down
when I tried to stand up, ~~we both fell.~~ *with me a second time.*

lay there flat on our backs howling with laughter.
We ~~were laughing so hard.~~ Then I heard the sound

of clapping. We sat up and saw the neighbor boy, Brayden,

standing at the edge of the pond. "this is better than the

circus!" he yelled. You should sell tickets!"

scooped up
Once I got over the embarasment, I ~~got~~ a handful of

snow from the edge of the pond. Maybe I can't skate very

well, but I can aim! Brayden got a snowball smack on his left

will never be able to remember that day without laughing.
shoulder. Sadie and me ~~laughed and laughed.~~

Specific details tell how Vivian and Sadie looked and sounded as they laughed.

A revised closing reveals what the writer gained from the experience—a happy memory that she and Sadie could share.

Use the following checklist as you revise your personal narrative.

Revising Checklist
My opening gets the reader's attention.
I told about the events in order.
I included dialogue that made my characters seem real.
I told enough details to make my experience clear.
I used time-order and spatial words.
I checked to see where I could use more descriptive words.
My closing tells what I learned or how I felt about what happened.

Proofreading Marks

∧∨ Add
⌐ Delete
≡ Capital letter
/ Lowercase
⟳→ Move

Personal Narrative: Proofread

Proofread your narrative carefully.

The Last Laugh

"Come on out on the ice, Vivian! It's easy!" shouted my

cousin Sadie. She glided over to me as though she had wings

under her feet instead of thin silver blades.

"I'm too scared," I said. "I've never done this before."

"Take my hand I'll help you," said Sadie.

carefully
I took Sadie's mittened hand and stepped ~~carfully~~

onto the ice of the pond. My feet wobbled under me. But at

least I was standing up! I braced my legs, and sadie started

skating. She pulled me slowly around the pond.

"Now start moving your feet," she said.

As soon as I tried to move my feet, my legs started

doing the splits! The bad thing about skating on a pond is

that there are no walls to grab if you lose your balance. So I

grabbed the only thing I could think of—Sadie.

We both screamed as I dragged her down with me.

Our feet flew up in the air when we landed, and somehow

blades
the ~~blads~~ of our skates got caught on each other. We slid

across the ice for several feet after we fell.

giggling
At first we were ~~gigling~~ so hard that we couldn't get

Continued

back up. We finally untangled our feet, [and] she stood up and

held out her hand. I grasped it with both of my hands. But

when I tried to stand up, my feet went out from under me. I

fell again, jerking her down with me a second time.

We lay there flat on our backs howling with

laughter. Then I heard the sound of clapping. We sat up

and saw the neighbor boy, Brayden, standing at the edge

of the pond. "[T]his is better than the circus!" he yelled. "You

should sell tickets!"

Once I got over the ~~embarasment~~, [embarrassment] I scooped up a

handful of snow from the edge of the pond. Maybe I can't

skate very well, but I can aim! Brayden got a snowball

smack on his left shoulder. Sadie and ~~me~~ [I] will never be able

to remember that day without laughing.

Use the following checklist as you proofread your personal narrative.

Proofreading Checklist

I used complete sentences (no comma splices, fused sentences, or fragments).
I began each sentence with a capital letter and ended it with a punctuation mark.
I used correct punctuation within sentences.
I wrote proper nouns correctly.
I used pronouns correctly.
I corrected misspelled words.

Proofreading Marks

∧∨ Add
⟋ Delete
≡ Capital letter
／ Lowercase
⟜→ Move

Reflection

Reread your personal narrative. What writing choices did you make to express your personality to the reader?

_____

_____

_____

_____

_____

_____

_____

_____

Cumulative Review

Put parentheses around each prepositional phrase.

1. Thirteen books in the New Testament were written by Paul.

2. God greatly used Paul for the spread of the gospel.

Mark the sentence that is written correctly.

3. ○ Pauls birthplace was Tarsus, which is in modern-day Turkey.
   ○ Paul's birthplace was Tarsus, which is in modern-day Turkey.

4. ○ Paul knew the Jewish law because of Gamaliel's good teaching.
   ○ Paul knew the Jewish law because of Gamaliel good teaching.

Underline the simple subject once and the correct past-tense helping verb twice.

5. Paul's family (have, had) obtained Roman citizenship.

6. Paul (do, did) violently persecute Christians.

7. Paul (was, were) dragging Christians off to prison.

8. Many Christians (do, did) fear Paul.

Write the correct past-tense form of the verb to complete the sentence.

9. Paul _____ to go to Damascus to put Christians in prison.
   rise

10. Paul _____ on the ground after hearing Jesus' voice from heaven.
    lie

Write *DO* if the underlined pronoun is a direct object. Write *OP* if the underlined pronoun is an object of a preposition.

_____ 11. Paul probably had a lot of fear within <u>himself</u>.

_____ 12. God commanded <u>him</u> to go to Damascus.

Circle the subordinating conjunction in the sentence. Write *I* if the underlined clause is independent. Write *D* if the underlined clause is dependent.

_____ 13. <u>After God instructed Ananias</u>, Ananias touched Paul's eyes, and then he could see.

_____ 14. God chose Paul <u>because he was to take the gospel to the Gentiles</u>.

_____ 15. <u>Paul preached and started churches</u> wherever he went.

Write *FS* if the group of words is a fused sentence. Write *CS* if the group of words is a comma splice. Write *C* if the sentence is correct.

_____ 16. Paul took three missionary trips, he was stoned once and shipwrecked three times.

_____ 17. The book of Acts describes Paul's trips thirteen New Testament books were written by Paul to the churches.

_____ 18. In the city of Lystra, Paul healed a man who could not walk.

_____ 19. Paul visited the cities of Derbe and Lystra, there Paul mentored Timothy.

_____ 20. Paul ministered in Ephesus for three years he left Timothy there to minister to the church.

Choose one of the comma splices and one of the fused sentences from the previous exercise and rewrite them correctly.

21. _____

_____

22. _____

_____

Use ⌄⌃ to add correct punctuation to the paragraph.

23. Young Timothy became the pastor of the church in Ephesus Because

Paul wanted to encourage him he wrote Timothy a letter Paul told him

Let no man despise thy youth; but be thou an example of the believers, in

word, in conversation, in charity, in spirit, in faith, in purity" (1 Timothy 4:12).

Imagine you are going on a mission trip. Write three sentences about your trip. Use one simple sentence, one compound sentence, and one complex sentence.

24. _____

_____

_____

_____

13

Developing Research Skills

Why is it important to have good sources of information?

Mentor Text

"Azerbaijan" excerpt from *My Librarian Is a Camel* by Margriet Ruurs

The children in the Kelenterli refugee settlement can't sit still when they know that the blue truck is coming! The blue truck library is here, thanks to the hard work of Relief International, an organization that provides relief to victims of natural disasters and civil conflicts.

These children live in poverty, but the blue library truck brings a surge of happiness and curiosity. "It's a big event when the library comes to town," says the librarian. "It's a bit of happiness for children who normally don't have much to look forward to."

This library-in-a-truck has been bringing books to children for several years. Designed to provide a wide variety of books to young people, two library trucks serve over sixteen hundred students in about twenty-three refugee schools. Their goal is simple: for a few hours each week, the children of Kelenterli and other settlements are given the opportunity to borrow books. In doing so, they may feel they are part of a new generation growing up in a new Azerbaijan. The trucks travel through only two regions of Azerbaijan. There are children in other areas of the country who would love to see the blue truck pay them a visit. But unfortunately, there are not enough trucks, or books, to reach them all. Relief International is working to change that.

"For us," says the librarian, "the mobile library is as important as air or water."

When the blue library truck arrives, Azerbaijanian children are eager to get their books.

Parts of a Book

Accurate sources help us answer our questions and understand things clearly. Many of these sources are books. Books are made up of different parts that can help you find information quickly.

Front of book:

The **title page** gives the title and author of the book, the illustrator, and the publishing company and city of publication.

The **table of contents** names the chapters and gives a page number for the first page of each chapter.

The **copyright page** tells the year the book was published.

Back of book:

The **index** contains page numbers for important topics in the book. The **glossary** is a dictionary that defines words used in the book.

The **bibliography** is a list of sources the author used that you could consult to find more information about the subject of the book.

Mark the best answer.

1. Where would you look to find the date a book was published?
   ○ copyright page   ○ index   ○ title page

2. Where would you look in the book to find the definition of an unfamiliar word?
   ○ bibliography   ○ glossary   ○ index

3. Where else besides the index could you look to find the location of a certain topic in the book?
   ○ bibliography   ○ glossary   ○ table of contents

4. Where would you look to find sources with more information on the subject of the book?
   ○ bibliography   ○ glossary   ○ index

5. Where would you look first if you were trying to find out whether a book was written before 2015?
   ○ bibliography   ○ glossary   ○ copyright page

Use the table of contents and index from a book about Alexandria, Egypt, to answer the question.

6. Which pages have information about Egyptian culture?

   ○ 4–8   ○ 6–7   ○ 73–75

7. Which chapter is most likely to have information about ancient statues?

   ○ Chapter 2   ○ Chapter 3   ○ Chapter 4

8. Which of these might be included in Chapter 3?

   ○ Eastern Orthodox Church

   ○ Napoleon's invasion

   ○ the search for Alexander's tomb

9. Which chapter has information about the library in ancient Alexandria?

   ○ Chapter 2   ○ Chapter 3   ○ Chapter 4

Contents	
1 Early History	4
2 Alexander's Conquest	11
3 Education and Religion	33
4 Art and Monuments	72
5 The Decline of Alexandria	97
6 Alexandria Reborn	110
7 Alexandria Today	130
Index	145

Index	
Alexander the Great	11–14
Cleopatra	67
culture	
Egyptian	4–8
Greek	14–22
Roman	33–36
education	
Library at Alexandria	36–38
University at Alexandria	39–45
monuments	
Pharos of Alexandria	73–75
Pompey's Pillar	78–81

Pompey's Pillar and sphinx in Alexandria, Egypt

Using the Library

A **library** contains fiction, nonfiction, biographies, and reference books.

Nonfiction books provide information about real people, places, or things. They are arranged by subject and have a **call number** that will help you find the book on the library shelves.

Fiction books tell stories that are made up, not real. They are arranged in alphabetical order by the author's last name.

Reference books, such as dictionaries, encyclopedias, thesauruses, and atlases, contain a specific type of information. They are arranged by volume in the reference section of the library.

Biographies contain the life stories of real people and are arranged alphabetically by the person's last name in a special section of the library.

The **library catalog** contains information about every book in the library. It can be searched by **title**, **author**, **subject**, or **keyword**.

Mark the most helpful source for answering the research question.

1. How is the word *sarcophagus* pronounced?
   - ○ atlas
   - ○ dictionary
   - ○ periodical

2. What were the first airplanes like?
   - ○ dictionary
   - ○ encyclopedia
   - ○ language arts textbook

3. What city had the largest population last year?
   - ○ almanac
   - ○ encyclopedia
   - ○ history textbook

4. Who won the Super Bowl last month?
   - ○ dictionary
   - ○ encyclopedia
   - ○ periodical

5. Which country in Africa has the most varied climate?
   - ○ almanac
   - ○ atlas
   - ○ periodical

Mark the best way to search for the book described.

6. You know the author's name but don't know the title of the book.

   ○ title   ○ author   ○ subject or keyword

7. You know the title of a book but don't know the author's name.

   ○ title   ○ author   ○ subject or keyword

8. You want a book about Egypt but don't know the title of the book or the author's name.

   ○ title   ○ author   ○ subject or keyword

Write the best word or words for the library search. Then mark the best type of search to use.

9. A biography of Alexander the Great

   Search: [   ]

   ○ title   ○ author   ○ subject or keyword

10. A book by Kellen Camfield about the Tuareg people of the Sahara Desert

   Search: [   ]

   ○ title   ○ author   ○ subject or keyword

11. A book about the history and culture of Morocco

   Search: [   ]

   ○ title   ○ author   ○ subject or keyword

12. A novel called *The Case of the Pyramid Puzzle*

   Search: [   ]

   ○ title   ○ author   ○ subject or keyword

13. A book of Mediterranean recipes

   Search: [   ]

   ○ title   ○ author   ○ subject or keyword

Dictionaries

If you come across an unfamiliar word or are not sure how to spell a word, look in a dictionary. A **dictionary** can give you the meaning of the word, help you pronounce it correctly, and tell you about its origin.

After each entry word is the **pronunciation** of the word. Accent marks or bold letters tell you which syllables to emphasize when you say the word. Online dictionaries usually include an audio recording of the word.

A **pronunciation guide** is found on every other page of most printed dictionaries to help you pronounce the words. Online dictionaries may provide a guide as well.

Guide words list the first and last words on the page.

Entry words are listed in alphabetical order and are divided into syllables.

The **etymology** tells what language the word came from and what other words are related to it. It is listed in brackets at the beginning or end of a dictionary entry.

spear   **spider**

spear |spîr|—*noun, plural* **spears** **1.** A weapon with a long shaft and a sharp head. **2.** A shoot or sprout: *a spear of asparagus.* [Middle English *spere,* from Old English.]

spe·cial |spĕsh ′ əl|—*adjective* **1.** Different from what is common or usual; extraordinary; exceptional. *Jenna baked a special cake for the birthday party.* **2.** Distinct in some way from others that are similar to it; particular: *Dad bought a special knife just for carving the turkey.* [Middle English, from Old French *especial,* from Latin *specialis,* from *species,* kind.]

speck |spĕk|—*noun, plural* **specks** **1.** A small spot or mark. *Each egg was light blue with some dark specks on one end.* **2.** A very small amount; a bit or particle. *He brushed a speck of dirt off his sleeve.* [Middle English *specke,* from Old English *specca.*]

spec·ta·tor |spĕk ′ tā ′ tər|— *noun, plural* **spectators** One who looks on; an observer: *The spectators cheered from the stands.* [Latin *spectator,* from *spectare,* to watch.]

The **part of speech** follows the pronunciation of the word. Parts of speech may be abbreviated.

You may see different forms of a verb or the plural form of a noun.

Mark the correct answer.

1. Which word could be found on a page with the guide words *discard* and *disgrace*?
   - ○ disdain
   - ○ disagree
   - ○ display

2. Which word would come after *headlong*?
   - ○ headfirst
   - ○ headway
   - ○ headache

Use a dictionary to look up the italicized word. Mark the best answer.

3. Which sentence uses the word *ideal* correctly?
   - ○ He broke his *ideal*.
   - ○ Dad is my *ideal* of a godly man.
   - ○ You should work hard and not be *ideal*.

4. Based on its syllable division, how would you hyphenate *identical* at the end of a line in a paragraph?
   - ○ id-entical
   - ○ ident-ical
   - ○ iden-tical

5. What part of speech is *identify*?
   - ○ noun
   - ○ verb
   - ○ adjective

6. Which word has the same *i* sound as the first *i* in *idiom*?
   - ○ bike
   - ○ oil
   - ○ pistol

7. Which is a correct form of *identify*?
   - ○ identifyed
   - ○ identifies
   - ○ identifys

8. Which syllable is most strongly accented in *identification*?
   - ○ second
   - ○ fifth
   - ○ sixth

Use a dictionary to find two definitions of *trim*. Write a sample sentence for each definition.

9. Definition 1: _____

   Sentence: _____

   _____

10. Definition 2: _____

   Sentence: _____

   _____

More about Dictionaries

Some words have more than one meaning. You can figure out the correct meaning through the context of the sentence.

We blew into our underline{recorders} softly.

Some words have **homographs**, or words that are spelled the same way but have different meanings. Homographs are two separate entries in the dictionary because they are different words. They are marked with a small number at the end of the word.

lock[1] |lŏk´|—*noun* **1.** A fastener for making something secure (such as a door or window), worked by a key, a combination, or other method. **2.** A part of a canal or river with gates at each end, used for raising and lowering boats. [Middle English *lok*, from Old English *loc*, bolt, bar.]

recorder |rĭ kôr´ der|—**1.** One that records. **2.** A type of flute with a mouthpiece on one end and finger holes for playing different notes.

lock[2] |lŏk´|—*noun* A portion of hair that hangs together; a curl or ringlet; tress. [Middle English *lok*, from Old English *loc*, *locc*.]

Write the number of the definition that fits the underlined word.

_____ 1. Our team had an underline{edge} over our younger opponents.

_____ 2. At the underline{edge} of the cliff was an ancient pine tree.

_____ 3. The cattle are grazing on the open underline{range}.

_____ 4. I will underline{save} my money to buy a bike.

_____ 5. God sent Jesus into the world to underline{save} sinners.

edge |ĕdj|—*noun* **1.** The line marking the end of something; boundary or border. **2.** The sharpened side of a blade of a cutting instrument or weapon. **3.** An advantage.

range |rānj|—*noun* **1.** The extent or distance within set limits. **2.** The longest distance something can reach or at which it is effective. **3.** A place for shooting practice. **4.** A stretch of land for the grazing of livestock. **5.** A cooking stove. **6.** A line or series of mountains.

save |sāv|—*verb* **1.** To rescue from danger or harm. **2.** To keep for the future; store or lay up. **3.** To avoid spending or wasting. **4.** To deliver from sin; redeem.

Write the number of the homograph used in the sentence.

_____ 6. He carried the toddler the <u>rest</u> of the way.

_____ 7. I was tired because I had not had enough <u>rest</u>.

_____ 8. The teacher kept a <u>file</u> on each student.

_____ 9. She used a <u>file</u> to smooth her nails.

Mark the sentence in which the underlined word means the same as it does in the given sentence.

10. He likes the taste of <u>mint</u>.
    - ○ We toured the <u>mint</u> in Denver.
    - ○ The shiny coins were right from the <u>mint</u>.
    - ○ Kai bought <u>mint</u> chocolate chip ice cream.

11. I had a muscle cramp in my <u>calf</u>.
    - ○ The <u>calf</u> stayed close to its mother.
    - ○ I hemmed the dress below the <u>calf</u>.
    - ○ The buffalo <u>calf</u> had a thick, woolly hide.

Use a dictionary to find two definitions of _prune_. Write a sample sentence for each definition.

12. Definition 1: _____

    Sentence: _____

    _____

13. Definition 2: _____

    Sentence: _____

    _____

rest¹ |rĕst|—_noun_ Sleep, a break in activity, or quiet.

rest² |rĕst|—_noun_ That which is left over; remainder.

file¹ |fīl|—_noun_ A collection of papers or other information arranged in order for reference.

file² |fīl|—_noun_ A tool with a rough surface for smoothing or scraping objects.

Practice

Mark the best answer.

1. Where would you look to find the chapter on fishing boats in the book *All about Boats*?

   ○ index ○ table of contents ○ title page

2. Where would you look to find the definition of *dinghy*?

   ○ index ○ copyright page ○ glossary

Use the table of contents and index from a book on George Washington to answer the question.

3. Which chapter will have information about the death of Washington's father when Washington was twelve?

   ○ 1 ○ 3 ○ 4

4. Which pages are most likely to have information about the Boston Tea Party?

   ○ 4–9 ○ 47–70 ○ 76–80

5. Which information might be included in Chapter 3?

   ○ The Declaration of Independence is signed.

   ○ General Cornwallis surrenders at Yorktown.

Contents	
1 His Childhood	4
2 His Civilian Life	10
3 His Military Life	35
4 His Political Life	75
Index	150

Index	
Constitution of the United States	
Constitutional Convention	77
ratification	79
military	
French and Indian War	37–45
Revolutionary War	47–70
President of the United States	
First Continental Congress	76–80
inaugural address	85
foreign conflicts	90–125
surveyor	8

Use a dictionary to look up the italicized word. Mark the best answer.

6. Which sentence uses the word *contrite* correctly?

   ○ He confessed his sin with a contrite spirit.

   ○ You should be contrite when you open your presents.

7. Which word has the same *o* sound as the *o* in *contain*?

   ○ bishop   ○ booth   ○ escort

Use a dictionary to find two definitions of *wave*. Write a sample sentence for each definition.

8. Definition 1: _____

   Sentence: _____

   _____

9. Definition 2: _____

   Sentence: _____

   _____

Mark the most helpful source for answering the research question.

10. What were the final scores for this year's world series games?

    ○ atlas   ○ dictionary   ○ periodical

11. How can I plan my cross-country trip from New York to San Francisco?

    ○ atlas   ○ encyclopedia   ○ periodical

Write the best word or words for the library search. Then mark the best type of search to use.

12. The myth of George Washington and the cherry tree

    Search: [   ]

    ○ title   ○ author   ○ subject or keyword

13. Lynn Cullen's book about George Washington

    Search: [   ]

    ○ title   ○ author   ○ subject or keyword

Internet Research

A **web browser** is a computer program that allows you to access the internet.

The **URL**, or web address, is the information at the top of a website that tells where the website can be found on the internet.

A **search engine** will help you locate websites about topics that interest you.

A **keyword search** tells the search engine what kind of information you want to find.

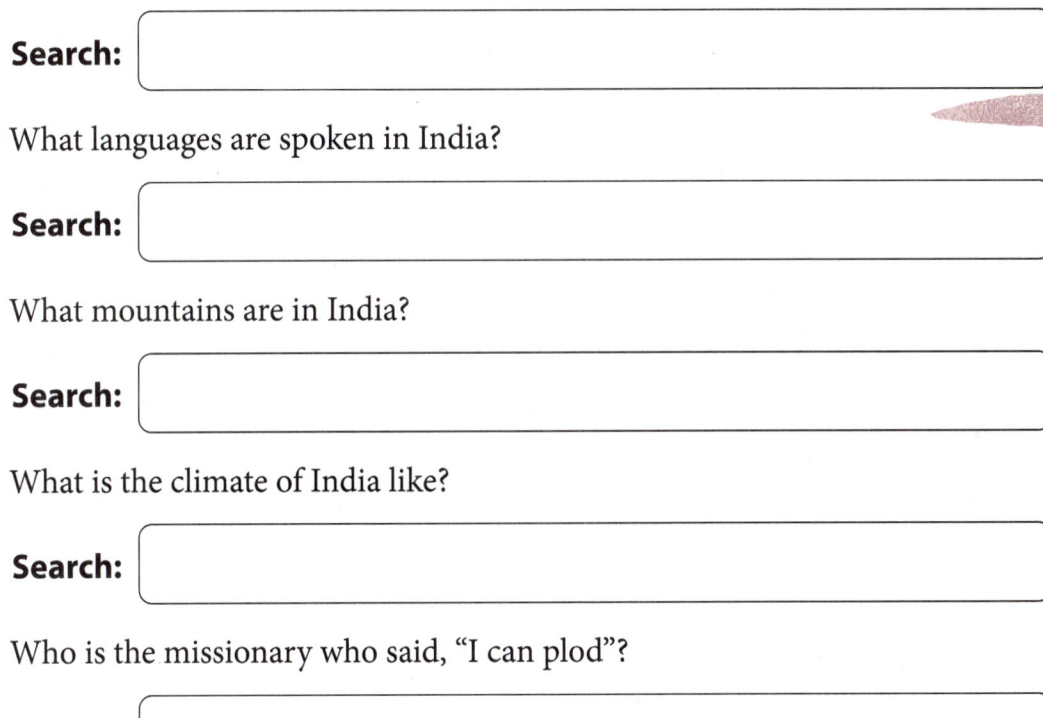

Think of a keyword search that you could use to help you find the answer to the research question. Write your keywords in the blank.

1. What is the traditional clothing of India?

   Search: [_____]

2. What languages are spoken in India?

   Search: [_____]

3. What mountains are in India?

   Search: [_____]

4. What is the climate of India like?

   Search: [_____]

5. Who is the missionary who said, "I can plod"?

   Search: [_____]

Write your own research question about a person or place you would like to learn more about. Think of a keyword search that you could use to help you find the answer. Write your keywords in the blank.

6. _____?

   Search: [_____]

Choose one of the questions from numbers 1–6. With help from an adult, go to a search engine and enter a keyword search using your keywords. Then complete numbers 7–9.

7. Look at the list of results from your keyword search. Was your search successful?

   ○ yes   ○ no

8. Think of another word or phrase to make your search more specific. Write your new keyword or words in the blank.

   Search: [   ]

9. Try your new keyword search. Did you get better results?

   ○ yes   ○ no

Follow the link to a website from your list of search results. Write down the bibliography information for that source.

Internet Sources

10. Author(s) _____

    Title of article _____

    Title of source (website) _____

    URL address _____

11. Author(s) _____

    Title of article _____

    Title of source (website) _____

    URL address _____

Internet Safety

Remember the following principles of internet **SAFETY** as you search for information online.

S — Serve and love others with technology.

A — Avoid websites that you do not have permission to visit.

F — Focus on words that please God.

E — Evaluate what you read.

T — Tell an adult if you see something that makes you feel uncomfortable.

Y — Your passwords, address, and phone number should not be shared online.

Decide what you should do in each situation. Discuss your answers with a partner.

1. A pop-up box appears on your computer asking for your phone number.

2. You open a website and see pictures that make you feel uneasy.

3. A friend sends you a link to a website your parents have warned you not to visit.

4. Someone you do not know asks you to post a picture of yourself.

5. A classmate posts a picture of someone with an unkind comment and asks you to comment as well.

6. You notice that an online conversation is disrespectful to God or what He has said in His Word.

Think of a way you could serve and love others with technology this week. Write at least two sentences describing your plan.

7. _____

_____

_____

_____

Be precise in how you choose sources and gather information. Each source you use should be **reliable**, or trustworthy.

Check the author, content, date, and website where you found the information.

As you look for facts, make sure you can find two or three sources that say the same thing.

Read the source description. Write *R* if the source is reliable or *U* if the source is unreliable. If you decide the source is unreliable, mark the problem or problems that you find.

_____ 8. An article about ancient ruins in the Alexandrian harbor written by a member of the Smithsonian research staff

    ○ author   ○ content   ○ date   ○ website

_____ 9. A weather forecast for Cairo, Egypt, posted January 19, 2010

    ○ author   ○ content   ○ date   ○ website

_____ 10. An article about Eratosthenes, the chief librarian of the Library of Alexandria, written by the director of a library association and posted on its website

    ○ author   ○ content   ○ date   ○ website

_____ 11. A map of Egypt drawn by eleven-year-old Oscar Kole and posted on his school website

    ○ author   ○ content   ○ date   ○ website

_____ 12. An article about sand rats by Professor Imogene Cubbins on the National Geographic website

    ○ author   ○ content   ○ date   ○ website

_____ 13. An infographic describing crowns of ancient Egyptian royalty on Costumez4Sale.biz

    ○ author   ○ content   ○ date   ○ website

_____ 14. A cartoon video about Alexander the Great based on the diary of Peritas, his favorite dog, on PenofPeritas.com

    ○ author   ○ content   ○ date   ○ website

Taking Notes: Outlining

An **outline** is a way to organize information as you take notes or plan a writing project.

Read the article about Jim Elliot. Write the missing information in the outline.

Something to Keep

Jim Elliot once wrote, "He is no fool who gives what he cannot keep to gain what he cannot lose." Jim Elliot's life proved that he really believed what he wrote.

Jim Elliot was born in Portland, Oregon, in 1927. He grew up with two brothers and one sister. When he was six, he trusted Christ as his Savior. He liked to have adventures with his friends, and he was good at drawing.

Jim went to Wheaton College. He majored in Greek to prepare himself to study and translate the Bible. He was a member of the wrestling team, and he was a leader among the students. But more than anything else, he was known for his love for God. While he was at college, he met Elisabeth. Later God led both of them to Ecuador to be missionaries. They served in different parts of the country before being married in Quito, Ecuador, on October 8, 1953.

Jim Elliot is best known for his work with the Huaorani people, then known as the Aucas, in the jungle of Ecuador. In 1955, he and four other men took an airplane into Huaorani territory. At first, they flew over Huaorani villages and dropped gifts, such as cooking pots and ribbons. Then they landed the plane and tried to talk to a group of the Huaorani in their own language.

The Huaorani seemed friendly at first. The five missionaries set up a camp in their territory. But then one day, Huaorani came to the camp and killed all five of the men. The men went to be with Jesus. But their story was told around the world. Thousands of people were influenced for Christ and missions.

Jim Elliot and his friends gave up something they could not keep. They gave up their lives. But they gained something they can keep for all eternity.

Jim Elliot

I. Introduction—Elliot's quote; his life showed he meant it

II. Elliot's childhood and salvation

___. Born in 1927 in Portland, Oregon

B. _____

___. Trusted Christ as Savior as a six-year-old

D. _____

III. _____

    A. Attended Wheaton College

        1. _____

        ___. Was on the wrestling team

        3. _____

    ___. Met Elisabeth at Wheaton

        1. _____

        ___. Married October 8, 1953, in Ecuador

IV. _____

    ___. Is most well known for his work with the Huaorani

    B. _____

        ___. Flew into Huaorani territory with four other men

        2. _____

        ___. Landed and attempted to speak with the Huaorani in their own language

V. Elliot's death and its results

    A. _____

    ___. Huaorani came there and killed all five men

        1. _____

        ___. Their story influenced thousands

VI. Conclusion—how Elliot's quote proved true

Taking Notes: Making Note Cards

Note cards can help you record and organize information for a research report.

Excerpt from *Free Indeed: Heroes of Black Christian History* by Mark Sidwell

Richard Allen was born a slave on February 14, 1760, in Philadelphia. In 1768 he was sold with his family to planter Stokely Sturgis who lived near Dover, Delaware. Allen's master was not a Christian, but he was "affectionate and tender-hearted," Allen said, "what the world called a good master." Unfortunately, Sturgis was also hard pressed financially. Somewhere around 1776, debts forced Sturgis to sell Allen's mother along with three of her children; Allen and one brother and one sister remained with Sturgis.

This wrenching event must have affected Allen deeply. He found comfort a year or so later, though, when he heard the gospel. Allen recalled, "I was awakened and brought to see myself, poor, wretched and undone, and without the mercy of God must be lost. Shortly after, I obtained mercy through the blood of Christ. . . ." Allen, his brother, and his sister were all converted. . . .

The change in Allen and his brother so impressed Sturgis that the planter asked Allen to have the Methodist preacher to come speak to him. After hearing the gospel, Sturgis was also converted. Furthermore, he embraced the Methodist opposition to slavery. The planter wanted to free his slaves, but he was in debt and could not easily do so. Therefore, he decided to let Allen and his brother earn the money to purchase their liberty.

Childhood
1. born February 14, 1760
2. born a slave
3. his mother and three of her children were sold in 1776
4. Allen, one brother, one sister not sold
<u>Free Indeed</u>, p. 31

Salvation
1. someone shared the gospel with Allen
2. he saw he was a sinner, came to Christ
3. his master was saved as well
<u>Free Indeed</u>, pp. 31–32

Read the following information. Take notes on the cards to help you remember the details. Write the information about the source.

Adapted from *Faith of Our Fathers: Scenes from Church History* edited by Mark Sidwell

John Wesley was born in England into a family that had known nineteen births (eight children died in infancy). His father was a minister, and both of his parents were very strict. When John was five, the Wesley home burned, but he escaped, and God spared his life.

John Wesley attended Oxford University. He was busy doing good works, especially as a member of a club at Oxford called the "Holy Club." He later said, "Doing so much, and living so good a life, I doubted not but I was a good Christian."

In keeping with his eager righteousness-by-works, he went with his brother Charles as a missionary to the new American colony of Georgia. He accomplished little and, after two years, returned to England a troubled man.

One night, after hearing an article by Martin Luther on the book of Romans, John's heart was moved as he trusted in Christ alone for his salvation. Now he knew that Christ had taken away his sins.

After receiving Christ, he preached about forty thousand sermons and traveled well over two hundred thousand miles, usually on horseback, during that half century. He averaged nearly five thousand miles a year and fifteen sermons a week. The Lord used John Wesley, his brother Charles, and George Whitefield to bring about revival in England.

Family and Childhood

1. _____

2. _____

3. _____

_____ *p. 140*

Education

1. _____

2. _____

_____ *p. 141*

Practice

Think of a keyword search that you could use to help you find the answer to the research question. Write your keywords in the blank.

1. Did George Washington have wooden teeth?

   Search: [ ]

2. Did George Washington go to school?

   Search: [ ]

Choose one of the questions from numbers 1–2. With help from an adult, go to a search engine and enter a keyword search. Follow the link to an appropriate website from your list of search results. Write down the bibliography information for that source.

Internet Sources

3. Author(s) _____

   Title of article _____

   Title of source (website) _____

   URL address _____

Read the source description. Write *R* if the source is reliable or *U* if the source is unreliable. If you decide the source is unreliable, mark the problem or problems that you find.

_____ 4. An infographic on a classmate's post listing the most popular dog names

        ○ author   ○ content   ○ date   ○ website

_____ 5. Photographic prints of buildings in Washington, DC, obtained from the Library of Congress website

        ○ author   ○ content   ○ date   ○ website

Read the article. Write the missing information in the outline.

Libraries of Learning

Alexander the Great founded Alexandria, Egypt, as the capital of his empire. His plan was to build a library there that would be a center of learning and knowledge. After his sudden death, Ptolemy I fulfilled Alexander's dream and completed the library. The purpose for the library was to store world knowledge and serve as a resource for Greek scholars.

In 2002 a new library was opened near the location of the first library. The books in the old library were mainly in Greek and Egyptian. The two million books in the new library are in many languages. The old library mainly contained knowledge in the form of documents and books. In addition to old maps and books, the new library has sections such as audio/visual, children's books, and resources for the blind.

Alexandrian Libraries

  I. Ancient library

     A. _____

        1. Planned by Alexander

       ____. _____

   ____. Purpose of the library

        1. _____

        2. As a resource for learning

  II. _____

   ____. Location of the library

     B. _____

        1. _____

       ____. Multiple sections

Chapter 13 Review

Mark the most helpful source for answering the research question.

1. What is the average temperature in Brazil?
   - ○ atlas
   - ○ history textbook
   - ○ science textbook

2. What is the etymology of *elephant*?
   - ○ almanac
   - ○ dictionary
   - ○ English textbook

3. Who became the new governor of Virginia last week?
   - ○ dictionary
   - ○ encyclopedia
   - ○ periodical

4. Where was King Tutankhamun's tomb located?
   - ○ atlas
   - ○ encyclopedia
   - ○ thesaurus

Use a dictionary to look up the italicized word. Mark the best answer.

5. Which syllable is most strongly accented in *abandon*?
   - ○ first
   - ○ second
   - ○ third

6. How would you hyphenate *abandon* at the end of a line?
   - ○ aban-don
   - ○ ab-andon
   - ○ aband-on

7. Which is the correct plural form of *abbey*?
   - ○ abbies
   - ○ abbeys

Think of a keyword search that you could use to help you find the answer to the research question. Write your keywords in the blank.

8. How tall is the Cape Charles Lighthouse?

   Search: [   ]

9. Who wrote the book *My Side of the Mountain*?

   Search: [   ]

10. What bird helps cattle?

    Search: [   ]

Read the source description. Write *R* if the source is reliable or *U* if the source is unreliable. If you decide the source is unreliable, mark the problem or problems that you find.

_____ 11. An article about brain surgery written by Dr. Henry Muilenberg of the Mayo Clinic
○ author   ○ content   ○ date   ○ website

_____ 12. A list of famous names from Alexander the Great's cell phone contact list posted on TimeTravel.com
○ author   ○ content   ○ date   ○ website

Read the article. Write the missing information in the outline.

A Famous Conqueror

Alexander the Great was the king of Macedonia. At an early age he showed great intelligence and skill. As an adult he created a world empire. He conquered most of Asia Minor and brought the entire Persian Empire and Egypt under his control. Alexander founded a new capital for Egypt and named it Alexandria after himself.

Alexander died of a fever at thirty-two. The effects of his short life have lasted for centuries. He extended the Greek empire, language, learning, and influence to the rest of the known world.

Alexander the Great

I. _____

____. His great ability

   B. _____

____. Asia Minor

      2. _____

____. Egypt

II. Effects of his life

   A. _____

____. Reached many countries

Read the following article from a website called *Ancient Wonders*. Take notes on the card to help you remember the details. Write the information about the source.

A Sunken Surprise

An entire sunken city was discovered off the coast of Alexandria. Cleopatra, the last of the Pharaohs, lived in this city. A palace that may have been hers has been found there, along with many well-preserved statues and other artifacts. Pieces of the Pharos lighthouse lie beneath the waters as well.

An Underwater City

1. _____

2. _____

3. _____

_____

Journal

You are getting ready to research a topic. What are some steps you should take to prepare for precise writing?

Cumulative Review

Write a complete subject or a complete predicate to finish the sentence.

1. _____ worked hard on his job.

2. The skilled fisherman _____.

Mark the sentence that is written correctly.

3. ○ Simon's fishing business was hard work.
   ○ Simons fishing business was hard work.

4. ○ The fisherman camed to Jesus after his brother invited him.
   ○ The fisherman came to Jesus after his brother invited him.

Choose a verb from the word bank. Use the past-participle form in a sentence.

> catch   choose   speak   tear   wear

5. _____

_____

Choose a word from the word bank. Write one expanded sentence using the word as an adverb and one expanded sentence using the word as a preposition.

> inside   out   over   under   up

Peter climbed.

6. Adverb: _____

7. Preposition: _____

Choose one of the sensory verbs. Write one sentence using the verb as an action verb and one sentence using it as a linking verb.

> feel   look   smell   sound   taste

8. Action: _____

_____

9. Linking: _____

_____

Write the pronoun that correctly renames the underlined antecedent.

10. <u>Peter</u>, <u>James</u>, and <u>John</u> were the three members of Jesus' inner circle. _____ witnessed many of Jesus' miracles.

11. After <u>Peter</u> witnessed Jesus' return to heaven, _____ obeyed Jesus' command to preach the gospel.

Combine the sentences. Use a coordinating conjunction for a compound sentence or a subordinating conjunction for a complex sentence. Remember to use a comma if necessary.

12. Complex: Peter went to the house of a Gentile named Cornelius. He helped Cornelius and his family to repent and trust in Christ.

_____

_____

13. Compound: The good news about Christ had gone only to the Jews. Peter explained that God has offered the gift of salvation to all.

_____

_____

Use ⌃ to add commas where they are needed.

14. Peter became a fisher of men didn't he?

15. Although he was arrested and beaten he continued to preach the gospel.

Use a dictionary to find two definitions of *second*. Write a sample sentence for each definition.

16. Definition 1: _____

    Sentence:_____

    _____

17. Definition 2: _____

    Sentence: _____

    _____

14

Writing a Research Report

How can I help someone else see the world more clearly?

Mentor Text

Excerpt from *Mary Slessor, Missionary Mother* by Terri B. Kelly

Nearly three years passed in Old Town. Some behaviors changed. The Egbo runners had announced the new law—death for anyone who killed twins. Yet Mary knew the natives were still killing twins but in secret. The mother, father, or another relative would shove the twins through a hole in the back of the hut for the animals to kill. She talked to the new Christians and asked them for help. "Will you alert me as soon as twins are born?"

Late every night, Mary kneeled and prayed. With God's help, she hoped one day she could convince the people that twins were not from an evil spirit. With the rescued children asleep around her, Mary opened her Bible to Psalms. "Bless the Lord, O my soul; and forget not all his benefits."

A thump sounded outside. "Run, Ma, run!"

"Oh, God, help me to get there," Mary prayed. Her bare feet pounded against the dirt path. "Get me there in time, Lord."

A crowd had gathered. Word traveled fast in villages. Arms waving frantically through the air, Mary screamed, "Get out of the way," hoping the noise would scare the people. She pushed past the women in the hut. No babies.

She ran to the back of the hut and found the twins lying on the ground below a hole in the hut. *Alive.* Mary gathered the babies in her arms and ran. She didn't dare look back to see if anyone followed her. As her foot crossed into the mission yard, she whispered, "Thank You, God."

Gently, she wiped each baby clean. Tiny cries erupted. "Hush now, sweet child." Mary slid a finger into the girl's tiny hand. "This reminds me of holding my baby sister, Janie, when she was born."

Mary looked at the scrawny little babies in her arms. "Wee girl, you will be Janie. And, young man, you shall be Robert." Mary spooned tea in each squalling baby's mouth. "Lord, please don't let the babies die."

Hut of Mary Slessor

Church in Okoyong

Research Reports

A **research report** gives facts about a topic. Your opinions, or how you feel about the topic, are not included.

A **biography** is a research report that gives facts about a person's life and accomplishments.

Charles Wesley: Preacher and Poet

Introduction
If you have ever sung the hymn "And Can It Be," you were singing the words of Charles Wesley. This great preacher and poet was amazed by the love of God, and he used his voice and his pen to tell others about that love.

Childhood
Charles Wesley was born in England on December 18, 1707. He was the eighteenth of nineteen children, but only eight of his brothers and sisters lived to be adults. His father was a minister, and his mother taught him at home.

Education
Although Charles's parents taught him many things about the Bible, he was not saved until he grew up. At Oxford University, he and a group of other students began the Holy Club. Members of the Holy Club tried to live very strict, disciplined lives.

Salvation
After college Charles and his brother John were both ordained as ministers and went to America to be missionaries. The work did not go well, and Charles became ill and returned to England. It was not until he was back at home that he realized he did not really know Christ and had not had his sins forgiven. After listening to a friend read Psalm 32, Charles put his faith in Christ to save him.

Ministry, marriage, and family
Charles became a minister in England. He visited in prisons and held open-air meetings. He and his brother John helped to form the Methodist movement. Charles married Sally Gwynne in 1749, and she traveled with him on many of his preaching trips. They had ten children, but only three of them survived.

Accomplishments
One of the first things Charles did after he was saved was to write a hymn. He continued to write hymns for the rest of his life. He wrote about 6,500 hymns, and many of them were published in collections. Some of his most famous hymns are "And Can It Be," "O for a Thousand Tongues to Sing," and "Hark, the Herald Angels Sing."

Continued

Conclusion

Charles Wesley wished he had a thousand tongues to sing the praise of Jesus. Although he had only one tongue, he gave us thousands of hymns to use in our worship.

Steps for Writing a Good Research Report

1. Choose your topic.

2. Decide what main ideas you want to write about.

3. Read and take notes about your main ideas from nonfiction sources.

4. Organize your information by writing an outline.

5. Write the first draft of your report from the outline.

6. Revise your report.

7. Proofread your report.

8. Make a bibliography listing all the sources you used in your report.

9. Publish your report.

Choose a Christian from the past to research. Then complete the chart.

I would like to write a biography about _____

What I already know:	What I would like to know:

Research Report: Taking Notes

Take notes using these five main ideas about the person you have chosen as your topic:

- *childhood*
- *education*
- *marriage and family*
- *salvation experience*
- *accomplishments*

Use at least three sources of information for your research report. Record full information about each source for your bibliography.

C. Wesley

Wesley, Charles (1707–1788) An English clergyman and hymnwriter who with his brother John founded the Methodist church. He was born in Epworth, Lincolnshire. Wesley attended Oxford University, where he formed a group who pursued spiritual and academic discipline. They were nicknamed "Methodists." Wesley was involved in missionary and preaching efforts in North America and Great Britain. Following his marriage in 1749, he settled in London. He wrote most of the Methodist *Collection of Hymns*, published in 1780. He is thought to have written over 6,500 hymns. Among the most well-known of these are "And Can It Be," "Christ the Lord Is Risen Today," "O for a Thousand Tongues to Sing," and "Hark, the Herald Angels Sing." He is buried in the churchyard of Marylebone Parish Church, London.

Richard Wexford

> Write each main idea at the top of a separate note card. Then make new note cards as you find more details about each main idea.

Wesley's accomplishments
1. *preacher and missionary*
2. *wrote 6,500 hymns*
3. *founded Methodism with brother John*
Hertford's Encyclopedia, Vol. 20, page 223

Wesley's childhood
1. *born in 1707*
2. *born in Epworth, Lincolnshire (England)*
Hertford's Encyclopedia, Vol. 20, page 223

Mark the item that does not belong on the note card.

1.

> *Wesley's marriage and family*
> ○ 1. *married Sarah Gwynne (called her "Sally")*
> ○ 2. *often preached in northern England*
> ○ 3. *three children lived to be adults*
> <u>*Our Heritage of Hymns*</u>*, p. 45*

2.

> *Wesley's education*
> ○ 1. *attended Oxford University*
> ○ 2. *started a student organization called the Holy Club*
> ○ 3. *son Samuel was a musician*
> *"Charles Wesley," www.hymhst.com/cw76*

Begin locating and reading information about the person of your choice. As you read, take notes on separate note cards. Write the information about the source at the bottom of each note card.

Think about ways the Christian you are researching has influenced others. List at least two of these ways below.

3. _____

_____

_____

_____

_____

Research Report: Writing an Outline

Organize your information under main points in an **outline** before you begin to write.

Wesley's salvation experience
1. recovering from illness in home of friend
2. listened to him read Psalm 32
3. later wrote that he had peace with God because of his faith in Christ
Church History Herald, page 18

Wesley's salvation experience
1. lived strict life but wasn't saved
2. tried to be missionary in America with his brother John—became ill
3. realized he didn't know Christ
4. talked with Moravian Christians
5. put faith in Christ
Our Heritage of Hymns, pages 21–23

Wesley's education
1. attended Oxford University
2. started a student organization—Holy Club
3. tried to live a very disciplined life
Church History Herald, page 17

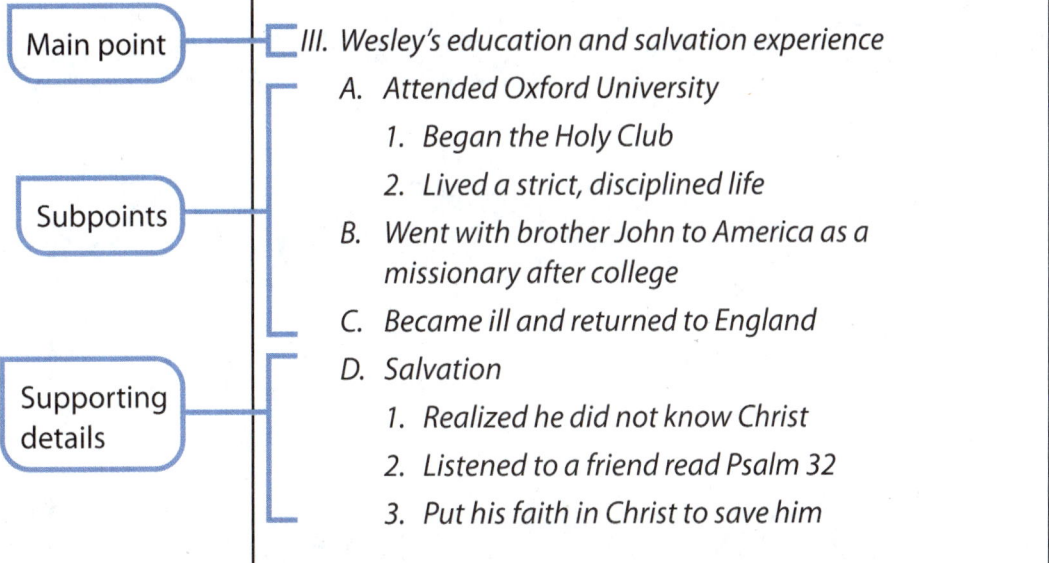

Main point
III. Wesley's education and salvation experience

Subpoints
A. Attended Oxford University
   1. Began the Holy Club
   2. Lived a strict, disciplined life
B. Went with brother John to America as a missionary after college
C. Became ill and returned to England

Supporting details
D. Salvation
   1. Realized he did not know Christ
   2. Listened to a friend read Psalm 32
   3. Put his faith in Christ to save him

Research Report Outline Guidelines

1. Plan an introduction.

2. Use your research to write at least four main points. You might want to combine some of your main ideas under one main point.

3. Support each main point with at least three lettered subpoints.

4. Some subpoints should have supporting details.

5. Remember that you might not use all the details from your note cards.

6. Plan a conclusion.

Write an outline to organize the information from your note cards for writing your research report. Follow the guidelines listed above.

Oxford University

Research Report: Draft

Use the main points, subpoints, and supporting details in your outline to draft your research report.

IV. Wesley's accomplishments as a minister and his marriage
  A. Became a minister in England
    1. Visited in prisons
    2. Held open-air meetings
  B. Helped brother John form the Methodist movement
  C. Married Sally Gwynne
    1. Traveled with him on preaching trips
    2. Had ten children, but only three survived
V. Wesley's accomplishments as a hymnwriter
  A. Wrote hymns right after he was saved
  B. Wrote about 6,500 hymns
  C. Most famous hymns
    1. "And Can It Be"
    2. "O for a Thousand Tongues to Sing"
    3. "Hark, the Herald Angels Sing"

Charles became a Minister in England. He visited in prisons. He held open-air meetings. He and his brother John helped to form the Methidist movement. He married Sally Gwynne in 1749. She traveled with him on many of his preaching trips. They had ten children, but only three of them survived.

Charles started writing hymns right after he was saved. He continued to write hymns for the rest of his life. He wrote about 6,500 hymns, and many of them were published in colections. Some of his most famous hymns are "And can It Be," "O for a Thousand Tongues to sing," and Hark, the Harold Angels Sing." "O for a Thousand Tongues to Sing" is my favorite hymn.

Use your outline to draft your research report. Follow the drafting guide, checking off each part of the research report as you write.

Drafting Guide		
Introduction	Write a short paragraph that leads into the report.	
Topic Sentence	Write a topic sentence about the first main idea.	
Details	Give details about the first main idea.	
Topic Sentence	Write a topic sentence about the second main idea.	
Details	Give details about the second main idea.	
Topic Sentence	Write a topic sentence about the third main idea.	
Details	Give details about the third main idea.	
Topic Sentence	Write a topic sentence about the fourth main idea.	
Details	Give details about the fourth main idea.	
Conclusion	Write a short paragraph that sums up the report.	

Research Report: Revise

As you revise your research report, check for a variety of sentence lengths. Consider combining short sentences or dividing long sentences.

The writer fixed an unclear pronoun reference.

Combining two short sentences adds variety.

Charles became a Minister in England. He visited in *and* prisons. He held open-air meetings. He and his brother John helped to form the Methidist movement. *Charles* He married *,and* Sally Gwynne in 1749. She traveled with him on many of his preaching trips. They had ten children, but only three of them survived.

This new topic sentence is more interesting.

One of the first things Charles did after he was saved were to write ~~Charles started writing hymns right after he was saved.~~ *a hymn.* He continued to write hymns for the rest of his life. He wrote about 6,500 hymns, and many of them were published in colections. Some of his most famous hymns are "And can It Be," "O for a Thousand Tongues to sing," and Hark, the Harold Angels Sing." ~~"O for a Thousand Tongues to Sing" is~~

The writer's opinion does not belong in a research report.

~~my favorite hymn.~~

A closer connection between the two sentences makes the meaning clearer.

Charles Wesley wished he had a thousand tongues to *Although he had only one tongue,* sing the praise of Jesus. He gave us thousands of hymns to use in our worship.

Use the following checklist as you revise your research report. If you need to search for additional details, reread your outline and look through your note cards again.

Revising Checklist	
My research report has an introduction that leads into the report.	
Each of my main paragraphs covers one main point in my outline.	
The sentences in each paragraph tell about the main point.	
My report gives a good amount of detail about each main point.	
I used sentences of various lengths in my report.	
I did not include any of my opinions about my topic in my report.	
My report has a conclusion that sums up the report.	

Proofreading Marks

∧∨ Add
       Delete
≡   Capital letter
/   Lowercase
     Move

Research Report: Proofread

Proofread your research report to find and correct mistakes. Read it through several times, looking for one or two types of mistakes each time.

Charles became a Minister in England. He visited in prisons and held open-air meetings. He and his brother John helped to form the ~~Methidist~~ Methodist movement. Charles married Sally Gwynne in 1749, and she traveled with him on many of his preaching trips. They had ten children, but only three of them survived.

One of the first things Charles did after he was saved ~~were~~ was to write a hymn. He continued to write hymns for the rest of his life. He wrote about 6,500 hymns, and many of them were published in ~~colections~~ collections. Some of his most famous hymns are "And can It Be," "O for a Thousand Tongues to sing," and Hark, the ~~Harold~~ Herald Angels Sing."

Charles Wesley wished he had a thousand tongues to sing the praise of Jesus. Although he had only one tongue, he gave us thousands of hymns to use in our worship.

Use the following checklist as you proofread your research report.

Proofreading Checklist	
I used complete sentences (no comma splices, fused sentences, or fragments).	
I began each sentence with a capital letter and ended it with a punctuation mark.	
I used correct punctuation with sentences.	
I used correct verb forms.	
I wrote proper nouns correctly.	
I corrected misspelled words.	

Proofreading Marks

∧∨ Add

⤸ Delete

≡ Capital letter

/ Lowercase

↻→ Move

The Bibliography

A **bibliography** is a list of all the sources you used in your report. This list may include books, encyclopedias, magazines, or internet sources.

The bibliography tells others where you found the information and gives proper credit to the authors.

The bibliography lists all the sources in alphabetical order by the authors' last names.

Bibliography

Chartel, Marie. Our Heritage of Hymns. Machen Press, 2020.

Finast, Paul. "Charles Wesley." Hymn Histories, www.hymhst.com/cw76.

Rider, Marsha. "The Wesley Brothers." Church History Herald, April 2022, pp. 16–19.

Wexford, Richard. "Charles Wesley." Hertford's Encyclopedia, 5th ed., vol. 20, Hertford House, 2021, p. 223.

The bibliography lists all the information needed for locating each source.

Basic format for a book

Last name, First name of author. Title of Book. Publisher, year of publication.

> Chartel, Marie. Our Heritage of Hymns. Machen Press, 2020.

Basic format for an encyclopedia

Last name, First name of author. "Title of Article." Title of Encyclopedia, edition number, volume number, Publisher, year of publication, page numbers of article.

> Wexford, Richard. "Charles Wesley." Hertford's Encyclopedia, 5th ed., vol. 20, Hertford House, 2021, p. 223.

Continued

Basic format for a magazine article

Last name, First name of author. "Title of Article." <u>Title of Magazine</u>, Date of publication, page numbers.

Rider, Marsha. "The Wesley Brothers." <u>Church History Herald</u>, April 2022, pp. 16–19.

Basic format for an internet article

Last name, First name of author. "Title of Article." <u>Name of Website</u>, URL.

Finast, Paul. "Charles Wesley." <u>Hymn Histories</u>, www.hymhst.com/cw76.

Write a bibliography for your report. List the sources alphabetically by the authors' last names and use the proper form.

Mark the checklist for each thing you remembered to do as you wrote. Then make any needed corrections to the bibliography.

My Bibliography Self-Check	
I listed my sources in alphabetical order by the authors' last names.	
I included all the elements needed for each type of source.	
I used correct capitalization and punctuation.	

Reflection

Answer the questions and complete the chart.

1. Do you want to be like the person you wrote about?

○ **Yes**

○ **No**

2. Why?

_____

_____

_____

_____

2. Why not?

_____

_____

_____

_____

3. What could you do to be like this person?

_____

_____

_____

_____

3. What could you do to be different from this person?

_____

_____

_____

_____

Cumulative Review

Make a compound subject or predicate by combining the sentences. Use the conjunction *and* or *or*.

1. "Honoring God" is a possible meaning of the name *Timothy*. "To fear God" is a possible meaning of the name *Timothy*.

   _____

   _____

2. The book 1 Timothy was written to Timothy by Paul. The book 2 Timothy was written to Timothy by Paul.

   _____

   _____

The following paragraph should be written in past tense. Circle the three incorrect verbs in the paragraph. Write the correct verb form to improve the paragraph.

Timothy lived in Lystra. When Paul comes to Lystra on his second missionary journey, he hears of Timothy's excellent reputation in the local church. Paul praises Timothy's mother and grandmother for faithfully teaching him. Timothy was selected by Paul to join him on the remainder of his journey.

3. _____

4. _____

5. _____

Add at least one adverb to expand the sentence.

6. Timothy joined Paul.

   _____

7. Timothy was faithful.

   _____

Timothy must have admired Paul. Write about a person you admire. Write one sentence for each pattern.

8. S-V-DO: _____

_____

9. S-LV-PA: _____

_____

Write the correct pronoun to complete the sentence.

10. Paul, Silas, and _____ traveled from one city to another.
    Timothy

11. The young churches of Galatia, Macedonia, and Achaia were discipled by Paul and

    _____.
    his companions

Use ⌃ to add commas where they are needed.

12. Because Timothy had demonstrated his growth in the faith Paul gave him important responsibilities.

13. Timothy ministered to the Thessalonian Corinthian and Philippian churches.

14. Paul planted a church in Ephesus and he sent Timothy there to continue ministering to the new believers.

Write *CS* if the group of words contains a comma splice. Write *C* if the sentence is correct.

_____ 15. In Paul's two letters to Timothy, Paul encourages him to "fight the good fight of faith" (1 Timothy 6:12).

_____ 16. Timothy was instructed to act with maturity, Paul challenged him to be an example to other believers.

Handbook

Thesaurus

A *thesaurus* contains a list of synonyms, words that have similar meanings. You can use a thesaurus to find a more exact word or a more interesting word when you write. A poet may use a thesaurus to find a word that fits better with a poem's sound or rhythm.

The *entry words* are arranged in alphabetical order. *Guidewords* can help you locate a word. Each entry gives a *definition* and uses the word in a *sample sentence*. A list of *synonyms* that can be used to replace the entry word is provided. The entry also tells the *part of speech*, how the word is used in a sentence. Some entries include *antonyms*, words that have the opposite meaning of the entry word.

This guideword is the first word on the page.

This guideword is the last word on the page.

hold(2)/last

Entry word

Part of speech

kind (1) *adjective*
friendly; having a helpful nature
Her kind *words show she cares.*
charitable, considerate, courteous, friendly, generous, gentle, helpful, thoughtful
antonyms: inconsiderate, mean, unkind

Definition

Sample sentence

Synonyms

Antonyms

The following sentence tells the reader what the person's words are like. Changing the word *kind* will give a more precise meaning to each sentence. When choosing a synonym, be careful not to change the meaning of the sentence.

Her **kind** *words show she cares.*

Her **charitable** *words show she cares.*
Her **considerate** *words show she cares.*
Her **courteous** *words show she cares.*
Her **friendly** *words show she cares.*
Her **generous** *words show she cares.*
Her **gentle** *words show she cares.*
Her **helpful** *words show she cares.*
Her **thoughtful** *words show she cares.*

afraid *adjective*
filled with fear
He is afraid *of the dark.*
fearful, frightened, nervous, panicky, terrified, timid, uneasy, worried **antonyms: bold, brave, confident, courageous, fearless, secure**

angry *adjective*
showing strong feeling that comes from believing one has been treated badly
She was angry *with him for reading her diary.*
cross, enraged, fuming, furious, infuriated, irate, offended, resentful, wrathful **antonyms: calm, peaceful, placid**

answer *noun*
a spoken or written reply to a question, statement, invitation, or letter
She knows the answer *to the question.*
reply, response **antonyms: inquiry, question**

argue *verb*
to quarrel or disagree
The boys argued *about who would go first.*
bicker, debate, dispute, oppose, quarrel, quibble, squabble **antonyms: agree, consent**

ask *verb*
to put a question to; to invite an answer to
Ask *the librarian for help.*
beg, inquire, interrogate, petition, question, request **antonyms: answer, reply, respond**

attack *verb*
to set upon with force or violence
The armies attack *the city.*
afflict, ambush, assault, harm, invade, raid **antonyms: defend, guard, protect**

bad *adjective*
not as it should be; of poor quality
His spelling is bad.
abominable, dreadful, evil, horrid, hurtful, nasty, poor, rotten, spoiled, wicked **antonyms: favorable, good, virtuous**

beautiful *adjective*
delightful to the senses or to the mind
The beautiful *song has lasted for hundreds of years.*
attractive, charming, dazzling, elegant, fair, gorgeous, lovely, pleasing, striking, stunning **antonyms: hideous, homely, ugly, unattractive**

before *adverb*
earlier; sooner
I read that book before.
ahead, already, earlier, preceding, previously, prior to **antonyms: after, behind, later**

beg *verb*
to ask for humbly or earnestly
The man begged *for forgiveness.*
beseech, entreat, persuade, plead, request, urge

big *adjective*
of great size, number, or amount
A redwood is a big *tree.*
colossal, enormous, gigantic, grand, great, huge, massive, sizable, vast **antonyms: microscopic, miniature, tiny**

bother *verb*
to annoy; to disturb
Please do not bother *your sister.*
agitate, annoy, disturb, harass, inconvenience, interrupt, irritate, perturb, pester, provoke, vex **antonym: comfort**

brave *adjective*
having or showing courage
The brave *man rescued the boy from the cave.*
bold, confident, courageous, daring, heroic, valiant **antonyms: cowardly, fearful**

break (1) *verb*
to cause to separate into parts
Break *the cookie in half.*
burst, crack, crush, damage, disjoin, fracture, separate, shatter, smash, split, wreck **antonyms: fix, mend, repair**

break (2) *noun*
an interruption; a rest or pause
When will we take a break?
disruption, intermission, interval, pause, recess, rest, retreat

bright *adjective*
giving off much light; brilliant in color
A lone star twinkled faintly above the bright *city lights.*
brilliant, dazzling, gleaming, glistening, glittering, illuminating, luminous, radiant, shining, vivid **antonyms: dim, dull**

build *verb*
to make or form by joining parts or materials together; to construct
We can build *a fence.*
assemble, construct, manufacture, remodel, shape **antonyms: break, demolish, destroy**

buy *verb*
to get goods or services for a payment
We will buy *fruit at the store.*
acquire, obtain, purchase **antonym: sell**

calm *adjective*
quiet; still; peaceful
The wind became calm *after the storm.*
peaceful, placid, relaxed, sedate, serene, still, tranquil, undisturbed **antonyms: agitated, frantic, troubled**

careful *adjective*
watchful; trying to avoid danger or harm
They are careful *when crossing the street.*
cautious, conscientious, meticulous, mindful, prudent, thorough, vigilant, watchful **antonyms: careless, thoughtless**

careless *adjective*
not using care; not paying attention
That was a careless *mistake.*
hasty, sloppy, thoughtless **antonyms: careful, cautious**

carry *verb*
to move or take from one place to another
The men carry *furniture into the house.*
deliver, haul, lug, tote, transfer, transport

change *verb*
to make or become different
The student changed *his answer to the question.*
adapt, adjust, alter, amend, modify, replace, shift, substitute, switch, transform, vary **antonyms: continue, remain**

cheat *verb*
to deceive or trick; to take something dishonestly
It is no fun to play with someone who cheats.
con, deceive, defraud, exploit, mislead, swindle, trick

chop *verb*
to cut by striking with a sharp instrument such as an ax or knife
Please chop *the onions.*
hack, mince, slice, split

clean (1) *adjective*
free from dirt, stain, or germs
The kitchen floor is clean.
immaculate, neat, pure, sanitary, spotless, stainless, tidy **antonyms: filthy, impure, soiled, stained**

clean (2) *verb*
to get rid of dirt, stain, or germs
You should clean *a wound to prevent infection.*
cleanse, disinfect, launder, polish, purify, sanitize, scour, scrub, wash **antonyms: pollute, soil, sully**

clear (1) *adjective*
free from cloudiness or anything that dims; transparent
She watched the fish swim through the clear *water.*
sheer, translucent, transparent **antonyms: cloudy, foggy, opaque**

clear (2) *adjective*
easy to understand, see, or hear
He gave a clear *explanation.*
apparent, legible, obvious, readable **antonyms: foggy, obscure**

clothes *noun*
coverings for the body
Mom bought me new clothes *for school.*
apparel, attire, costume, dress, garments, outfit, wardrobe

cold (1) *adjective*
having a low temperature
Today the weather is snowy and cold.
arctic, chilly, frigid, frosty, frozen, icy, wintry **antonyms: scorching, searing, sweltering**

cold (2) *adjective*
not friendly
He gave me a cold *look and turned away.*
aloof, hostile, standoffish **antonyms: cordial, friendly, warm**

collect *verb*
to come or bring together in a group
The girls collect *stickers.*
accumulate, assemble, bunch, compile, gather, reserve, store **antonyms: disperse, distribute, scatter**

common (1) *adjective*
belonging to or shared by more than one
The two houses share a common *driveway.*
joint, mutual **antonym: varying**

common (2) *adjective*
occurring frequently; usual; ordinary
It was only a common *cold.*
average, customary, familiar, ordinary, usual
antonyms: unusual, rare

confuse *verb*
to mix up; to bewilder
The unclear directions confused *the students.*
baffle, bewilder, mystify, perplex, puzzle
antonym: clarify

copy (1) *noun*
a reproduction or duplicate
Make a copy *of this letter.*
duplicate, imitation, model, replica, reproduction **antonym: original**

copy (2) *verb*
to make a copy or copies of
Copy *the sentence onto your paper.*
duplicate, replicate, reproduce

courage *noun*
the quality of mind that enables one to meet danger and difficulty with firmness or without fear; bravery
It takes courage *to speak the truth.*
boldness, bravery, gallantry, heroism, valiancy, valor **antonyms: cowardice, dread**

cry *verb*
to shed tears because of a feeling of pain or sorrow
I sometimes cry *when I am hurt.*
bawl, moan, mourn, sob, wail, weep, whimper, whine **antonyms: chuckle, giggle, laugh**

cut *verb*
to separate into pieces with a sharp-edged tool
Mom cut *the apple with a knife.*
carve, chop, dice, gash, rip, shred, slash, slice, slit, snip, tear, trim

dangerous *adjective*
threatening harm or injury; unsafe
The weatherman described the dangerous *winds of the hurricane.*
hazardous, perilous, risky, treacherous, unsafe **antonyms: harmless, secure**

dark *adjective*
having little or no light
No moon rose on that dark *night.*
cloudy, dim, dull, foggy, gloomy, murky, overcast, shadowy, shady **antonyms: bright, light**

destroy *verb*
to completely ruin or break into pieces
The tornado destroyed *many buildings.*
abolish, annihilate, demolish, devastate, exterminate, pulverize, wreck **antonyms: build, construct, make**

different *adjective*
unlike; not the same
A frog is different *from a toad.*
distinct, unique, unlike, unusual **antonyms: alike, same, similar**

dirty *adjective*
unclean; not pure
My shirt was dirty *after I played with the dog.*
filthy, foul, grimy, impure, muddy, nasty, polluted, rancid, soiled, stained, vile
antonyms: clean, pure, sanitary

disappear *verb*
to pass from sight
The chocolate cookies always disappear *first.*
evaporate, fade, vanish **antonyms: appear, emerge, materialize**

discover *verb*
to find, see, or learn of something for the first time
The diver discovered *sunken treasure.*
encounter, locate, pinpoint, uncover, unravel

do *verb*
to perform or carry out
What will you do *this summer?*
achieve, complete, execute, practice, undertake

eager *adjective*
having keen or impatient desire; wanting something very much
We're eager *to visit Grandma's house.*
enthusiastic, excited **antonyms: indifferent, unenthusiastic**

English 5

easy *adjective*
needing little effort or thought
This book is easy to read.
effortless, simple, uncomplicated **antonyms: complicated, difficult**

empty *adjective*
containing nothing; not occupied
The house was empty when we left.
abandoned, bare, barren, deserted, hollow, unoccupied, vacant, void **antonyms: crammed, crowded, occupied, packed**

enough *adjective*
as much or as many as needed
I earned enough money for a new bike.
abundant, adequate, ample, plenty, sufficient **antonyms: deficient, inadequate, insufficient**

excited *adjective*
aroused to strong emotion; stirred up
The excited puppy licked my face.
agitated, animated, eager, energized, enthusiastic, roused, stirred, thrilled **antonyms: bored, calm, uninterested**

expect *verb*
to look forward to as likely to occur
We expect a snowstorm tonight.
anticipate, await, foresee, predict

explore *verb*
to inquire into; to investigate or examine
Researchers explore ways to treat cancer.
investigate, probe, research, search, study

fair *adjective*
just; honest
The judge made a fair decision.
consistent, equitable, honest, impartial, just, lawful, legal, right **antonyms: partial, unfair**

fake *adjective*
false; not genuine
The criminal tried to spend fake money.
artificial, counterfeit, false, fraudulent, imitation, phony **antonyms: genuine, real**

famous *adjective*
celebrated; widely known
The astronaut is famous for landing on the moon.
celebrated, distinguished, illustrious, legendary, notable, recognized, renowned **antonyms: obscure, unknown**

fast *adverb*
quickly; rapidly; swiftly
He ran as fast as he could.
hastily, promptly, rapidly, speedily, swiftly **antonyms: leisurely, slowly**

fat *adjective*
having a great amount of fat; plump
That is a very fat cat.
bulky, chubby, large, obese, overweight, plump, stocky, sturdy **antonyms: skinny, slender, thin**

fear *noun*
a strong feeling that danger may be near
She has a fear of dogs.
alarm, anxiety, dismay, dread, fright, horror, panic, terror, timidity **antonyms: bravery, courage**

find *verb*
to come upon; to discover by searching
Did you find my keys?
detect, discover, encounter, locate, recover, uncover, unearth **antonyms: lose, misplace**

finish *verb*
to come to the end of
Did you finish your science project?
accomplish, complete, conclude, terminate **antonyms: begin, commence**

fix *verb*
to make stable; to repair
Could you fix the broken faucet?
bind, mend, repair, restore **antonym: break**

funny *adjective*
causing laughter; humorous
The funny joke made us laugh.
amusing, comical, entertaining, hilarious, humorous, jolly, laughable, silly **antonyms: boring, sad, serious**

get *verb*
to receive; to come to have
Will we get a puppy?
acquire, fetch, gain, obtain **antonyms: give, lose**

give *verb*
to hand over or present to someone
We give money to the missionaries.
bestow, confer, contribute, distribute, donate, grant, impart, offer, present, provide, supply **antonyms: get, receive**

giving *adjective*
having an attitude of generosity
Her giving *neighbors brought meals when she was ill.*
charitable, generous, hospitable **antonyms: greedy, stingy**

gloomy *adjective*
a state of mind or atmosphere that is dark or discouraging
The day was gloomy *because of the dark clouds.*
bleak, depressing, dismal, dreary, glum, miserable, overcast, somber **antonyms: cheerful, happy, light**

go *verb*
to move or travel to a place
We go *to Washington State every year.*
advance, depart, leave, move, proceed, race, run, travel **antonyms: remain, stay**

good (1) *adjective*
high in quality
He used a good *map for the trip.*
favorable, helpful, suitable, superb, terrific, useful, wonderful **antonyms: harmful, horrible, poor, terrible**

good (2) *adjective*
pleasing; agreeable
The cookies are good *to eat.*
delightful, enjoyable, fabulous, pleasant **antonyms: bad, dull, unpleasant**

great *adjective*
remarkable; very skillful
George Washington was a great *leader.*
awesome, excellent, exceptional, fantastic, grand, magnificent, majestic, marvelous, outstanding, stupendous, terrific, tremendous **antonyms: awful, bad, terrible**

group *noun*
a number of persons or things together
The state of Hawaii is made up of a group *of islands in the Pacific Ocean.*
assembly, bunch, clump, cluster, collection, gathering, section, set, team **antonym: individual**

grow (1) *verb*
to increase in size
The trees grow *every year.*
accumulate, develop, expand, increase, mature **antonyms: decrease, shrink**

grow (2) *verb*
to cause to grow; to produce; to raise
Joe grows *tomatoes in his garden.*
cultivate, raise, vegetate

guard *verb*
to keep safe; to protect
Two big dogs guard *the house.*
defend, keep, preserve, protect, shield **antonym: neglect**

happy *adjective*
cheerful; showing pleasure
The happy *children played and sang.*
blissful, carefree, cheery, content, delighted, jolly, jovial, joyful, jubilant, merry, pleased **antonyms: depressed, gloomy**

hard *adjective*
difficult to do; requiring great effort
A police officer has a hard *job to do.*
challenging, complicated, difficult, tough, trying **antonyms: easy, effortless**

hate *verb*
to dislike greatly
I hate *asparagus.*
abhor, despise, detest, dislike, loathe **antonym: love**

hide *verb*
to put out of sight
I will hide *Mom's gift.*
conceal, cover, disguise, mask **antonyms: reveal, show**

high *adjective*
extending far upward or being at a great height
Only Dad can reach that high *shelf.*
elevated, towering **antonym: low**

hit *verb*
to strike a blow
He hit *the nail with a hammer.*
bang, knock, pound, punch, slug, smack, smite, strike, thump, whack

hold (1) *verb*
to grasp with the arms or hands
Hold the rope tightly.
brace, clasp, cling, clutch, cradle, cuddle, embrace, grasp, grip **antonym: release**

hold (2)   *verb*
to keep in place or possess; to maintain
The museum holds *rare artwork.*
contain, harbor, house, lodge, maintain, reserve, shelter **antonym: remove**

honest (1)   *adjective*
truthful; trustworthy
The honest *boy would not lie.*
honorable, respectable, sincere, trustworthy, truthful, upright **antonyms: corrupt, crooked, dishonest, dishonorable**

honest (2)   *adjective*
open or frank; sincere
Give me your honest *opinion.*
forthright, frank, genuine, sincere **antonyms: deceitful, deceptive, unreliable**

hot (1)   *adjective*
having a high temperature
The bread bakes in a hot *oven.*
burning, fiery, roasting, scorching, searing, sizzling, smoldering, steaming, sweltering **antonyms: cold, frigid, icy**

hot (2)   *adjective*
having a burning taste; spicy or biting
That was a hot *chili pepper!*
fiery, peppery, sharp, spicy **antonyms: bland, mild**

hurry   *verb*
to move or act with haste
Hurry *to get your shoes on!*
accelerate, hasten, hustle, rush **antonyms: dawdle, delay, linger, plod**

hurt   *verb*
to cause pain or harm
The boy fell and hurt *his knee.*
abuse, damage, harm, impair, injure, wound **antonym: help**

important   *adjective*
having significant value or meaning
He had an important *message to give the president.*
essential, impressive, influential, meaningful, momentous, significant, valuable, vital **antonyms: trivial, unimportant, worthless**

interesting   *adjective*
exciting curiosity or interest; engaging attention
This book has interesting *characters.*
absorbing, amusing, entertaining, fascinating, mesmerizing, riveting, thrilling **antonym: boring**

job   *noun*
a chore, usually done on a regular schedule; an occupation
My job *is to feed the cat every day.*
career, chore, duty, employment, livelihood, occupation, profession, task, trade, work

join   *verb*
to put or bring together
He joined *the pieces of the puzzle.*
attach, combine, connect, fasten, link, unite **antonyms: disassemble, disconnect**

jump   *verb*
to use the legs to spring from the ground
Our cat jumps *from the ground to the porch.*
bounce, bound, hop, hurdle, leap, pounce, spring up, vault

kind (1)   *adjective*
friendly; having a helpful nature
Her kind *words show she cares.*
charitable, considerate, courteous, friendly, generous, gentle, helpful, thoughtful **antonyms: inconsiderate, mean, unkind**

kind (2)   *noun*
a group of things that are the same in some way
Lions and tigers are the same kind *of animal.*
brand, category, group, sort, type

large   *adjective*
of great size, number, or quantity
The large *van holds fifteen passengers.*
colossal, considerable, enormous, generous, gigantic, grand, great, huge, immense, massive, sizable, substantial, vast **antonyms: diminutive, minute, slight**

last   *adjective*
after all others; coming at the end
We had a picnic on the last *day of school.*
closing, concluding, final **antonyms: beginning, first**

laugh *verb*
to express joy or amusement with sounds and movements
I always laugh *at Grandpa's funny stories.*
cackle, chuckle, giggle, guffaw, howl, roar, snicker **antonyms: bawl, cry, mourn**

leave *verb*
to go away from
Don't leave *the house without your backpack.*
abandon, depart, desert, disappear, evacuate, exit, forsake, quit, retreat **antonyms: remain, stay**

let *verb*
to permit; to allow
My brother let *me bat first.*
authorize, consent, license, permit, sanction **antonyms: forbid, prohibit**

lift *verb*
to move from a lower to a higher position
She will lift *the box.*
boost, elevate, hoist, raise **antonyms: drop, lower**

like *verb*
to enjoy; to find pleasing
Our family likes *to camp in a tent.*
admire, enjoy, favor, prefer **antonyms: abhor, dislike, hate**

little *adjective*
small in size or amount
Our little *table seats only three people.*
diminutive, insignificant, microscopic, miniature, minute, petite, short, slight, tiny **antonyms: gigantic, huge, large**

live (1) *verb*
to make one's home
I live *in a brick house.*
abide, dwell, inhabit, occupy, remain, reside

live (2) *verb*
to be alive
Noah lived *at the time of the Flood.*
exist, survive **antonyms: die, expire, terminate**

look (1) *verb*
to use one's eyesight
Look at the beautiful sunset.
behold, gaze, glance, glare, observe, peek, peer, scan, stare, view, watch

look (2) *verb*
to search
Look everywhere for the kitten.
check, explore, hunt, investigate, search, seek, survey

love (1) *noun*
strong affection; devotion; unselfish desire for the good of another
Jesus showed His love *for mankind by dying on the cross.*
adoration, affection, charity, devotion, endearment, fondness, friendship, kindness, tenderness **antonyms: animosity, hatred**

love (2) *verb*
to have love for; to hold dear
I'll love *you forever.*
adore, cherish, desire, treasure, value **antonyms: despise, hate**

main *adjective*
most important
What is the main *idea of the paragraph?*
central, chief, core, dominant, key, major, primary, principal **antonym: minor**

make *verb*
to cause to exist or happen
I will make *a gift for you.*
assemble, build, compose, construct, craft, create, develop, form, manufacture, mold, produce, shape **antonyms: dismantle, destroy**

many *adjective*
consisting of a large number; not few
He has many *friends.*
abundant, countless, multiple, numerous, plentiful **antonym: few**

mix *verb*
to put together and combine
Mix the butter and sugar first.
blend, combine, scramble, stir **antonym: separate**

move *verb*
to change position or location; to go in a certain direction
My grandparents will move *to Ohio.*
budge, relocate, reposition, scoot, shift, transfer, transport **antonyms: remain, stay**

neat *adjective*
clean; tidy; orderly
He has a neat *desk.*
orderly, organized, tidy, uncluttered
antonyms: cluttered, messy, unkempt, unorganized

needed *adjective*
necessary
We don't have the needed *tools to fix the car.*
essential, necessary, required **antonym: unnecessary**

nervous *adjective*
easily upset or excited; anxious or jumpy
She feels nervous *around dogs.*
anxious, edgy, jittery, panicky, restless, skittish, tense, worried **antonyms: calm, relaxed**

new *adjective*
not existing or made until recently
Don't walk on the new *grass.*
fresh, immature, modern, novel, recent
antonyms: ancient, old

nice *adjective*
pleasant
The weather is nice *and sunny today.*
agreeable, blissful, delightful, fine, lovely, pleasant, pleasing **antonyms: nasty, offensive**

noise *noun*
any sound, especially a sound that is loud, unpleasant, or unwanted
We can hear the noise *of the traffic.*
clamor, commotion, racket, ruckus, sound, uproar **antonyms: quiet, silence**

obey *verb*
to follow instructions or commands
She gladly obeyed *the Lord.*
conform, follow, submit **antonyms: disobey, rebel**

often *adverb*
frequently; many times
Kate often *rides her bike to school.*
frequently, habitually, regularly **antonym: rarely**

old *adjective*
having lived for many years; made long ago
They visited a very old *castle.*
aged, ancient, antique, elderly, obsolete, worn **antonyms: new, young**

outside *noun*
the outer part, side, or surface
Dad painted the outside *of the shed.*
covering, exterior, shell **antonym: inside**

package *noun*
an item or items boxed or wrapped together; parcel
The mail truck has delivered a package.
bundle, carton, packet, parcel

part *noun*
a section or piece of a whole
The bottom part *of the garage door is missing.*
chunk, component, division, element, fraction, fragment, piece, portion, section, segment, slice **antonym: whole**

path *noun*
a way, course, or track along which something moves
We walked in a single line along the path.
channel, course, opening, pass, passage, pathway, route

perfect *adjective*
without fault or flaw
Cal threw a perfect *pitch across the plate.*
accurate, exact, faultless, flawless, immaculate, impeccable, precise, pure, spotless **antonyms: blemished, defective, marred**

pick *verb*
to decide on or prefer something
She will pick *a leader.*
choose, decide, elect, select **antonyms: overlook, refuse**

piece *noun*
a part or portion that has been separated from a whole
May I have a piece *of cake?*
bit, chunk, fragment, portion, segment, slice **antonym: whole**

polite *adjective*
showing careful thought for others
We are polite *to the store workers.*
civil, courteous, gracious, mannerly, pleasant, respectful, tactful **antonyms: impolite, rude**

pour *verb*
to flow or cause to flow in a steady stream
Pour *hot water into the mugs.*
discharge, dispense, empty, spill

praise *verb*
to express approval of; to speak well or highly of
The officer *praised* the boy for his quick thinking.
admire, applaud, esteem, exalt, flatter, glorify, honor, worship **antonyms: belittle, criticize**

pretty *adjective*
delightful to look at, listen to, or think about
That is a *pretty* painting.
appealing, attractive, beautiful, gorgeous, lovely, marvelous, pleasing, radiant, stunning **antonyms: hideous, repulsive**

promise (1) *verb*
to give one's word to do or not to do something
I *promise* to obey.
agree, commit, declare, guarantee, pledge, swear, vow

promise (2) *noun*
a statement giving one's word to do or not to do something
I kept my *promise* to finish the work today.
agreement, commitment, contract, covenant, guarantee, oath, pledge, vow, warrant

protect *verb*
to keep from injury or damage; to guard
These sports goggles *protect* my eyes.
defend, guard, preserve, screen, shelter, shield **antonym: attack**

proud (1) *adjective*
overly satisfied with oneself
The *proud* boy bragged about his family's money.
arrogant, conceited, haughty, pompous, vain **antonym: humble**

proud (2) *adjective*
feeling very pleased or satisfied over something accomplished or owned
I am *proud* of the A I got on my test.
contented, delighted, fulfilled, pleased, satisfied, thrilled **antonym: ashamed**

pull *verb*
to use force to move something toward oneself
Pull *the rope harder.*
drag, jerk, tow, tug **antonym: push**

punishment *noun*
a penalty for doing wrong
The *punishment* for cheating is a zero on the test.
penalty, retribution, sentence **antonym: reward**

push (1) *verb*
to press against in order to move
He could not *push* the rock into the hole.
nudge, press, propel, shove, thrust **antonym: pull**

push (2) *verb*
to urge or pressure
Dad *pushed* him to join the soccer team.
coerce, compel, encourage, inspire, persuade, press, prod, urge **antonyms: discourage, prevent**

put *verb*
to set in a certain place or position
Put *the towels in the closet.*
arrange, assign, establish, lay, place, set **antonym: remove**

quick *adjective*
speedy; done in a short time
Mom made a *quick* trip to the grocery store.
accelerated, brief, hasty, hurried, rapid, speedy, swift **antonyms: gradual, slow**

quiet *adjective*
having little or no noise or activity
A farm is *quiet* in the early morning hours.
calm, hushed, mute, peaceful, restful, silent, still, tranquil **antonyms: loud, noisy**

real *adjective*
genuine; not artificial
Real *gems sparkled in his crown.*
actual, authentic, genuine **antonyms: fake, phony**

reason *noun*
explanation or cause
What is his *reason* for going to church?
basis, cause, grounds, intention, logic, motive, purpose

report   *noun*
an account or description
Did you hear today's weather report?
account, announcement, bulletin, explanation, statement, testimony

respect   *noun*
a high opinion; honor; esteem
A good citizen has respect *for the law.*
admiration, consideration, courtesy, esteem, honor, reverence, tribute
antonyms: irreverence, rudeness

rich   *adjective*
having great or abundant wealth
The rich *man used his money to help others.*
affluent, prosperous, wealthy **antonyms: destitute, needy, penniless, poor**

right   *adjective*
correct; appropriate or proper
She wrote the right *answer to the question.*
accurate, correct, exact, precise, proper, true **antonyms: incorrect, wrong**

rough (1)   *adjective*
having a surface that is uneven or not smooth
Our truck bounced over the rough *road.*
bumpy, coarse, harsh, jagged, rugged, scaly, uneven **antonym: smooth**

rough (2)   *adjective*
difficult, unpleasant, or challenging
He had a rough *day.*
burdensome, difficult, severe, tough, trying

run   *verb*
to move quickly using the legs, not touching the ground with both or all feet at the same time
The soccer players run *after the ball.*
canter, dart, dash, flee, gallop, jog, race, scurry, sprint **antonyms: saunter, stroll**

sad   *adjective*
feeling or showing sorrow or unhappiness
He was sad *when it was time to leave.*
depressed, distressed, downcast, gloomy, glum, heartbroken, miserable, sorrowful, unhappy **antonyms: joyful, jubilant**

same   *adjective*
just like or identical to something else
My friend and I have the same *shoes.*
duplicate, equivalent, exact, identical, similar **antonym: different**

save (1)   *verb*
to keep for use in the future; to store up
Chad saved *money for a new trumpet.*
conserve, preserve, reserve, store **antonym: spend**

save (2)   *verb*
to rescue from danger or harm
The firefighter saved *the child from the fire.*
deliver, liberate, rescue, salvage **antonym: abandon**

say   *verb*
to speak words aloud
Can you say *that more clearly?*
announce, communicate, declare, exclaim, express, pronounce, remark, state, utter, verbalize

scary   *adjective*
causing alarm; frightening
Scary *stories keep me awake at night.*
alarming, fearful, frightening, horrifying, terrifying **antonyms: pleasant, unalarming**

see   *verb*
to look at with the eyes
I see *mountains up ahead.*
behold, distinguish, spot, view, witness

serious (1)   *adjective*
acting or looking thoughtful or grave
Dad looked serious *when he heard about the accident.*
earnest, grave, grim, solemn, somber **antonyms: comical, humorous**

serious (2)   *adjective*
not joking; in earnest
He is serious *about his work.*
earnest, sober **antonyms: carefree, frivolous**

shake   *verb*
to move quickly up and down or back and forth
Did your house shake *during the earthquake?*
agitate, jiggle, quake, quiver, rock, shiver, shudder, tremble, vibrate, wiggle

shiny *adjective*
  reflecting light; bright
  Mother has a shiny *jewel in her ring.*
  bright, brilliant, gleaming, glistening, glossy, polished, radiant **antonym: dull**

short (1) *adjective*
  happening for a brief time
  I'm going for a short *walk.*
  abrupt, brief, condensed, quick **antonyms: lengthy, long**

short (2) *adjective*
  having little length or height; low
  The rope is too short.
  miniature, petite, stunted, tiny, undersized **antonym: long**

shout *verb*
  to call or cry out loudly
  Don't shout *in the library.*
  bellow, cheer, holler, roar, scream, shriek, whoop, yammer, yell **antonyms: murmur, whisper**

show *verb*
  to cause to be seen
  Please show *your science project to the judge.*
  demonstrate, display, exhibit, present, reveal **antonyms: conceal, hide**

silent *adjective*
  perfectly quiet; noiseless
  He remained silent *while the others spoke.*
  hushed, mute, quiet, speechless **antonyms: loud, noisy**

smart *adjective*
  intelligent; having an alert mind
  The smart *doctor helped me get well.*
  bright, clever, ingenious, intelligent, shrewd, skillful **antonyms: foolish, unintelligent**

smell *noun*
  the sense by which odors are recognized; an odor or scent
  I love the smell *of pine trees.*
  aroma, fragrance, odor, reek, scent, stench, stink

smile *verb*
  to show happiness, amusement, pleasure, or friendliness by an expression on the face
  The teacher smiled *kindly at the new student.*
  beam, grin, smirk **antonym: frown**

special *adjective*
  different from what is common or usual
  She uses special *tools to make her crafts.*
  distinguished, exceptional, extraordinary, noteworthy, particular, unique, unusual **antonyms: normal, ordinary, usual**

start *verb*
  to begin a movement or activity
  The game will start *after lunch.*
  activate, begin, commence, embark, initiate **antonyms: conclude, discontinue, finish**

stop *verb*
  to cease a movement or activity
  The workers will stop *to rest and drink water.*
  break, cease, halt, pause **antonyms: begin, go**

strange *adjective*
  not known before; not familiar
  Their dog has a strange *name.*
  abnormal, bizarre, different, odd, peculiar, unfamiliar, unusual, weird **antonyms: familiar, normal, ordinary**

strengthen *verb*
  to make or become stronger
  The exercises strengthened *her arms.*
  brace, fortify, reinforce, rejuvenate, toughen **antonym: weaken**

strict *adjective*
  firm or severe
  Our principal is strict *about silence during fire drills.*
  authoritarian, firm, rigid, severe, stern **antonyms: flexible, lenient**

strong *adjective*
  having much physical power
  The strong *elephant lifted the tree trunk.*
  durable, fortified, mighty, muscular, powerful, sturdy **antonym: weak**

sure *adjective*
  feeling certain, confident; having no doubt
  I'm sure *he will be at school.*
  certain, confident, convinced, definite, positive **antonyms: doubtful, uncertain**

surprise *verb*
  to cause to feel wonder at something unexpected
  I will surprise *my mother on her birthday.*
  amaze, astonish, shock, startle, stun

take *verb*
to get or seize
Take *a book from the shelf.*
acquire, grab, grasp, seize, snatch, sneak, steal **antonym: give**

teach *verb*
to show how; to instruct
I'll teach *you how to play the game.*
acquaint, counsel, direct, educate, guide, inform, instruct, train, tutor

territory *noun*
an area of land; a region
There are lions in that territory.
domain, neighborhood, quarter, zone

thankful *adjective*
full of gratitude; showing appreciation
The boy was thankful *for what his parents taught him.*
appreciative, grateful, indebted **antonyms: unappreciative, unthankful**

thin *adjective*
skinny; not thick
That board is too thin *for our project.*
bony, gaunt, lean, scrawny, slender, slight, slim **antonyms: thick, wide**

think *verb*
to use the mind
Think *before you act.*
consider, contemplate, imagine, meditate, muse, ponder, reflect, wonder

throw *verb*
to cause to move through the air with a forward motion of the arm
Throw *the ball to Lance.*
cast, fling, heave, hurl, launch, lob, pass, pitch, shoot, sling, toss, volley **antonym: catch**

tie *verb*
to bind together or fasten with a cord, rope, or something similar
He tied *the twigs together with string.*
bind, fasten, lash, link, secure, wrap **antonyms: loosen, untie**

tired *adjective*
having lost strength or energy
Emma was tired *after raking the leaves.*
drowsy, exhausted, fatigued, sleepy, sluggish, weary **antonyms: alert, energetic**

trade *verb*
to exchange one thing for another
They often trade *baseball cards.*
barter, swap, switch

travel *verb*
to make a journey; to go from one place to another
He will travel *across the country.*
commute, journey, roam, sojourn, tour, traverse, trek, venture, voyage

trip *noun*
a journey
Dad packed the car for our trip *to the mountains.*
excursion, journey, vacation, voyage

trouble *noun*
a difficult situation; a need
The flood caused trouble *for the family.*
affliction, danger, difficulty, distress, grief, misery, trial **antonym: safety**

turn *verb*
to move or cause to move around a center or an axis; rotate
She turned *the steering wheel to the left.*
revolve, roll, rotate, spin, twist

ugly *adjective*
not pleasing to the eye; unsightly
We finally got rid of the ugly *brown carpet.*
gross, grotesque, hideous, homely, odious, repulsive, revolting, unattractive **antonyms: beautiful, gorgeous**

understand *verb*
to get the meaning of
Now I understand *what this word means.*
comprehend, discern, fathom, grasp, know, perceive, realize **antonym: confuse, misunderstand**

unlikely *adjective*
not likely; not probable
That is an unlikely *story.*
farfetched, improbable, inconceivable **antonyms: likely, probable**

unusual *adjective*
not usual; uncommon; rare
It's unusual *to see that bird in winter.*
abnormal, alien, irregular, odd, rare, unique, weird **antonyms: common, ordinary, usual**

upset *adjective*
sad or unsettled; distressed
The upset *child could not be comforted.*
alarmed, annoyed, anxious, bothered, distraught, disturbed, flustered, perturbed, troubled **antonyms: happy, pleased, satisfied**

useful *adjective*
capable of being used in a helpful way
The small scissors are useful *for snipping threads.*
beneficial, effective, handy, helpful, practical, profitable **antonyms: useless, worthless**

usual *adjective*
commonly used; ordinary
I ate my usual *breakfast.*
common, customary, expected, normal, ordinary, predictable, regular, typical, unvarying **antonyms: extraordinary, unusual**

very *adverb*
in a high degree
That part of the lake is very *deep.*
absolutely, considerably, entirely, extremely, fully, genuinely, truly **antonyms: moderately, slightly**

walk *verb*
to go on foot
We walked *through the woods.*
amble, hike, march, plod, saunter, step, stride, stroll, strut, tread, trek, trudge **antonyms: race, run, skip**

want *verb*
to have a desire for
I want *to play outside.*
crave, desire, wish, yearn

waste *verb*
to spend or use up carelessly or without valuable result
Don't waste *so much time playing video games.*
misuse, squander **antonym: save**

weak *adjective*
without strength or energy
He was weak *after his illness.*
feeble, frail, powerless **antonym: strong**

wet *adjective*
full of moisture
The wet *towels soon dried in the sun.*
damp, drenched, humid, moist, saturated, soaked, soggy **antonyms: arid, dehydrated, dry, parched**

whole *adjective*
complete; including all parts
They ate the whole *cake.*
complete, entire, total, unbroken, undivided **antonyms: incomplete, partial**

wicked *adjective*
evil; very sinful; morally bad
God destroyed the wicked *city of Sodom.*
corrupt, criminal, depraved, godless, immoral, perverted, sinful, vile **antonyms: moral, righteous**

wish *verb*
to have a desire; to long for or want
I wish *I could fly.*
aim, crave, desire, hunger, yearn

work (1) *noun*
that which is done to accomplish something or to earn money
He has almost finished his work *in the yard.*
chore, duty, effort, employment, job, livelihood, occupation, profession, task, trade

work (2) *verb*
to put forth effort to make or accomplish something
We worked *in the cornfield all day.*
labor, perform, strive, struggle, sweat, toil **antonyms: play, rest**

worker *noun*
one that works
She is a diligent worker.
employee, laborer

worried *adjective*
uneasy or anxious
We are worried *about the recent robberies.*
anxious, distracted, frantic, nervous, troubled **antonyms: calm, trusting**

Verbs

In a sentence, the **verb** tells what the subject does or is.

An **action verb** tells what the subject does.

> *Bryson ate a chocolate chip cookie.*

A **linking verb** tells what the subject is by connecting the subject to a noun or an adjective in the complete predicate.

> *The cookie was delicious.*

A **helping verb** helps the <u>main verb</u> in the sentence. Helping verbs come before the main verb.

> *Bryson will <u>share</u> the rest of the cookies with his friends.*

Helping Verbs				
am	be	had	will	must
is	being	do	would	can
are	been	does	should	could
was	have	did	may	
were	has	shall	might	

Forms of the **verb** *be* can be linking verbs or helping verbs.

Forms of Be			
am	is	are	was
were	be	being	been

Sensory verbs can be action verbs or linking verbs.

Sensory Verbs				
feel	look	smell	sound	taste

Prepositions

A **prepositional phrase** begins with a preposition and ends with the object of the preposition.

A **preposition** shows the relationship between a noun or pronoun and the other words in a sentence.

The noun or pronoun that comes after the preposition is called the **object of the preposition**.

Jasmine found her missing homework assignment behind the bookshelf.

She wrote her name at the top of the page.

Common Prepositions		
about	by	on
above	down	out
across	for	outside
after	from	over
around	in	through
at	inside	to
before	into	under
behind	near	until
below	of	up
beside	off	with

Capitalizing Proper Nouns

1. Capitalize the names and initials of people, titles of respect, and abbreviations of titles.

Mrs. Davis   **Rev. James C. White**   **President Lincoln**

2. Capitalize the names and titles of God.

Father   **Holy Spirit**   **Son of God**   **Shepherd**

3. Capitalize the names of groups, teams, businesses, and organizations.

Frontier Girls   **Parkview Panthers**   **Sam's Quickmart**   **American Red Cross**

4. Capitalize the names of specific days of the week, months, holidays, and their abbreviations.

Sunday   **Sun.**   **January**   **Jan.**   **Thanksgiving Day**

5. Capitalize the names of streets, cities, states, countries, continents, rivers, lakes, oceans, buildings, ships, and submarines.

Oak St.   **Atlanta, GA**   **North Carolina**   **USA**   **Asia**   **Nile River**

Lake Erie   **Indian Ocean**   **Empire State Building**   **USS *Enterprise***   **USS *Seawolf***

6. Capitalize the names of languages.

Chinese   **English**   **French**

Capitalizing Titles

1. Capitalize the first, last, and all important words in the titles of books, newspapers, magazines, stories, poems, and songs.

   Where the Red Fern Grows   *The Greenville News*   Highlights

   "Ali Baba and the Forty Thieves"   "I Hear America Singing"   "Amazing Grace"

2. Book, newspaper, and magazine titles should be underlined when handwritten or put in italics when typed on a computer.

   Blue Willow   *The New York Times*   The Horse and His Boy   *Brady*

3. Use quotation marks around the titles of stories, poems, and songs.

   (story) "The Wind and the Sun"

   (poem) "The Eagle"

   (song) "The Star-Spangled Banner"

4. Capitalize names of the Bible, its divisions, and its books.

   God's Word   Holy Bible   New Testament   John 3:16

Abbreviations

United States Postal Abbreviations

The United States Postal Service gives abbreviations for states and territories as two capital letters with no periods.

Alabama	**AL**	Montana	**MT**
Alaska	**AK**	Nebraska	**NE**
American Samoa	**AS**	Nevada	**NV**
Arizona	**AZ**	New Hampshire	**NH**
Arkansas	**AR**	New Jersey	**NJ**
California	**CA**	New Mexico	**NM**
Colorado	**CO**	New York	**NY**
Connecticut	**CT**	North Carolina	**NC**
Delaware	**DE**	North Dakota	**ND**
District of Columbia	**DC**	Northern Mariana Islands	**MP**
Florida	**FL**	Ohio	**OH**
Georgia	**GA**	Oklahoma	**OK**
Guam	**GU**	Oregon	**OR**
Hawaii	**HI**	Pennsylvania	**PA**
Idaho	**ID**	Puerto Rico	**PR**
Illinois	**IL**	Rhode Island	**RI**
Indiana	**IN**	South Carolina	**SC**
Iowa	**IA**	South Dakota	**SD**
Kansas	**KS**	Tennessee	**TN**
Kentucky	**KY**	Texas	**TX**
Louisiana	**LA**	Utah	**UT**
Maine	**ME**	Vermont	**VT**
Maryland	**MD**	Virgin Islands	**VI**
Massachusetts	**MA**	Virginia	**VA**
Michigan	**MI**	Washington	**WA**
Minnesota	**MN**	West Virginia	**WV**
Mississippi	**MS**	Wisconsin	**WI**
Missouri	**MO**	Wyoming	**WY**

More Abbreviations

Days of the Week

Sunday	**Sun.**
Monday	**Mon.**
Tuesday	**Tues.**
Wednesday	**Wed.**
Thursday	**Thurs.**
Friday	**Fri.**
Saturday	**Sat.**

Months

January	**Jan.**
February	**Feb.**
March	**Mar.**
April	**Apr.**
August	**Aug.**
September	**Sept.**
October	**Oct.**
November	**Nov.**
December	**Dec.**

May, *June*, and *July* have no abbreviations because they are short words.

Titles of People

Titles are special words used with people's names to show respect. The names and titles of people are capitalized. Abbreviations are used for most titles. The title *Miss* does not have an abbreviation.

adult man	**Mr.**
married adult woman	**Mrs.**
adult woman	**Ms.**
unmarried adult woman	**Miss**
doctor	**Dr.**
ordained preacher	**Rev.**
president	**Pres.**
senator	**Sen.**
governor	**Gov.**
professor	**Prof.**
captain	**Capt.**
junior	**Jr.**
senior	**Sr.**

Address Abbreviations

Apartment	**Apt.**	Drive	**Dr.**
Avenue	**Ave.**	Lane	**Ln.**
Boulevard	**Blvd.**	Post Office	**PO**
Circle	**Cir.**	Road	**Rd.**
Court	**Ct.**	Street	**St.**

Measurement Abbreviations

Metric Measurement Units

meter(s)	m
centimeter(s)	cm
millimeter(s)	mm
gram(s)	g
kilogram(s)	kg
liter(s)	l or L
milliliter(s)	ml or mL

Customary Measurement Units

inch(es)	in.
foot (feet)	ft.
yard(s)	yd.
pound(s)	lb.
ounce(s)	oz.
gallon(s)	gal.

Times

morning	*a.m.
afternoon, night	*p.m.
before Christ	BC
after Christ's birth	*AD
minute(s)	min(s).
second(s)	sec(s).
hour(s)	hr(s).

*Latin. a.m. = ante meridiem, "before noon."

p.m. = post meridiem, "after noon."

AD = anno Domini, or "in the year of our Lord."

Prefixes and Suffixes

A **prefix** is a group of letters added to the beginning of a base word to make a new word.

Prefix	Meaning	Example	Meaning
bi-	having two of; twice	bicycle	having two wheels
dis-	not; opposite of	distrust	to not trust
un-		unwanted	not wanted
im-	not	imperfect	not perfect
in-		inaccurate	not accurate
non-		nonfiction	not fiction
mis-	wrong; incorrectly	misunderstood	understand incorrectly
out-	greater; better	outdo	to do better than
pre-	before	preview	to view before
re-	again or back	reprint	to print again

A **suffix** is a group of letters added to the end of a base word to make a new word.

Suffix	Meaning	Example	Meaning
-able	capable or worthy of	likable	worthy to be liked
-ible		flexible	capable of being flexed
-en	to make	brighten	to make bright
-er, -or	one who does	painter, collector	one who paints
-ist		artist	one who collects
			one who does art
-ful	full of	truthful	full of truth
-ish	like; somewhat	girlish	like a girl
-less	without; not having	penniless	without money
-ly	like in nature or manner	gladly	in a glad manner
-ment	the act, state, quality, or result of	adjustment	the act of adjusting
-ness	state, condition, or quality of	neatness	state of being neat

Homophones

Homophones are words that sound alike but have different meanings and usually different spellings.

air	a mixture of gases on Earth	The fresh *air* feels good.
heir	someone who receives money or property of another person after his death	Mother was my grandparents' only *heir*.
allowed	permitted	Mom *allowed* us to have a snack.
aloud	loud enough to be heard	I read the story *aloud*.
ate	past tense of eat	We *ate* hot dogs for lunch.
eight	a number; 8	I found *eight* coins.
bill	money	I have a dollar *bill*.
bill	statement of money owed	The company sent me a *bill*.
bill	beak	The duck had an orange *bill*.
blew	past tense of *blow*	The wind *blew* the door shut.
blue	a color	She wore a *blue* skirt.
brake	a device to slow or stop a vehicle	Dad pressed his foot on the *brake*.
break	crack, split, or burst into pieces	Be careful not to *break* that teacup!
buy	to pay money for something	I'd like to *buy* that bicycle.
by	through the action or effort of	We traveled *by* train.
bye	a short form of "good-bye"	"*Bye*, Mom!" I called.
can	to be able to	I *can* play the flute.
can	metal container	I opened a *can* of soup.
chord	three or more musical notes played together	I played a *chord* on the piano.
cord	a thin rope or bundle of electric wire	Please plug in the computer *cord*.
close	to shut	*Close* the door quietly.
clothes	articles of dress	Tim has new *clothes*.
dear	loved or respected	A *dear* friend gave me a gift.
deer	an animal	The *deer* leaped over the brook.
fair	honest	The referee made a *fair* call.
fair	a carnival	Did you go the *fair*?
fare	toll	The taxi *fare* was expensive.
file	collection of papers	Put that document in the *file*.
file	tool for smoothing	I used the *file* for my nails.
flour	processed grain	Add *flour* to the dough.
flower	colorful plant petals	This *flower* is a daisy.

Homophones (continued)

for	purpose	Mom made a cake *for* the party.
for	destination	We headed *for* the beach.
four	a number; 4	I wrote *four* sentences.
hair	grows on the head	Andy has red *hair*.
hare	rabbit	The *hare* twitched his ears.
heal	cure	My cut will *heal* quickly.
heel	bottom of the foot	My *heel* is sore.
hear	understand by listening	Can you *hear* him talking?
here	in this place	Please sit *here*.
heard	past tense of hear	I *heard* the bird singing.
herd	a group of animals	The *herd* of cows grazed in the pasture.
him	a masculine pronoun	I sat next to *him*.
hymn	a song to God	We sang my favorite *hymn*.
hoarse	husky-voiced	He was *hoarse* from yelling.
horse	an animal	The cowboy rode a *horse*.
hole	tear, opening	There is a *hole* in my jacket.
whole	entire	We ate the *whole* pizza.
I'll	contraction of *I will*	*I'll* bring my baseball glove.
aisle	a narrow passage	The bride walked up the *aisle*.
its	the possessive form of *it*	Return the book to *its* shelf.
it's	contraction of *it is*	I think *it's* going to rain.
knew	was aware of	I *knew* the answer.
new	just made or bought	Mike has *new* shoes.
new	different	We have a *new* teacher.
knot	a twist or tangle	My shoelaces are in a *knot*.
not	negation of a word	I will *not* forget the assignment.
knows	is aware of	He *knows* about the surprise.
nose	organ of smelling	My *nose* is stuffy.
lock	a curl of hair	A *lock* of hair fell over her eyes.
lock	a fastener	Dad put a *lock* on the door.
mail	letters and packages sent through a postal system	Did we get any cards in the *mail* today?
male	a boy or man	Is the new baby a *male* or female?
main	most important	Write down the *main* idea of the book.

Homophones (continued)

mane	long hair that grows from the head and neck of some animals	I combed the horse's *mane*.
might	power	Our God is a God of *might*.
might	will possibly happen	We *might* have to cancel the game.
mint	plant with fresh flavor	You can crush *mint* leaves to make tea.
mint	place where coins are made	We visited the Denver *Mint*.
our	possessive form of *we*	*Our* house is around the corner.
hour	a unit of time	Dad will be home in one *hour*.
pair	couple; two things	I bought a *pair* of shoes.
pare	cut or peel	Will you *pare* the apples?
pear	juicy, grainy fruit	The *pear* was delicious.
peace	freedom from war	The two countries are at *peace*.
piece	part of a whole	He ate a *piece* of pie.
plain	ordinary; nothing added	Grandpa wore a *plain* red tie.
plane	airplane	We flew on a *plane*.
rest	sleep	I did not get enough *rest* last night.
rest	the remainder	The *rest* of us will wait here.
right	the opposite of left	My house is on the *right*.
right	correct	He gave the *right* answers.
write	make letters or words	Please *write* neatly.
sail	strong material attached to a mast on a ship or boat to catch the wind	The *sail* fluttered in the breeze.
sale	the exchange of goods for money	We held a garage *sale*.
sea	body of water	The *sea* was still and blue.
see	to look	I *see* birds flying.
sent	past tense of *send*	I *sent* the letter to him.
cent	penny	The groceries cost seven dollars and one *cent*.
scent	a smell	Hunting dogs can track by *scent*.
shed	a building	Dan put the lawnmower back in the *shed*.
shed	to take off	Snakes *shed* their skin.
stair	a step	The toddler sat on the *stair*.
stare	to gaze steadfastly	It is not polite to *stare*.

Homophones (continued)

tail	part attached to the back of an animal	The puppy wagged his *tail*.
tale	a story	"Paul Bunyan" is a tall *tale*.
their	possessive form of *they*	I'm going to *their* house.
there	at that place	Look over *there*.
they're	contraction of *they are*	*They're* coming with us.
to	direction of or toward	We drove *to* Washington.
too	also	I can play the piano *too*.
too	very	You worked *too* quickly.
two	a number; 2	He has *two* cookies.
vain	without success	I tried in *vain* to stay awake.
vein	a blood vessel	I could see the *veins* in Grandma's hands.
waist	section of the body between the ribs and the hips	Her dress had a bow tied at the *waist*.
waste	to spend or use foolishly	Don't *waste* your allowance.
wait	to stay in place	*Wait* for me outside the front door.
weight	the measure of the heaviness of something	The *weight* of the suitcase was ten pounds.
way	path or direction	Which *way* should we go?
way	habit of doing things	That is the *way* we do things.
weigh	heaviness of something	I will *weigh* the apples.
weak	lack of strength	He was *weak* from hunger.
week	seven days	We spent a *week* at the beach.
well	a deep hole	She carried a bucket of water from the *well*.
well	correctly	You did *well* on the spelling test.
won	the past tense of *win*	They *won* the championship!
one	a number; 1	I have only *one* math problem left.
wood	part of a tree	We cut the *wood* to make a treehouse.
would	past tense of *will*	He said we *would* go today.
yoke	a bar with two U-shaped pieces that fit around the necks of a team of animals	The farmer slipped the *yoke* over the heads of the oxen.
yolk	the yellow part of the inside of an egg	Add two egg *yolks* to that cake mix.
your	possessive form of *you*	*Your* ice cream is melting.
you're	contraction of *you are*	*You're* invited to my party.

Photo Credits

Key: (t) top; (c) center; (b) bottom; (l) left; (r) right; (bg) background; (i) inset

Chapter 1

5 GETSARA/Shutterstock.com; 10 virtu studio/Shutterstock.com; 12 maspriy/Shutterstock.com; 13 Romiana Lee/Shutterstock.com; 19 ALEAIMAGE/E+ via Getty Images; 20 cdrin/Shutterstock.com; 22 IrinaK/Shutterstock.com; 24t Paulrommer SL/Shutterstock.com; 24b cynoclub/Shutterstock.com; 25 JeniFoto/Shutterstock.com; 26 Ortis/Shutterstock.com

Chapter 2

32c PTZ Pictures/Shutterstock.com; 32b Andrey_Kuzmin/Shutterstock.com; 34 Joseph Sohm/Shutterstock.com; 35tr BERNATSKAIA OKSANA/Shutterstock.com; 35br moosehenderson/Shutterstock.com; 35c ElenaPhotos/Shutterstock.com/vladoleg/Shutterstock.com; 35l M88/Shutterstock.com; 45 lenakorzh/Shutterstock.com; 46 Tiplyashina Evgeniya/Shutterstock.com

Chapter 3

52b National Audubon Society/Public Domain; 53t © Panupong Ponchai | Dreamstime.com; 53b Merlin74/Shutterstock.com; 56 YUSHENG HSU/Shutterstock.com; 59t Vuk Varuna/Shutterstock.com; 59b Roman Barkov/Shutterstock.com; 60 Scott Delony/Shutterstock.com; 62t Anke van Wyk/Shutterstock.com; 62b My name is boy/Shutterstock.com; 64 Yuval Navot/Shutterstock.com; 66t Betty Ann Killgoar/Shutterstock.com; 66b Dean Pennala/Shutterstock.com; 72t Jason Swalwell/Shutterstock.com; 72b © Anastasiia Guseva | Dreamstime.com; 76 Katsumi Murouchi/Moment via Getty Images

Chapter 4

85 Nancybelle Gonzaga Villarroya/Moment via Getty Images; 86 Lucky-photographer/Shutterstock.com; 86i "The Metropolitan Museum of Art, New York," Fletcher Fund, 1931/Public Domain; 89 osafus/Shutterstock.com; 90 © Biathlonua | Dreamstime.com; 92t Ivan Smuk/Shutterstock.com; 92b Terryfic3D/iStock/Getty Images Plus via Getty Images; 93t Niday Picture Library/Alamy Stock Photo; 93b Gift of the Rhode Island Society for the Encouragement of Domestic Industry, Division of Cultural and Community Life, National Museum of American History, Smithsonian Institution; 96 StompingGirl/Shutterstock.com

Chapter 5

117 matimix/Shutterstock.com; 126 88studio/Shutterstock.com

Chapter 6

140 Gregory_DUBUS/iStock/Getty Images Plus via Getty Images; 142 Jason Persoff Stormdoctor/Image Source via Getty Images; 143 Photography by Deb Snelson/Moment via Getty Images; 146 Dennis W Donohue/Shutterstock.com; 149 Alex Izeman/Shutterstock.com; 150t tunasalmon/Shutterstock.com; 150b Stocktrek Images/Richard Roscoe via Getty Images; 152 Antonio S/Shutterstock.com; 156l alex7370/Shutterstock.com; 156r Stefan Neumann/Shutterstock.com

Chapter 7

166t Adam Pretty/Getty Images Sport via Getty Images; 166b © Christian Jones | Dreamstime.com; 168 Click Images/Shutterstock.com; 170 Catherine Leblanc/Godong/The Image Bank Unreleased via Getty Images; 176l Bruce Bennett via Getty Images; 176r Steve Babineau/National Hockey League via Getty Images; 178 Bruce Bennett/Getty Images Sport via Getty Images

Chapter 8

194 Teresa Otto/Shutterstock.com; 197l ayzek/Shutterstock.com; 197r railway fx/Shutterstock.com; 199 © Judy Kennamer | Dreamstime.com; 200 Sovereign Images/Shutterstock.com

Chapter 9

210t Photo courtesy of Schmidt Ocean Institute; 210b Aaron Bull/iStock/Getty Images Plus via Getty Images; 212 Alexander Lysenko/Shutterstock.com; 213 Eric Isselee/Shutterstock.com; 214 SA Tourist/Shutterstock.com; 216 EMiddelkoop/iStock/Getty Images Plus via Getty Images; 217l Sean Pavone/Shutterstock.com; 217r Jesse Kunerth/Shutterstock.com

Chapter 10

242bg Petrov Stanislav/Shutterstock.com; 244 beats1/Shutterstock.com; 251 Moussa81/iStock/Getty Images Plus via Getty Images; 253 Peter Devlin/Alamy Stock Photo

Chapter 11

268 Bill Chizek/iStock Editorial/Getty Images Plus via Getty Images; 270 Grant Faint/The Image Bank via Getty Images; 271 Travelpix Ltd/The Image Bank Unreleased via Getty Images; 274 Johner Images/Johner Images Royalty-Free via Getty Images; 276 Alon Adika/Shutterstock.com; 277 (art reference) Science History Images/Alamy Stock Photo; 282 f11photo/Shutterstock.com

Chapter 12

299t © Cadifor | Dreamstime.com; 299b © Geoffrey Kuchera | Dreamstime.com

Chapter 13

311 Eshma/iStock/Getty Images Plus via Getty Images; 312 Mister_Knight/Shutterstock.com; 323 FG Trade/E+ via Getty Images

Chapter 14

338bl, 338br (frames) jamessnazell/iStock/Getty Images Plus via Getty Images; 338bli, 338bri Courtesy of the Mary Slessor Foundation/http://maryslessor.org; 341 Archive Photos/Stringer via Getty Images; 344 Matthew Chattle/Alamy Stock Photo; 351 Andrey Lobachev/Shutterstock.com; 352l FG Trade/E+ via Getty Images; 352r sirikorn thamniyom/Shutterstock.com

Acknowledgments

Chapter 1

Illustrations, by John O'Brien, copyright © 1999 by John O'Brien; and book cover image and excerpt from EAT YOUR WORDS: A FASCINATING LOOK AT THE LANGUAGE OF FOOD by Charlotte Foltz Jones, text copyright © 1999 by Charlotte Foltz Jones. Used by permission of Random House Children's Books, a division of Penguin Random House LLC. All rights reserved. (2)

Chapter 2

"Tent" and "Dragon" from *Words with Wings* by Nikki Grimes. Copyright © 2013 by Nikki Grimes. Published by Wordsong, an imprint of Astra Publishing House. Book cover image used by permission of Astra Publishing House. Reprinted by permission. (32)

Chapter 3

Excerpts from pages 8–9 of "America, My Country." *This Strange Wilderness: The Life and Art of John James Audubon* by Nancy Plain. University of Nebraska Press, 2015. Book cover image used by permission of the University of Nebraska Press. (52)

Chapter 4

Illustrations, by John O'Brien, copyright © 1991 by John O'Brien; and book cover image and excerpt from MISTAKES THAT WORKED by Charlotte Foltz Jones, text copyright © 1991 by Charlotte Foltz Jones. Used by permission of Doubleday, an imprint of Random House Children's Books, a division of Penguin Random House LLC. All rights reserved. (84)

Chapter 5

Excerpts from pages 241–242 of THE WHEEL ON THE SCHOOL by Meindert DeJong - Illustrated by: Maurice Sendak. Text copyright © 1954 by Meindert DeJong. Illustrations copyright © 1954 by Maurice Sendak. Used by permission of HarperCollins Publishers. (116)

Chapter 6

Book cover image and excerpt from *You Wouldn't Want to Live Without Extreme Weather!* © The Salariya Book Company Ltd, 2015. (138)

Chapter 7

Excerpt from "Queen of the Slopes" by Emily Cambias, *Cobblestone*, February 2021 © by Cricket Media, Inc. Reproduced with permission. All Cricket Media material is copyrighted by Cricket Media and/or various authors and illustrators. Any commercial use or distribution of material without permission is strictly prohibited. Please visit http://www.cricketmedia.com/info/licensing2 for licensing and http://www.cricketmedia.com for subscriptions. (166)

Chapter 8

Book cover image and excerpt from *Children of the Storm: The Autobiography of Natasha Vins* translated by Jane Vins Comden. Copyright © 2002 BJU Press. All rights reserved. (190)

Chapter 9

Excerpt from "Nosy News: Hide and Reef" by Elizabeth Preston, *Ask*, April 2021 © by Cricket Media, Inc. Reproduced with permission. All Cricket Media material is copyrighted by Cricket Media and/or various authors and illustrators. Any commercial use or distribution of material without permission is strictly prohibited. Please visit http://www.cricketmedia.com/info/licensing2 for licensing and http://www.cricketmedia.com for subscriptions. (210)

Chapter 10

Book cover image, title page art, and excerpt from *The Mysterious Benedict Society* by Trenton Lee Stewart, copyright © 2007. Reprinted by permission of Little, Brown, an imprint of Hachette Book Group, Inc. (US) Reproduced with permission of Chicken House Ltd. All rights reserved. (UK/BC) (242)

Chapter 11

Illustrations, by John Hinderliter, copyright © 2016 by Penguin Random House LLC; book cover image and excerpt from WHERE IS STONEHENGE? by True Kelley, text copyright © 2016 by True Kelley. Used by permission of Grosset & Dunlap, an imprint of Penguin Young Readers Group, a division of Penguin Random House LLC. All rights reserved. (264)

Chapter 12

Book cover image, illustration, and excerpt from *Frances Ridley Havergal: A Poet for the King* by Eileen M. Berry. Copyright © 2019 BJU Press. All rights reserved. (292)

Chapter 13

"Azerbaijan" from *My Librarian Is a Camel* by Margriet Ruurs. Copyright © 2005 by Margriet Ruurs. Published by Boyds Mills Press, an imprint of Astra Publishing House. Jacket photograph and additional photograph used by permission of Boyds Mills Press. Reprinted by permission. (310)

Excerpt from *Free Indeed: Heroes of Black Christian History* by Mark Sidwell. Copyright © 2001 BJU Press. All rights reserved. (327)

Excerpt from *Faith of Our Fathers: Scenes from Church History* edited by Mark Sidwell. Copyright © 1989 BJU Press. All rights reserved. (328)

Chapter 14

Book cover image and excerpt from *Mary Slessor: Missionary Mother* by Terri B. Kelly. Copyright © 2014 BJU Press. All rights reserved. (338)